INNOVATIONS IN TAX COMPLIANCE

INNOVATIONS IN TAX COMPLIANCE

BUILDING TRUST, NAVIGATING POLITICS, AND TAILORING REFORM

Roel Dom, Anna Custers, Stephen Davenport, and Wilson Prichard

 WORLD BANK GROUP

CONTENTS

Boxes

Figures

Tables

FOREWORD

Protecting people's health, income, and jobs from the worst of the pandemic has required substantive increases in public expenditures. As levels of debt in lower- and middle-income countries continue along the upward trajectory that began well before the pandemic, fiscal space for development spending is shrinking. Hence, strengthening domestic resource mobilization has become an urgent priority in the political and economic agendas of governments everywhere.

Yet empirical evidence shows that tax reforms have not always yielded higher revenue. How governments go about collecting tax is integral to how the state is financed. But it also determines how taxpayers view state institutions, because paying tax is a major point of interaction between citizens and the state. Although the need to simply raise more revenue is clear, the need to raise revenue in a better way is important as well. Efforts to raise revenue should be strengthened to address the biases of tax systems that exacerbate inequality. Accelerating the move to a digital revenue administration will underlie this undertaking.

At the Bill & Melinda Gates Foundation and the World Bank, we believe tax systems should be equitable and deliver for all citizens. To that end, this report develops a new avenue for delivering country tax reform by setting out a novel, integrated framework for strengthening tax compliance and reform, especially in low-income countries. In the past, tax reform leaned heavily toward strengthening tax enforcement and facilitating tax compliance. However, as this report demonstrates, improving the trustworthiness of the tax system is equally important to strengthening tax compliance. It is also key to building the political sustainability of reform and the social contract more broadly. Building trust also helps mobilize political support for tax reform, prompting initially skeptical citizens to demand the changes to the tax system needed to ensure that everyone pays their fair share.

Substantial evidence across countries and regions indicates that the willingness to pay taxes and support reform is higher when trust in the state is strong. For example, a recent World Bank survey found that both anticorruption and participatory budgeting measures led to improvements in tax compliance. It also found that improving service provision—a sign that governments are holding up their end of the social contract—predicts more positive attitudes toward compliance. It should not be a surprise that citizens are more willing to pay taxes when they know that their money is being well spent on services they want. What is surprising is that more tax authorities have not made building citizens' trust a central plank of their compliance strategies. Building trust and boosting accountability are fundamental to providing countries with a stable, predictable, and sustainable fiscal environment and to promoting inclusive growth.

As highlighted in this report, tax reform could benefit from this broader perspective on the drivers of tax compliance and reform. Governments face consequences from how well citizens believe their taxes are being spent, from whether they feel they are treated fairly by tax officials, from how well tax laws and decisions are communicated, and from how equitable the tax system is. The key is to recognize both the importance of more effective engagement between the state and citizens and the pivotal role played by the tax system in this relationship. More holistic approaches to reform that consider both politics and ways to enhance trust could achieve more sustainable improvements in revenue raising that are fair and equitable and translate into benefits for citizens.

By unpacking trust into four drivers—fairness, equity, reciprocity, and accountability—this report offers readers clear-cut paths to operationalizing trust-building in the tax system in practice. More important, it urges reformers to focus on how to more effectively tailor reform strategies to local contexts and constraints, reflecting the distinctive technical capacity and political challenges policy makers face when building trust with taxpayers.

We hope this report will serve as an essential reference for the tax policy makers, administrators, and practitioners who will lead the way in shifting the paradigm from taxing more to taxing better. It is our hope that the framework is adopted and used across the World Bank country network, building on the successful pilots conducted in Albania, Georgia, Nigeria, Pakistan, and Tajikistan. But adoption of this framework should not stop there. Through actions such as the Addis Tax Initiative, international partners have pledged to increase their capacity-building programs to continue to spur tax reform. As they work to mobilize extra resources, they can use the framework laid out in this report to guide their own advice and interventions. Doing so will not only provide sustainable finance for vital public services, but also build trust in the very institutions that we all are attempting to support. We extend our thanks to our partners, the Global Tax Program and the International Centre for Tax and Development, for their crucial support of this important endeavor.

Marcello Estevão
Global Director, Macroeconomics,
Trade, and Investment
Equitable Growth, Finance, and Institutions
The World Bank

Kalpana Kochhar
Director, Development
Policy and Finance
Bill & Melinda Gates
Foundation

Edward Olowo-Okere
Global Director, Governance
Equitable Growth, Finance, and Institutions
The World Bank

ACKNOWLEDGMENTS

This report was overseen by a team led by Anna Custers, Economist, in the Macroeconomics, Trade, and Investment (MTI) Global Practice at the World Bank; and Stephen Davenport, Global Lead, Anticorruption, Openness, and Transparency, in the Governance Global Practice at the World Bank. Other core team members were Roel Dom, Economist, Fiscal Policy and Sustainable Growth Unit, World Bank; Wilson Prichard, Associate Professor, Munk School of Global Affairs and Public Policy at the University of Toronto; Benjamin Holzman, Consultant, Equitable Growth, Finance, and Institutions Global Practice, World Bank; and Moyo Arewa, Program and Research Officer, International Centre for Tax and Development. Excellent research support was provided by Emily Kallaur, Tanya Bandula-Irwin, and Joseph Paul Massad.

The work was carried out under the guidance of Chiara Bronchi, Practice Manager, MTI; Jens Kromann Kristensen, Practice Manager, Governance; William Maloney, Chief Economist, Equitable Growth, Finance, and Institutions; Marcello Estevão, Global Director, MTI; Edward Olowo-Okere, Global Director, Governance; and James Brumby, Senior Adviser, Governance. Special thanks go to Marijn Verhoeven for the support and strategic leadership in conceptualizing this work.

Chapters were written by Moyo Arewa, Anna Custers, Stephen Davenport, Roel Dom, and Wilson Prichard. A special thanks to Michael Roscitt, who contributed to the early stages of the project. Nursena Acar and Matthew Collin provided important inputs.

The team has also benefited enormously from the discussions with and feedback from our peer reviewers at the concept stage and during the quality enhancement and decision reviews: Anders Agerskov, James Alm, Daniel Alvarez, James Anderson, Josh Aslett, James Brumby, Oscar Calvo-Gonzalez, Blanca Moreno Dodson, Peter Hurst, Gabriela Inchauste, Leif Jensen, Moses Kajubi, Steve Knack, Jens Kristensen, Jonathan Leigh Pemberton, Alberto Leyton, Jan Loeprick, Roland Lomme, Giulia Mascagni, Oyebola Okunogbe, Tiago Peixoto, Jaffar Al Rikabi, Stephen Rimmer, Michael Roscitt, Luis Serven, Mahvish Shaukat, Emilia Skrok, Joseph Stead, Benno Torgler, and Marijn Verhoeven.

ABOUT THE AUTHORS

Anna Custers is an Economist in the Macroeconomics, Trade, and Investment Global Practice at the World Bank, where she focuses on fiscal policy in low- and middle-income countries. She works on macrofiscal issues in Afghanistan and has provided technical assistance to revenue and customs administrations in Georgia, Nigeria, Pakistan, Tajikistan, Uganda, and Uzbekistan. Before joining the World Bank, she worked with the Jameel Poverty Action Lab (J-PAL) in France and India. She holds a PhD in management research from the University of Oxford and an MSc in development studies from the London School of Economics.

Stephen Davenport is the Global Lead for Anticorruption, Openness, and Transparency in the Governance Global Practice at the World Bank. He works on various projects related to Open Government and GovTech and co-leads the Innovation in Tax Compliance program, which promotes strategies to engender greater trust in tax administrations. He has more than 20 years of experience in program innovation, development, fundraising, communications, client relationship management, and delivery of e-government services. He has worked in partnership with the United States Agency for International Development, International Aid Transparency Initiative, Open Aid Partnership, Open Contracting Partnership, and Open Government Partnership to accomplish his goals for greater transparency in international development. He has also led breakthrough innovations, including the Open Gov Hub, FeedBack Labs, and AidData.

Roel Dom is a Fiscal Policy Adviser with Open Vld. At the time of the writing of this publication, he was an Economist with the Fiscal Policy and Sustainable Growth Unit at the World Bank, focusing on tax and customs, and in particular on the role of trust and digitalization in tax systems. Before joining the World Bank, he worked as a research fellow for the International Centre for Tax and Development and for the Overseas Development Institute, where he worked closely with revenue administrations in low-income countries and fragile states. He holds a PhD in development economics from the University of Nottingham and an MSc in development studies from the London School of Economics.

Wilson Prichard is an Associate Professor at the Munk School of Global Affairs and Public Policy at the University of Toronto and is CEO of the International Centre for Tax and Development and research fellow at the Institute of Development Studies (IDS). His research focuses on the political economy of tax reform and the relationship between taxation and citizens' demands for improved governance in Sub-Saharan Africa. He has published widely in academic outlets and works regularly with governments and international and civil society organizations to support stronger tax systems. He is a graduate of IDS and Harvard University.

ABBREVIATIONS

AEOI	Automatic Exchange of Information
AI	artificial intelligence
AMT	alternative minimum tax
API	application programming interface
ASYCUDA	Automated System for Customs Data
B2G	business-to-government
BEPS	Base Erosion and Profit Shifting (OECD)
CAMA	computer-assisted mass appraisal
CIT	corporate income taxation
COTS	commercial off-the-shelf
DMFAS	Debt Management and Financial Analysis System
EBM	electronic billing machine
EFD	electronic fiscal device
ERCA	Ethiopian Revenue and Customs Authority
ETI	electronic tax invoice
FCC	Freetown City Council (Sierra Leone)
FIRS	Federal Inland Revenue Service (Nigeria)
G2B	government-to-business
G2P	government-to-person
G20	Group of 20
G-24	Intergovernmental Group of Twenty-Four
GDP	gross domestic product

GIS	geographic information system
GSMA	GSM Association (Cambodia)
HICs	high-income countries
HNWI	high-net-worth individual
HTS	HomeTax Service (Republic of Korea)
HTT	hard-to-tax
ICT	information and communication technology
ICTD	International Centre for Tax and Development
ID	identification
IGC	International Growth Centre
ILO	International Labour Organization
IMF	International Monetary Fund
IT	information technology
JCC	Joint Compliance Committee (Uganda)
KADGIS	Kaduna Geographic Information Service (Nigeria)
KCCA	Kampala Capital City Authority (Uganda)
LICs	low-income countries
LMICs	lower-middle-income countries
LTU	large taxpayer unit
MLI	Multilateral Instrument (OECD)
MNC	multinational corporation
MTRS	medium-term revenue strategy
NTS	National Tax Service (Republic of Korea)
OECD	Organisation for Economic Co-operation and Development
OGP	Open Government Partnership
OSS	open-source software
P2G	person-to-government
PAYE	pay-as-you-earn
PDIA	problem-driven iterative adaptation
PIT	personal income tax
RFP	request for proposal
RRA	Rwanda Revenue Authority

SAS	Self-Assessment System (Malaysia)
SMEs	small and medium enterprises
SMS	short message service
SRM	sales registration machine
SSC	social security contribution
TADAT	Tax Administration Diagnostic Assessment Tool (IMF)
TEVIES	temporary road user licensing database (Uganda)
TIETP	Tax Incentives for Electronically Traceable Payments
TIN	tax identification number
TIS	Tax Information System (Republic of Korea)
TIWB	Tax Inspectors Without Borders
TREP	Taxpayer Register Expansion Program (Uganda)
UMICs	upper-middle-income countries
UN	United Nations
UNCTAD	United Nations Conference on Trade and Development
URA	Uganda Revenue Authority
URSB	Uganda Registration Services Bureau
VAT	value added tax

CHAPTER 1

Introduction

Tax Compliance: A Persistent Challenge

Questions of how to effectively reform and strengthen tax systems have moved to the center of development debates. On the one hand, recent successes present opportunities for emulation and further progress. In many low- and middle-income countries, governments have achieved significant administrative and policy modernization as well as meaningful improvements in revenue mobilization. On the other hand, successes have been uneven, and major challenges remain. Tax revenue in many countries continues to be well below the level needed to finance achievement of the United Nations' Sustainable Development Goals (figure 1.1)—15 percent of the gross domestic product (GDP) is often cited as a rough minimum annual target (Gaspar, Jaramillo, and Wingender 2016). Meanwhile, revenue collection is frequently characterized by much unfairness and inequity, with especially weak compliance and enforcement among the rich and significant, though overlooked, formal and informal burdens on lower-income groups. There is a growing consensus that these persistent challenges reflect not only technical challenges, but also persistent political barriers to reform (Moore and Prichard 2017).

Observers have likewise questioned whether recent improvements in revenue collection have contributed adequately to the construction of broader social contracts.[1] Revenue collection is not an end in itself. It only becomes socially desirable if it results in efficient, productive spending. Extensive research now documents the ways in which the expansion of taxation may spur greater

FIGURE 1.1 **Total Tax Collection as a Share of GDP, by Region, 1990–2018**

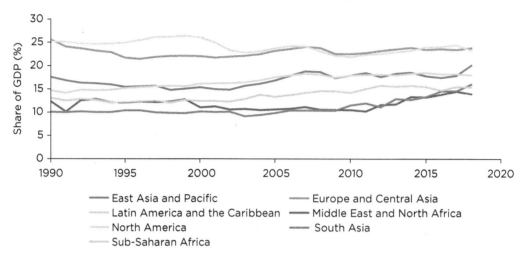

Source: Government Revenue Dataset of the International Centre for Tax and Development, United Nations University World Institute for Development Economics Research (UNU-WIDER), https://www.wider.unu.edu /project/government-revenue-dataset.
Note: "North America" follows the World Bank regional definition, comprising Bermuda, Canada, and the United States.

accountability and contribute to state-building. Yet that research makes clear that, despite success stories, strong connections among taxation, responsiveness, accountability, and state-building are far from guaranteed (PCT 2017; Prichard 2015). This uncertainty has, in part, motivated creation of medium-term revenue strategies (MTRSs)—that is, a medium-term, whole-of-government approach to tax reform. Meanwhile, questions remain about whether current reform efforts are sufficiently aimed at fostering broader development gains (Prichard 2010, 2015, 2016b).

The limited attention paid to building social contracts is evident in, among other things, the scant fiscal redistribution in many low-income countries, reflecting, in part, the weakness of both progressive taxation and redistributive public spending (Lustig 2017). Although the impact of taxes on poverty reduction may look more encouraging when the in-kind value of all government-funded services is considered, there is ample evidence that service delivery targeting the poor is frequently ineffective (Hirvonen, Mascagni, and Roelen 2018). In fact, perception surveys indicate that many citizens of lower-income countries, particularly across Africa, think the taxes they pay do not improve public services (Bratton and Gyimah-Boadi 2016; Isbell 2017).

It is not surprising that inequitable tax burdens, questionable interactions with tax officials, and the poor translation of revenue into services are reflected in the limited trust that much of the low-income world has in tax systems. In the majority of African countries, less than half of taxpayers trust their tax administration, with levels of trust falling below 30 percent in some countries (Isbell 2017). Across Latin America and the Caribbean, trust in government can be as low as 26 percent (Argentina) and 17 percent (Brazil)—see OECD (2020).

This analysis suggests that the central challenge facing reformers lies in both identifying innovative technical strategies to strengthen revenue mobilization and improving trust to enhance compliance, build political support for reform, and reinforce stronger social contracts. Recent research points to possible elements of a strategy, including strengthening the morale of taxpayers, paying more attention to the political challenges of reform, tailoring reform to local contexts and needs, and empowering taxpayers. However, these strands of research have yet to be consistently applied in practice or translated into an overarching vision for reform.

This report develops an integrated framework for strengthening tax compliance and tax reform, especially in lower-income countries. The framework combines three related dimensions of reform: enforcement, facilitation, and trust. This is best understood not as an effort to fundamentally rethink what is known about tax reform, but rather as an attempt to provide policy makers, practitioners, and researchers with a coherent framework to guide reform efforts. By bringing together recent research and lessons from the field about the drivers of tax compliance, this report aims to guide thinking in holistic ways about how to overcome persistent barriers to successful reform. It reviews the main technical and political challenges of reform and outlines approaches to overcoming them—all while emphasizing the importance of solutions tailored to specific national and subnational contexts. Central to the framework is an emphasis on strengthening social contracts as a way to improve tax compliance, but also as a way to build political support for sustainable reform.

The remainder of this chapter reviews traditional approaches to tax reform and summarizes the conceptual framework that underpins this report. In the chapters that follow, this conceptual framework is applied in greater detail to reform challenges related to specific tax instruments and to taxpayer segments. The aim is not to be exhaustive in either the topics covered or in the treatment of those topics. Instead, each chapter applies the framework to specific tax challenges to highlight the value of the overall framework and identify specific opportunities and strategies to strengthen tax compliance and reform.

Traditional Approaches to Tax Reform

Traditionally, approaches to tax reform have stressed the importance of technical measures to strengthen enforcement and, more recently, facilitate tax compliance. This view of reform reflects early models of tax compliance in which the decision to comply took the form of a rational economic calculus: a taxpayer's perceived probability of an audit, exposure to penalties, and risk aversion. Stronger enforcement—increased detection and higher penalties—was thus the key to inducing compliance (Cummings et al. 2009). Over time, these models were complemented by a greater emphasis on *facilitating* tax compliance, recognizing that taxpayers were more likely to comply when doing so was straightforward and low-cost, thereby shifting the rational economic calculus in favor of compliance (Alm et al. 2010; Alm and Torgler 2011).

The corresponding logic of reform has been relatively straightforward: (1) identify contexts where political support for reform appears to exist; (2) invest in strengthening enforcement and facilitation, often heavily informed by international experience (Fjeldstad and Moore 2008; Sanchez 2006); and (3) trust

FIGURE 1.2 **Traditional Theory of Change for Tax Reform**

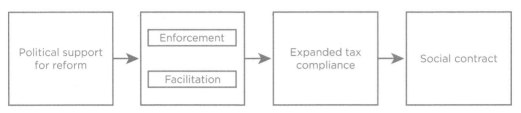

Source: World Bank.

that expanded revenue collection will ultimately translate into broader public benefits. This stylized, and admittedly highly simplified, traditional model of reform is illustrated in figure 1.2.

This dual focus on enforcement and facilitation has underpinned a range of desirable reforms in low- and middle-income countries along with modest, but consistent, revenue gains. Efforts to strengthen enforcement have included investments to expand assessment and audit capacities, new information technology (IT) systems designed to reduce the scope for avoidance, improved collection methods, expanded access to third-party information, and policy changes to reduce the scope for evasion (Slemrod 2018).

Meanwhile, efforts to facilitate compliance—and emphasize "customer service"—have sought, among other things, to simplify reporting requirements; provide easy access to information, support, and advice; offer simple ways to make tax payments, including online, at banks, and via mobile phones; and reduce face-to-face interactions with tax collectors (Fjeldstad and Moore 2008).

Finally, reform efforts have not only targeted taxpayers but also sought to improve the efforts and performance of tax officials to emphasize a customer-oriented approach and reduce collusion, corruption, and simple shirking. These reforms have included pay increases and better career paths, performance-based contracts, increased monitoring of results, efforts to reduce opportunities for corruption and collusion, and a broad emphasis on strengthening the customer orientation of tax administrations (Fjeldstad 2003; Mookherjee 1998; Raballand et al. 2017).

Reform: Progress and Challenges

Despite important successes, efforts to strengthen enforcement and facilitation have not been sufficient to consistently deliver more effective, equitable, and accountable tax systems. In general, taxation of the wealthy remains highly ineffective in many low- and middle-income countries, where the share of revenue from personal income taxes (PIT) is less than half of the share of PIT revenue in high-income countries—one of the largest gaps in revenue mobilization between the two groups of countries (figure 1.3). Subnational tax systems generally fail to generate significant revenues, especially from property taxes, while in areas of weak governance there is mounting evidence of heavy burdens that user fees and demands for informal payments are placing on lower-income groups (Bird 2011; Franzsen and McCluskey 2017; van den Boogaard, Prichard, and Jibao 2019).

FIGURE 1.3 **Composition of Tax Revenue, by Country Income Group, 1990–2018**

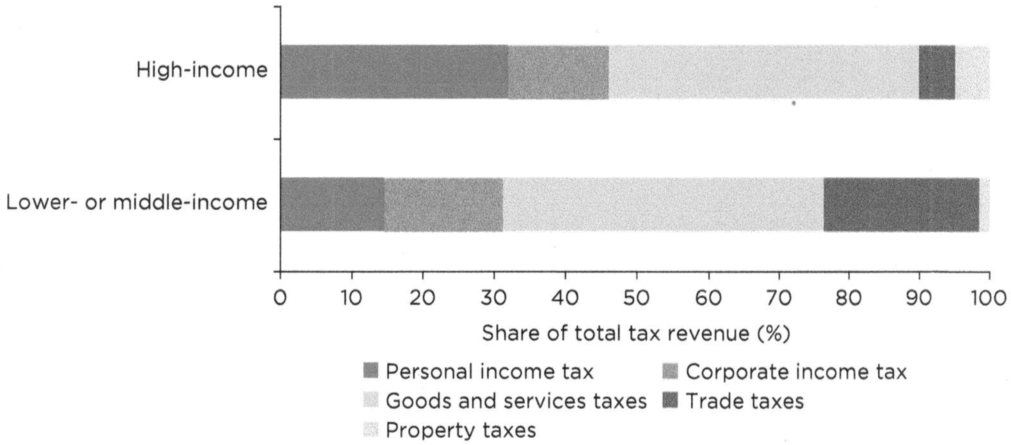

Source: Government Revenue Dataset of the International Centre for Tax and Development, United Nations University World Institute for Development Economics Research (UNU-WIDER), https://www.wider.unu.edu /project/government-revenue-dataset.

Although the value added tax (VAT) has been hailed as a relative success, in lower-income countries its performance has lagged expectations (Baunsgaard and Keen 2010). Corporate tax collection continues to be plagued by extensive and poorly managed exemptions, despite decades of international pressure for better transparency. Meanwhile, recent estimates suggest that revenue losses from international tax avoidance and evasion[2] are larger (as a share of GDP) in low- and middle-income countries than in Organisation for Economic Co-operation and Development (OECD) member states (Cobham and Jansky 2017). In turn, institutional reforms aimed at strengthening IT systems, limiting political interference, reducing corruption, improving transparency, and expanding engagement have frequently underperformed (Ahlerup, Baskaran, and Bigsten 2015; Bird and Zolt 2008; Dom 2019; Moore 2014).

Considerations in Developing Reform Strategies

For those seeking strategies to strengthen reform efforts, four sets of considerations are particularly important: (1) proactively navigating the political challenges of reform; (2) fostering quasi-voluntary tax compliance through trust-building; (3) strengthening social contracts; and (4) tailoring reform strategies to local contexts and constraints. The conceptual framework developed in this report addresses these broad challenges.

Political support. Ample evidence now suggests that, consistent with its role in other aspects of public sector performance, political support is most often the critical factor in the success of tax reform—see box 1.1 (Andrews 2013; McCulloch and Piron 2019; Prichard 2019; World Bank 2017). Many opportunities for reform in low- and middle-income countries have been consistently frustrated, despite being both relatively low-cost and technically straightforward. Although in some cases failures may have been driven by a lack of understanding, particularly among the senior officials who need to sign off on reforms, in most cases lack of political will is the most compelling explanation.

World Development Report 2017

Recognition of the growing importance of politics to tax reform is consistent with the role of politics in other aspects of public sector performance. *World Development Report 2017: Governance and the Law* (WDR 2017) (World Bank 2017) argues that the asymmetries of power that lead to exclusion, capture, and clientelism are at the root of a wide range of development challenges. Tax reform inevitably creates winners and losers and confronts strong vested interests, but it cannot succeed without political support. Even so, broad-based political support is frequently absent owing to perceptions that the system is unfair and to the lack of clear reciprocity and benefits from expanded tax collection. WDR 2017 proposes that it is possible to make progress by

- Transforming incentive structures to enable commitment in the policy arena
- Shifting the preferences and beliefs of those with power
- Enhancing the contestability of the decision-making process.

As in the framework developed here, WDR 2017 ascribes a central role to building trust and expanding fairness: "delivering on commitments feeds ... back into building trust in institutions and strengthening outcome legitimacy." This is most likely where government actions "resonat[e] with peoples' needs and perceptions of fairness." Operationally, more effectively navigating the political barriers to reform by explicitly considering power a relevant factor is likely to involve a combination of opportunism in identifying political opportunities for reform, strategies designed to build a sustainable political foundation for reform, and more effective approaches to assessing the extent of political commitments to reform.

For example, many governments fail to engage in even basic data sharing within tax administrations to identify the most obvious and egregious examples of tax evasion by elite groups, despite clear evidence that such data sharing can yield immediate gains (Kangave et al. 2016, 2018). In other contexts, tax policies have been written in ways that provide obvious opportunities for avoidance and evasion, or that generate poorly justified tax exemptions for certain firms or individuals (Prichard and Moore 2018).

Tax reform inevitably creates winners and losers. It also often threatens the interests of political leaders or tax administrators who may benefit from weak systems that allow for evasion, politicization, and various forms of informality, collusion, and corruption. Because losses tend to be concentrated among a relatively few stakeholders and gains tend to be dispersed across many, it is usually easier for the losers to mobilize against reform, despite the aggregate gains from reform outweighing the losses. Mobilizing the winners of reform to generate broad-based political support is further complicated because of perceptions that the tax system is unfair, without clear reciprocity and benefits from expanded tax collection (Hassan and Prichard 2016; Moore 2017). Mobilizing pro-reform coalitions among taxpayers and within government to overcome staunch political opposition is thus central to successful reform. Yet traditional models of change largely treat political support as exogenous instead of seeking concrete strategies for building support.

Despite the centrality of politics to successful reform, reform strategies have historically been relatively silent on how to identify politically viable reform opportunities, align reform to local political constraints, and build targeted political support for reform. In each area, recent research has provided useful guidance. First, identifying genuine political support for reform can be difficult because governments may express support for reform, but in practice be unable or unwilling to confront vested interests. Recent research suggests that relatively low-cost, technically straightforward but politically costly reform measures, such as improving data sharing, increasing transparency, pursuing existing tax arrears, or tackling obvious sites of tax abuses, may indicate a genuine commitment to reform. The willingness of reformers to tackle such politically costly challenges can be a strong signal of a commitment to reform—and vice versa (Jibao and Prichard 2016). Second, even where broad political support for reform exists, reform must be tailored to the particular constraints that exist in particular contexts, reflecting specific policies, institutions, and power dynamics (Hassan and Prichard 2016). Finally, it is important to identify potential supporters of reform and specific strategies for building their engagement in the reform processes, which, too, are likely to differ across contexts (Fairfield 2010, 2013).

Trust and quasi-voluntary compliance. A growing body of research has highlighted the potential for investments in strengthening trust to foster both quasi-voluntary compliance and broader political support for reform. Yet in practice efforts to build trust have been relatively ad hoc and low priority within many reform programs. In thinking about the drivers of tax compliance, a useful distinction can be drawn between "enforced compliance," which results from the state's enforcement power, and "voluntary" (or "quasi-voluntary") compliance, which is driven by values, social norms, and levels of trust in the fairness, equity, reciprocity, and accountability of tax systems (often collectively referred to as tax morale). The "slippery slope" framework developed by Kirchler, Hoelzl, and Wahl (2008) predicts that compliance will be highest when both enforcement power and trust are high. At the same time, compliance may decline rapidly when either trust or enforcement declines to very low levels. This dynamic reflects the deep interdependence of the two. Trust and voluntary compliance are unlikely in the absence of complementary investments in enforcement, while stronger enforcement is less likely to be politically feasible in the absence of trust, especially in the medium to long term.

Social contracts. A legitimate, responsive state is an essential precondition for raising adequate revenue (Bird, Martinez-Vazquez, and Torgler 2006). Yet it cannot be assumed that tax revenue will be used for public purposes. Ideally, then, strategies to strengthen accountability should be part of tax reform efforts. A broad literature highlights the potential for expanded taxation to spur greater accountability by prompting taxpayers to demand results and generating incentives for governments to make concessions to encourage quasi-voluntary compliance (Dom 2018; Prichard 2015). This process may, in turn, provide the basis for the construction of durable fiscal contracts, which contribute in important ways to social outcomes, strengthening the overall social contract (which includes more than just taxation). However, such positive outcomes are not guaranteed. Although tax authorities will never have direct control over the extent of government reciprocity and accountability, there may be specific aspects of tax reform design that could enhance accountability by empowering popular engagement and demand making. Recent research has referred to these aspects as a "governance-focused tax reform agenda." It would place greater weight on increasing the political salience of taxation (including through direct taxation), increasing horizontal equity in tax enforcement, expanding meaningful transparency around taxation and budgets, and directly supporting popular engagement by giving people more opportunities to have a voice in tax reform (Prichard 2016b).

Contextually appropriate reform strategies. Finally, reform strategies have historically been heavily guided by international best practices, leading researchers to refer to a "global tax reform agenda" (Fjeldstad and Moore 2008). Although this approach has had important benefits, there is growing recognition of the need to also tailor solutions to local needs, capacities, and constraints (Dom and Miller 2018). A growing body of research has highlighted a disconnect between international reform models and the local capacity constraints in lower-income countries, as well as the need to offer simplified reform strategies tailored to local capacities (see, for example, Best et al. 2015; Jibao and Prichard 2015; Prichard and Moore 2018). Similarly, a focus on politics, trust, and social contracts requires strategies for understanding the unique political barriers to reform and the unique drivers of (mis)trust in different contexts.

Toward a Holistic Tax Reform Framework: Integrating Tax Morale and Trust

The main value of the tax reform framework lies in the way it coalesces relatively siloed and fragmented strands of research and practical insight into a coherent approach to tax reform. In recognition of the need for a more holistic way to think about the design of tax reforms, the framework places politics, quasi-voluntary compliance, and the construction of stronger social contracts front and center (figure 1.4). No individual component of this framework is particularly novel or transformative. The best reform programs already do much of what is proposed here, though often in more ad hoc ways. By translating research insights into operational guidance and

FIGURE 1.4 Theory of Change for Innovations in Tax Compliance

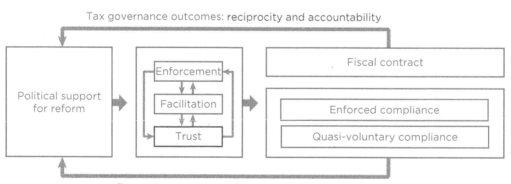

Source: World Bank.

Innovations in Tax Compliance

tools, the framework provides a holistic platform for reform and for conducting systematic research on the effectiveness of these approaches for improving reform outcomes (for a more detailed presentation of the framework and the research that informs it, see Prichard et al. 2019).

The framework is centered on a belief that the effectiveness of reform efforts can be strengthened by emphasizing trust-building alongside a more conventional focus on enforcement and facilitation. By combining complementary investments in enforcement, facilitation, and trust, reformers not only strengthen enforced compliance but also (1) encourage quasi-voluntary compliance; (2) create conditions conducive to strengthening social contracts; and (3) generate sustained political support for reform.

The box in the center of the model in figure 1.4 captures the interconnected nature of investments in enforcement, facilitation, and trust. A key component of trust in the tax system is a belief that everyone pays their fair share and is punished fairly if they do not. This belief depends on adequate enforcement (Touchton, Wampler, and Peixoto 2019). Meanwhile, where there is little trust, it may be impossible to mobilize the necessary political commitment to strengthen enforcement capacity. Investing in measures to strengthen trust is thus also about creating a supportive political environment for expanded enforcement. Ideally, these interconnected investments can set the stage for virtuous circles of reform: successful investments in building trust provide the political capital needed to pursue further reform, while translation of the resulting revenue into public benefits further builds trust and compliance among taxpayers.

Historically, reform programs have often treated political support for reform as largely exogenous, whereas investments in building trust are a concrete strategy for building political support for sustaining and advancing reform. Making political support endogenous through trust-building can occur through two broad channels, reflecting the different dimensions of trust. First, reformers may seek to emphasize the fairness and equity of tax systems ("tax system outcomes"). Second, reformers may seek to strengthen the extent of reciprocity and accountability ("tax governance outcomes"). When taxpayers see visible gains in both dimensions, they will be more willing to support future reform, thus potentially ensuring a virtuous circle of reform. Although such trust-building strategies are not a substitute for the need for committed political leadership, they can reinforce that political support and make it more sustainable over time so that reform reversals are less likely.

Meanwhile, trust-building measures are likely to improve the quality of governance in two broad ways. First, increasing trust in the tax system often goes together with improvements in equity, reciprocity, and accountability—that is, focusing on building trust makes strengthening public benefits an explicit part of reform design. Second, investments in building trust—particularly efforts to introduce meaningful transparency and consultation, to increase the political salience of taxation, to ensure more equitable tax policy and enforcement, and to strengthen taxpayer engagement—can empower taxpayers to successfully demand public benefits from tax revenues.

Although trust has the potential to expand quasi-voluntary compliance, mobilize additional political support for reform, and strengthen the social contract, it also introduces new points of potential resistance to reform. A push for greater fairness in tax implementation may be resisted by tax officials who fear fewer opportunities for collusion and corruption. An expanded emphasis on equity is also likely to be met by resistance from wealthy taxpayers, who often escape their full tax liabilities. Finally, governments themselves may be supportive of increasing revenue collection but resistant to constraints on their spending or to demands for accountability. More narrow technocratic approaches to reform have often been adopted because they have been expedient in the short term. However, both research and experience increasingly indicate that tackling many of the most important reform challenges requires a more holistic approach to shifting the existing political constraints on reform. Reflecting that reality, the model in figure 1.4 is underpinned by broader strategies for navigating political resistance to reform and tailoring reform to specific contexts.

Elements of the Tax Reform Framework: Enforcement, Facilitation, and Trust

This section develops the elements of the conceptual framework—and the role of trust-building, in particular—in greater detail. First, it reviews recent research and evidence on the roles of enforcement and facilitation in strengthening tax systems. It then expands on the role of trust-building as part of strategies for strengthening tax compliance and tax reform. The goal is to highlight potential directions for reform and to provide a framework for prioritizing different reform strategies in different contexts.

The discussion aims to move beyond a singular focus on technical effectiveness. Instead, any approach to reform should be technically effective, politically feasible, and socially desirable. *Technical effectiveness* implies that each intervention—whether related to enforcement, facilitation, or building trust—should be shown to be an effective strategy for improving compliance. *Political feasibility* implies that the reform strategy must either enjoy political support or include a clear strategy for mobilizing it in a sustainable way. *Social desirability* implies that any tax reform should be designed not only to increase revenue but also to do so in a way that is equitable, engages and empowers taxpayers, and creates conditions favorable to the construction of stronger social contracts.

Enforcement

Dominant models of tax compliance have long taken enforcement as the starting point, with research progressively expanding understanding of enforcement tools available to governments. The benchmark model of individual tax compliance developed by Allingham and Sandmo (1972) treats taxpayers as welfare-maximizing economic actors, with their compliance decisions reflecting both the likelihood that noncompliance will be detected and the extent of penalties. Their original model assumed that individual taxpayers would declare their own income, subject to audit, and predicted levels of compliance far lower than those observed in OECD countries (Cummings et al. 2009). Subsequent research has begun to explain this higher-than-expected compliance, focusing especially on the ways in which (third-party) information and tax withholding can dramatically improve enforcement outcomes (Pomeranz 2015). Given this potential, effective and equitable enforcement is likely to remain the bedrock of any successful reform strategy.

Two elements are common among efforts to strengthen enforcement: (1) measures to increase *monitoring of taxpayers* and (2) measures to improve *tax collectors' performance*. Most models of tax compliance, particularly in OECD contexts, have focused on strategies to improve the monitoring of taxpayers. This reflects an assumption that tax collectors are committed to enforcing tax compliance but lack the necessary tools. However, in low- and middle-income country settings some tax collectors may not be fully committed to enforcement, reflecting some combination of shirking behavior, collusion, corruption, or political interference. Networks based on collusion and corruption are often deeply embedded in tax administrations, with rents flowing upward or, in some cases, helping to finance broader state patronage (Hassan and Prichard 2016; Khan, Khwaja, and Olken 2016; Piracha and Moore 2015). In these contexts, improvements in enforced compliance may depend not only on deploying new tools to monitor taxpayers, but also on strengthening rules-based enforcement efforts by tax collectors.

In response to persistent challenges, including capacity constraints in lower-income countries, some researchers and practitioners have advocated simplification to strengthen enforcement, such as streamlining excessively complex business processes (Prichard and Moore 2018). Moreover, simplification could benefit taxpayers by making it easier for them to comply with their tax obligations, facilitating quasi-voluntary tax compliance. Simplifying approaches to taxing income may also reduce the scope for abuse. For example, based on research in Pakistan, Best et al. (2015) present evidence that shifting corporate income taxation away from profits (which are more easily manipulated) in favor of turnover taxes may reduce evasion by 70 percent or more while creating relatively little economic distortion.

Facilitation
Although enforcement remains the bedrock of most reform strategies, efforts to facilitate compliance have become a standard feature of reform programs over the past couple of decades. Reforms aimed at facilitation recognize the role of the tax administration as a provider of services and information that should make compliance as easy as possible. Noncompliance is not solely a function of purposeful evasion (intent). It also may result from taxpayer ignorance, inability to pay, or transaction costs that tip the scales against compliance. Facilitation is often presented as making tax administrations customer friendly, with taxpayers treated as clients rather than potential criminals. The intuition is clear: at the margin, a taxpayer is more likely to comply if the government does not erect hurdles to doing so.

Initially, facilitation efforts were viewed in primarily technical terms. While enforcement efforts sought to raise the cost of noncompliance, facilitation measures aimed to reduce the cost of complying. These kinds of reforms had several key elements, including improving access to information (so that taxpayers understand what is required); cost reduction (via simplification of policies and filing requirements); and reduction of interaction with tax officials (to help reduce compliance time, but also to reduce corruption). Reforms aimed at simplification have reduced unnecessary regulations and the (sometimes large) number of taxes businesses must pay (especially small businesses). In most cases, national governments now collect a relatively small number of taxes (income taxes, VAT, and customs duties, most notably) for which the discretion of tax collectors is comparatively limited and payments can be made in a variety of ways.

Although much remains to be done, in general the costs of compliance have fallen, and the scope for day-to-day corruption and collusion has similarly declined. Globally, the average time required for companies to comply with their tax obligations fell from 324 hours in 2006 to 205 hours in 2019, while the average number of required payments dropped from 34 to 24. However, significant regional differences remain (World Bank 2019). A partial exception to this progress seems to be at the subnational level in many lower-income countries, where revenue systems frequently continue to be characterized by significant complexity, extensive face-to-face interactions between tax collectors and taxpayers, and a wide range of "nuisance taxes" and informal payments. That said, there, too, reforms to simplify tax systems and facilitate compliance appear to be taking root.[3]

Although these facilitation reforms have enjoyed significant success, their impact on compliance is less clear. At some level, there is no doubt that facilitation reforms have led to concrete gains in tax receipts: psychological research makes clear that reducing costs virtually guarantees increased compliance (Alm et al. 2010). In addition, there is some evidence that, for example, the introduction of "one-stop shops" for small-business registration has aided formalization and compliance (Devas and Kelly 2001). Yet there have been few systematic efforts to study the magnitude of these effects, especially in low- and middle-income countries. Additional evidence could help tax agencies allocate resources and confront institutional inertia—or the vested interests slowing implementation of useful reforms.

Trust

Recent research has increasingly stressed the importance of building trust to strengthen tax morale and encourage tax compliance (Chang, Supriyadi, and Torgler 2018). Tax morale is generally defined as capturing "nonpecuniary motivations for tax compliance" (Luttmer and Singhal 2014, 150)—that is, all of the factors other than enforcement and facilitation that may drive tax compliance. Tax morale reflects individual ethics and values, social norms, and the extent of trust in tax systems—and more broadly, fiscal systems. Some of these factors, such as ethics, values, and social norms, vary across individuals and are relatively unrelated to and unconditional on government performance. Trust, on the other hand, is more conditional and depends on the extent to which taxpayers believe they are treated fairly, tax systems are equitable, they receive services in return, and governments are broadly accountable (Prichard, forthcoming). Improvements in trust can thus improve tax morale and contribute to enhanced tax compliance, offering the most immediate target for prospective reformers.

Less frequently emphasized is the importance of building trust to strengthen political support for reform. The conventional view from research is that governments should enhance trust to encourage individual taxpayers to comply with taxes quasi-voluntarily. This narrow focus makes better sense in high-income countries, where the core features of well-functioning tax systems are already in place. By contrast, in most low- and middle-income countries a lack of political support for tax reform is the most immediate barrier to progress. There is even some evidence that tax administrators themselves may be less committed to enforcement where there is little trust in government (Prichard 2016a). In most countries, political leaders have, for example, been unwilling to bear the political costs of expanding revenue collection among elites via income or property taxes. By increasing trust in the tax system, it may be possible to encourage compliance by those elites and equally to mobilize the political support needed for expanded enforcement more broadly. Building trust is thus not a substitute for enforcement; it is a complement. Consistent with this view, research has highlighted the political payoffs from crackdowns on illegal tax evasion (Casaburi and Troiano 2016) and from linking public services more clearly to new revenue collection (Jibao and Prichard 2015; Prichard 2015).

Finally, where governments invest in building trust in tax systems, such a step can directly and indirectly help strengthen the broader social contract. Strategies that focus exclusively on strengthening enforcement and facilitation run the risk of ignoring the broader social objectives of tax systems because they offer no mechanism for increasing the likelihood that revenue will be used to provide public benefits. Strengthening trust implies improving fairness, equity, reciprocity, and accountability. By making expanded trust central to reform, these broader goals are given greater prominence as well. Meanwhile, investments in trust-building—such as efforts to expand transparency or the space for accountability—can also empower taxpayers, increasing their ability over time to demand responsiveness and accountability from governments (Prichard 2015).

Building trust as part of tax reform strategies seems likely to be especially important in low- and middle-income countries, where trust in tax authorities is limited, compliance is poor, and political support for taxation is low. Across 36 countries in 2014–15, Africans expressed more trust in informal institutions such as religious leaders (72 percent) and traditional leaders (61 percent) than in the tax department (on average, 44 percent). More than one-third of Africans report believing that all or some people working for domestic tax agencies are corrupt (Bratton and Gyimah-Boadi 2016; Isbell 2017).

One way to conceptualize the importance of trust-building in lower-income countries is to view it as a strategy for escaping a low-level equilibrium in tax collection. In theory, taxpayers would be willing to pay more taxes in exchange for more effective government services. However, a lack of trust leads to noncompliance and little support for expanded enforcement. Meanwhile, governments would like to collect more revenue, but they are unwilling to bear the short-term political costs of increasing enforcement and do not trust that taxpayers will reward them politically, even if new revenue translates into better services. Neither side wants to move first. Building trust could help to break this impasse by making tax reform more popular, thereby generating both short- and long-term political payoffs to reform.[4]

Conceptualizing Trust

Converting the growing interest in building trust into practice requires clearer definitions, concepts, and strategies that lead to understanding what it means to strengthen trust in tax systems and how that might be achieved. Definitions of trust vary across disciplines, but they generally refer to whether governments are behaving "in accordance with normative expectations" and whether they will continue to do so (Miller and Listhaug 1990). As important, an individual's degree of trust is consistently understood to be a learned behavior, shaped by changing experiences and social norms, rather than a stable personality trait. Levels of trust in government fluctuate in response to who is in power, which policies are adopted, and how they are implemented. More simply, concrete government action can drive greater trust, expanded compliance, and broader support for tax reform.

Although research has conceptualized trust in diverse ways, the framework described here deepens the "trust" component of the overarching conceptual framework presented in figure 1.4 by breaking it down into four key drivers, capturing the extent of perceived

- *Fairness,* whereby tax systems are fairly and competently designed and administered

- *Equity,* whereby burdens are equitably distributed, and everyone pays their share

- *Reciprocity,* whereby tax revenues are translated into reciprocal publicly provided goods and services

- *Accountability,* whereby governments administering tax systems are accountable to taxpayers.

This framework does not capture every possible dimension of trust, but it does focus attention on elements that map naturally onto specific objectives of tax reform efforts. As noted earlier, these components of trust can be usefully divided into two broad types: (1) elements specifically related to the functioning of the tax system (fairness and equity); and (2) elements related to the broader use of tax revenue by the government (reciprocity and accountability). The first set—tax system outcomes—fall within the traditional remit of tax reform efforts. Those responsible for tax policy and administration can, with the political license to do so, directly improve fairness and equity in both policy and administration.

By contrast, the second set—tax governance outcomes—are not directly under the control of tax authorities. Although tax administrations are accountable to taxpayers (for example, by acting on their concerns), there is a broader element of accountability involved in building trust with the government at large. In these cases, tax governance outcomes depend on the broader actions of government in delivering reciprocal services or expanding political accountability. Even a politically empowered tax agency cannot guarantee improved reciprocity in service delivery because it depends on the engagement of a broader set of government actors.

When trust is expanded—which implies that governments have both the positive intent (integrity) and the technical competence to increase fairness, equity, reciprocity, and accountability—this leads to expanded tax morale while also shaping norms of compliance. Tax morale, in turn, drives two broad outcomes: enhanced quasi-voluntary tax compliance and enhanced political support for current and future reform.

Ultimately, it is important to understand the construction of trust around tax compliance in active, reciprocal terms. Trust is not, in and of itself, socially beneficial. Blind trust in government can undermine long-term reform by reducing citizens' demands for improved outcomes (Hardin 1999). Trust is, instead, something built through reciprocal action by taxpayers and governments. In the language of political science and sociology, the goal is not simply to foster trust among citizens but to foster the trustworthiness of governments (Levi and Stoker 2000).

The next subsections explore each component of trust in greater detail for both individuals and businesses.

Fairness

Fairness captures the extent to which taxpayers believe the process for paying taxes is fairly designed and administered. This includes taxpayers understanding, among other things, the system itself, their treatment by tax collectors, the fairness of penalties, and the availability of recourse in cases of abuse. This component of trust broadly combines the categories of procedural justice and retributive justice from economic psychology and is fundamentally about how individual taxpayers experience tax administrators and the tax system. Taxpayers (either individuals or businesses) are more likely to comply if they feel that they have been treated respectfully, honestly, and impartially (Fjeldstad and Tungodden 2003; Picciotto 2007; Shapiro and Slemrod 2003).

Limitations to taxpayer knowledge. One source of perceived unfairness in many low- and middle-income countries is the limited understanding of both individuals and some (particularly small) businesses of the taxes they are required to pay and how to pay them. According to the Afrobarometer surveys, over 55 percent of taxpayers reported that it was "difficult" or "very difficult" to find out what taxes they are supposed to pay to the government.[5]

Arbitrary or abusive tax enforcement. Another source of unfairness is arbitrary or abusive enforcement, and extraction, by tax collectors. Surveys indicate that tax agencies are frequently among the least-trusted institutions—and those most likely to be involved in corruption—in many low- and middle-income countries (see, for example, Fjeldstad 2005).

Arbitrary or punitive penalties. Yet another source of unfairness is the arbitrary or highly punitive penalties related to some taxes, both formal and informal. In some low-income countries, enforcement can be highly punitive for infractions related to smaller taxes (Fjeldstad and Semboja 2001; Fjeldstad and Therkildsen 2008). Even for somewhat larger businesses, however, punitive enforcement measures (such as closing businesses) can be a double-edged sword. Here the reform goal is, in principle, simple: put in place penalties that are sufficient to encourage compliance but not excessive and, critically, that are consistently applied.

Tax uncertainty for businesses. Especially for businesses, the predictability of tax enforcement likely figures centrally in compliance decisions. Research suggests that predictability—and not only related to taxation (Campos, Lien, and Pradhan 1999)—is important for businesses because it facilitates planning and investment, while predictably equitable enforcement ensures a level competitive playing field (Hassan and Prichard 2016). Reflecting this logic, a recent OECD study goes so far as to use measures of "tax certainty" as a direct proxy for business tax morale because of the current absence of alternative measures and survey data (OECD 2019).

Links with tax policy and forecasting. Inappropriate tax policies and problems with revenue forecasting sometimes are at the root of unfair tax administration. This may be true where tax policies offer significant subjectivity in the assessment of tax liabilities—such as the "market value" systems of property tax assessment or presumptive tax systems based on administrative estimation of turnover. A different problem can arise at the level of revenue forecasting. In many if not most cases, revenue forecasting is highly imprecise, which can expand incentives for tax collectors to engage in arbitrary extraction to meet targets (Piracha and Moore 2015).

Equity

Equity captures the extent to which the tax burden is believed to be fairly distributed across taxpayers. There is now considerable evidence that taxpayers are less likely to comply—or to support higher taxes—when they feel that the distribution is unfair. Put differently, although taxpayers may be willing to pay their "fair share," they are more likely to oppose taxation when they feel others are not paying enough. The term *equity* captures two distinct dimensions: horizontal and vertical equity.

Horizontal equity. Horizontal equity asks whether there are large differences in tax burdens among otherwise similar taxpayers owing to unequal tax policies or unequal enforcement. The most conspicuous, and problematic, horizontal inequity in most countries appears to result from unequal enforcement of many taxes. If the enforcement efforts of tax administrations are selectively targeting, or selectively ignoring, certain classes of taxpayers that otherwise have the same income, the principle of horizontal equity will be violated. To some extent, this violation is inevitable because risk management usually includes factors beyond income believed to be associated with evasion and avoidance (Carfora, Pansini, and Pisani 2017; Scotchmer 1987). More problematic, but more difficult to document precisely, is the perception that those with strong connections within government and the administration are better able to minimize or avoid taxes (Lin et al. 2018).

Vertical equity. Vertical equity asks whether the distribution of the tax burden is equitable across the income and wealth spectrum. This depends to an important degree on societal beliefs about what a "fair" vertical distribution of the tax burden looks like. In most countries, there is a broad belief that individual tax burdens should be progressive—in other words, that the rich should pay more, as a share of income or wealth, than those who are less well off. To achieve the goal of vertical equity, most tax systems rely on a subset of progressive tax policies such as income taxes with progressive rates. Whether tax systems as a whole are vertically equitable will depend on the balance between progressive taxes and other taxes and fees that may be less progressive or impose relatively heavier burdens on lower-income groups. It will also depend on the effectiveness of the tax administration, which can be a source of vertical inequities if administrative efforts—or the government's willingness to collect tax—vary along the income distribution (Bachas, Jaef, and Jensen 2019).

Reciprocity

Reciprocity, perhaps the most intuitive of the four elements underlying trust in tax systems, lies at the core of the social contract. It is the idea that tax revenues will contribute to the provision of valued public goods and services. This concept is frequently at the heart of government outreach and education campaigns, which stress the need for taxes to fund national development. The operational question for governments is whether taxpayers believe that taxes are, in fact, used for national development and, if not, how to build greater trust.

Taxpayers' beliefs. Surveys in low- and middle-income countries suggest that taxpayers are, at least in principle, strong believers in the importance of taxation to fund government. Afrobarometer survey data find that two-thirds of respondents on average believe that citizens should pay their taxes to support national development (Aiko and Logan 2014). Accordingly, there is mounting empirical evidence that the use of tax revenue for public goods is associated with higher levels of tax morale and compliance (Ali, Fjeldstad, and Sjursen 2013; Ortega, Ronconi, and Sanguinetti 2016). The core challenge facing governments is thus to demonstrate to taxpayers that tax revenues are in fact being used to fund national development.

Increasing transparency. Assuming that governments are genuinely committed to improving services, increasing transparency is one strategy for achieving improvements in public trust. At the local government level, this may mean publishing documents detailing revenue raised and public expenditure by project and category. At the national level, a growing number of countries publish (sometimes in newspapers) all public spending projects, thereby allowing more targeted monitoring of public expenditures. In Kenya, for example, civil society groups have sought to explicitly link citizens' status as taxpayers to their expenditure tracking advocacy (Prichard 2015). However, there are important concerns about the efficacy of transparency initiatives alone. The availability of information is only likely to encourage trust if taxpayers can access, understand, and use the information, and if it proves that the government's performance is indeed meeting popular expectations (van den Boogaard et al., forthcoming). Transparency about poor performance may, in fact, reinforce a lack of trust in public authorities.

Earmarking tax revenue. If transparency or communication-based initiatives seem inadequate for increasing trust, earmarking revenues may be an option. Earmarking is a way to link specific revenue collection more explicitly to specific public expenditures, either formally or informally. Experiences from Norway suggest that earmarking may significantly heighten political support for tax increases (Sælen and Kallbekken 2011). Ghana has produced similar evidence as well (Prichard 2015). However, there are important trade-offs in explicitly linking taxes to services. Conceptually, taxes are generally intended to be unrequited payments to government, and such earmarking risks creating expectations—particularly among the wealthy—that they should receive quite narrow and direct benefits from tax payments. More pragmatically, the expansion of earmarks can create problematic budget rigidity, while budget fungibility means that earmarks can become political theater and complicate budget processes without actually driving improvements in service delivery (Bird and Jun 2005). These risks are a reminder that earmarking almost certainly should be used cautiously and with clear justification.

Accountability
While the desire for reciprocity captures taxpayers' interest in receiving public goods and services, a demand for accountability captures their desire for an institutionalized voice in shaping how tax and spending decisions are made. The goals of reciprocity and accountability do, however, overlap: the goal of accountability is often to provide an institutionalized way for taxpayers to demand and ensure reciprocity. But the goals are also meaningfully distinct: whereas reciprocity implies that governments are making potentially time-limited concessions to taxpayers, institutionalized accountability is intended to ensure that reciprocity is sustained. To an extent, ensuring accountability can help to address time inconsistencies in promises to increase reciprocity in exchange for higher taxation (Aidt and Magris 2006). As important, accountability may have an independent value to those who are granted a voice in shaping tax and spending decisions.

Citizen participation. Evidence suggests that lower corruption, as well as participatory budgeting and other forms of direct democracy, are associated with higher tax compliance. Two studies from Brazil support these ideas. One finds that evidence of corruption reduces property tax receipts and increases demands for participatory budgeting (Timmons and Garfias 2015). The other, a World Bank study, demonstrates that the presence of participatory governance institutions is closely associated with the ability of municipal governments to raise local tax revenue (Touchton, Wampler, and Peixoto 2019).

Private sector engagement. The importance of accountability in shaping trust and tax compliance among business taxpayers has been underresearched, although some key messages have begun to emerge. In general, businesses appear more involved than individuals in the creation of specific narrow forums for participation in shaping government action because these forums may most directly address their core interests and concerns.

Summary: Targeted Approaches to Building Trust
A critical challenge for reformers thus lies in identifying the right kinds of local strategies for building trust among groups of taxpayers who are significant contributors to revenue or political support for reform. There are likely to be distinct drivers of (mis)trust among groups of taxpayers, and the taxpayers who are most important to reform objectives will likewise vary, depending on reform objectives and the dynamics of particular contexts. The best strategies will be able to identify the specific concerns of targeted groups, as well as tailored solutions for addressing them. Taxpayers will increasingly trust the government if the government can successfully deliver fairness, equity, reciprocity, and accountability. Governments will increasingly trust taxpayers if taxpayers increase their tax compliance in response to improved government performance and openness. Because of the limited public trust in public authorities, improvements are likely to be incremental. The payoff for governments is clear: not only greater tax compliance but also greater political support for continued reform and expanded enforcement.

Tailoring Reform: Combining Enforcement, Facilitation, and Trust to Strengthen Social Contracts
A key challenge for governments lies in finding the right combination of enforcement, facilitation, and trust-building measures to achieve both revenue gains and broader development goals. Here, the research thus far has comparatively

little to say. Although all of these factors clearly matter, it is less clear how to best combine, prioritize, or sequence them. Most likely, the answer will depend on identifying the specific objectives and constraints in various contexts, while viewing enforcement, facilitation, and trust as complementary, rather than distinct, strategies. This approach requires carefully defining local reform priorities, analyzing the local politics of reform, identifying the binding constraints to improved outcomes, and focusing on developing evidence-based paths to trust-building.

Successful implementation of the framework laid out here is likely to depend on tailoring reform to local contexts, but this report does not spell out specific tax reform strategies or trajectories. Instead, it reviews key challenges and barriers to tax reform and, drawing on discrete research findings, describes how investments in enforcement, facilitation, and trust have been used in the past to provide a more holistic framework for thinking about future reform. It also lays the groundwork for developing tools to consistently transform research findings into operational outcomes and provides a platform for conducting systematic research on the effectiveness of these approaches to reform.

Reflecting this commitment to translating research evidence into practice, an operational toolkit has been developed to complement this report. It is designed to support assessments of challenges to tax compliance and tax reform in particular contexts and to help identify contextually appropriate and politically informed reform strategies. While beyond the scope of what is discussed here, the operational toolkit is built around a four-part analysis: (1) a technical assessment; (2) an assessment of taxpayer trust; (3) a political economy analysis; and (4) a binding constraints analysis. The technical assessment explores the underlying challenges of tax policy and administration that limit progress on reform. The technical assessment is complemented by a taxpayer survey intended to dive deeper into taxpayers' relationships with the tax administration to uncover trust bottlenecks. The political economy analysis seeks to understand the political barriers to reform, assess what kinds of reform may be politically feasible, and suggest strategies for designing incentive-compatible reform, minimizing political resistance and building more sustainable political support for reform. Finally, the binding constraints analysis pulls together those distinct elements to support governments in identifying the most immediate priorities for unlocking improved performance in particular contexts. The operational toolkit and conceptual framework complement existing frameworks and diagnostics such as the MTRS and the Tax Administration Diagnostic Assessment Tool (TADAT) by explicitly integrating political economy, the role of trust, and an emphasis on targeting binding constraints to reform (box 1.2).

In emphasizing the role of trust-building in reform design, the goal is not only about taxing more, but taxing better. Research has provided a broad picture of strategies to empower taxpayer voices as part of tax reform, including expanding the political salience of taxation, improving horizontal equity in enforcement, strengthening transparency and the links between revenue and expenditures, and supporting institutional space for engagement between taxpayers and governments (Prichard 2015; van den Boogaard et al., forthcoming). All of these approaches overlap closely with strategies for increasing trust, compliance, and political support for reform. Thus there is a clear

BOX 1.2

Diagnostics and Programmatic Approaches to Tax Reform

A medium-term revenue strategy (MTRS) aims to strengthen political ownership of tax reform and provide a comprehensive medium-term perspective on reform objectives. It presents an overarching vision of the objectives of tax system reform, while establishing an appropriate institutional setting and stakeholder engagement. The Tax Administration Diagnostic Assessment Tool (TADAT) is a technical "health" assessment of the effectiveness of critical tax administration functions, processes, and institutions.

The framework developed here draws on these resources and provides insights into how to concretely advance reform efforts. An MTRS helps to define what government reformers want to achieve. TADAT is a detailed assessment of what currently works well and less well. In turn, the framework described here seeks to answer this question: What should governments prioritize concretely to advance in their reform objectives? The MTRS objectives and TADAT technical assessment—when available—are taken as starting points. The framework then, after considering the political constraints to reform and exploring the role of (mis)trust in shaping compliance and support for reform, combines the technical, political, and trust diagnostics in order to assess what reform strategies and priorities are most appropriate in specific local contexts.

argument for reformers to place greater emphasis on trust-building, not only to increase revenue collection but also to support the translation of new revenues into broader social benefits.

Organization of This Report

The remainder of this report is organized as follows. Chapters 2–6 apply the reform framework to specific tax topics. Each chapter introduces the compliance challenges and barriers to reform common to the taxation of a taxpayer segment—individuals and households, high-net-worth individuals, large corporations, small and medium enterprises (SMEs), and subnational taxpayers—and considers options for improving quasi-voluntary compliance and building political support for reform by combining reforms targeting enforcement, facilitation, and trust.

The focus on specific groups of taxpayers, rather than tax types, reflects the logic of the framework developed here. Each group of taxpayers presents distinctive political challenges, needs, and opportunities for trust-building. The focus on compliance implies an emphasis on tax administration as opposed to tax policy, because that is where the largest operational compliance problems tend to be. However, that does not mean tax policy is not addressed. In fact, the link between policy and administration is a key part of the framework. Tax policy choices directly affect the distribution of the tax burden and therefore perceptions of the trustworthiness of the tax system. Tax policy choices also shape the nature of administrative challenges. Although the emphasis is on administration of the tax system, links with tax policy are highlighted where they are important for understanding the challenges to improving tax compliance.

Chapters 2–6 are structured as follows:

- *The tax compliance challenge.* The first section spells out the key challenges to improving tax compliance in a particular segment of taxpayer.

- *Barriers to reform.* This section identifies the binding technical and political barriers that complicate progress on reform.

- *Reform progress—and future options.* Based on a review of the academic and policy literature, this section revisits reform options across the enforcement, facilitation, and trust dimensions.

- *Conclusion.* The final section brings together the different parts and highlights the key messages.

Chapter 7, the final thematic chapter, focuses on the crosscutting role of technology, reflecting the centrality of technology across many reform initiatives. Technology plays an important role not only in strengthening enforcement and facilitation, but also in building trust. Chapter 8 offers conclusions.

The aim is not to be exhaustive in either the set of topics covered or the treatment of those topics. Instead, the goal of the thematic chapters is threefold: (1) to illustrate the ways in which the conceptual framework developed here may shift understanding of tax reform challenges; (2) to reflect on how that understanding can support the development of reform strategies that contribute not only to expanded revenue collection but also to strengthening the social contract; and (3) to offer concrete illustrations of the ways in which an expanded focus on trust-building, political analysis, tailored approaches to reform and strengthening of the social contract can drive distinctive, and hopefully more effective, approaches to designing and implementing reform programs.

Notes

1. Taxation is an integral part of many social contracts. It contributes to state-building through "tax bargaining" between citizens and governments, which underpins an exchange between citizens and governments. In tax bargaining, increased tax collection is exchanged for greater responsiveness and accountability. This process may, in turn, provide the basis for the construction of durable fiscal contracts, which contribute in important ways to social outcomes, strengthening the overall social contract (which includes more than just taxation).

2. Tax avoidance refers to the use of legal methods to minimize one's tax liability. Tax evasion refers to the illegal concealment of income or information from tax authorities.

3. For example, Englebert and Kasongo (2014) and Paler et al. (2017) document the huge range of subnational taxes and fees that exist in the Democratic Republic of Congo, as well as tentative government efforts to begin to reduce the range of such payments.

4. Lagos, Nigeria, offers an interesting example of this kind of positive dynamic (Cheeseman and de Gramont 2017).

5. Afrobarometer, Round 6, 2014/15, http://www.afrobarometer.org.

References

Ahlerup, P., T. Baskaran, and R. Bigsten. 2015. "Tax Innovations and Public Revenues in Sub-Saharan Africa." *Journal of Development Studies* 51 (6): 689–706.

Aidt, T. S., and F. Magris. 2006. "Capital Taxation and Electoral Accountability." *European Journal of Political Economy* 22 (2): 277–91.

Aiko, R., and C. Logan. 2014. "Africa's Willing Taxpayers Thwarted by Opaque Tax Systems, Corruption." Policy Paper No. 7, Afrobarometer, Accra, Ghana.

Ali, M., O-H. Fjeldstad, and I. Sjursen. 2013. "To Pay or Not to Pay? Citizens' Attitudes toward Taxation in Kenya, Tanzania, Uganda, and South Africa." *World Development* 64: 828–42.

Allingham, M. G., and A. Sandmo. 1972. "Income Tax Evasion: A Theoretical Analysis." *Journal of Public Economics* 1 (3–4): 323–38.

Alm, J., T. Cherry, M. Jones, and M. McKee. 2010. "Taxpayer Information Assistance Services and Tax Compliance Behavior." *Journal of Economic Psychology* 31 (4): 577–86.

Alm, J., and B. Torgler. 2011. "Do Ethics Matter? Tax Compliance and Morality." *Journal of Business Ethics* 101 (4): 635–51.

Andrews, M. 2013. *The Limits of Institutional Reform in Development: Changing Rules for Realistic Solutions*. Cambridge, UK: Cambridge University Press.

Bachas, P., R. N. F. Jaef, and A. Jensen. 2019. "Size-Dependent Tax Enforcement and Compliance: Global Evidence and Aggregate Implications." *Journal of Development Economics* 140: 203–22.

Baunsgaard, T., and M. Keen. 2010. "Tax Revenue and (or?) Trade Liberalization." *Journal of Public Economics* 94 (9–10): 563–77.

Best, M., A. Brockmeyer, H. Jacobsen Kleven, J. Spinnewijn, and M. Waseem. 2015. "Production versus Revenue Efficiency with Limited Tax Capacity: Theory and Evidence from Pakistan." *Journal of Political Economy* 123 (6): 131–55.

Bird, R. 2011. "Subnational Taxation in Developing Countries: A Review of the Literature." *Journal of International Commerce, Economics and Policy* 2 (1): 139–61.

Bird, R., and J. Jun. 2005. "Earmarking in Theory and Korean Practice." International Studies Program Working Paper No. 05-15, Andrew Young School of Policy Studies, Georgia State University, Atlanta.

Bird, R., J. Martinez-Vazquez, and B. Torgler. 2006. "Societal Institutions and Tax Effort in Developing Countries." In *The Challenges of Tax Reform in the Global Economy*, edited by J. Alm, J. Martinez-Vazquez, and M. Rider, 283–338. New York: Springer.

Bird, R., and E. Zolt. 2008. "Technology and Taxation in Developing Countries: From Hand to Mouse." *National Tax Journal* 61 (4): 791–821.

Bratton, M., and E. Gyimah-Boadi. 2016. "Do Trustworthy Institutions Matter for Development? Corruption, Trust, and Government Performance in Africa." Dispatch No. 112, Afrobarometer, Accra, Ghana.

Campos, J. E., D. Lien, and S. Pradhan. 1999. "The Impact of Corruption on Investment: Predictability Matters." *World Development* 27 (6): 1059–67.

Carfora, A., R. V. Pansini, and S. Pisani. 2017. "Regional Tax Evasion and Audit Enforcement." *Regional Studies* 52 (3): 362–73.

Casaburi, L., and U. Troiano. 2016. "Ghost-House Busters: The Electoral Response to a Large Anti Tax Evasion Program." *Quarterly Journal of Economics* 131 (1): 273–314.

Chang, H. F., M. W. Supriyadi, and B. Torgler. 2018. "Trust and Tax Morale." In *The Oxford Handbook of Social and Political Trust,* edited by E. M. Uslaner. Oxford, UK: Oxford University Press.

Cheeseman, N., and D. de Gramont. 2017. "Managing a Mega-City: Learning the Lessons from Lagos." *Oxford Review of Economic Policy* 33 (3): 457–77.

Cobham, A., and P. Jansky. 2017. "Global Distribution of Revenue Loss from Tax Avoidance: Re-Estimation and Country Results." Working Paper No. 2017/55, United Nations University World Institute for Development Economics Research (UNU-WIDER), Helsinki.

Cummings, R. G., J. Martinez-Vazquez, M. McKee, and B. Torgler. 2009. "Tax Morale Affects Tax Compliance: Evidence from Surveys and an Artefactual Field Experiment." *Journal of Economic Behavior and Organization* 70 (3): 447–57.

Devas, N., and R. Kelly. 2001. "Regulation or Revenues? An Analysis of Local Business Licences, with a Case Study of the Single Business Permit Reform in Kenya." *Public Administration and Development* 21 (5): 381–91.

Dom, R. 2018. "Taxation and Accountability in Sub-Saharan Africa: New Evidence for a Governance Dividend." Working Paper No. 544, Overseas Development Institute, London.

Dom, R. 2019. "Semi-Autonomous Revenue Authorities in Sub-Saharan Africa: Silver Bullet or White Elephant." *Journal of Development Studies* 55 (7): 1418–35.

Dom, R., and M. Miller. 2018. "Reforming Tax Systems in the Developing World: What Can We Learn from the Past?" ODI Report, Overseas Development Institute, London.

Englebert, P., and E. Kasongo. 2014. "Essor provincial et asphyxie locale: Paradoxe des réformes de décentralisation en RD Congo." *Décentralisation et espaces de pouvoir* (2014): 51–63.

Fairfield, T. 2010. "Business Power and Tax Reform: Taxing Income and Profits in Chile and Argentina." *Latin American Politics and Society* 52 (2): 37–71.

Fairfield, T. 2013. "Going Where the Money Is: Strategies for Taxing Economic Elites in Unequal Democracies." *World Development* 47: 42–57.

Fjeldstad, O.-H. 2003. "Fighting Fiscal Corruption: Lessons from the Tanzania Revenue Authority." *Public Administration and Development* 23 (2): 165–75.

Fjeldstad, O-H. 2005. "Corruption in Tax Administration: Lessons from Institutional Reforms in Uganda." Working Paper No. 2005:10, Chr. Michelsen Institute, Bergen, Norway.

Fjeldstad, O.-H., and M. Moore. 2008. "Tax Reform and State-Building in a Globalised World." In *Taxation and State-Building in Developing Countries: Capacity and Consent*, edited by D. Brautigam, O.-H. Fjeldstad, and M. Moore, 235–60. Cambridge, UK: Cambridge University Press.

Fjeldstad, O-H., and J. Semboja. 2001. "Why People Pay Taxes: The Case of the Development Levy in Tanzania." *World Development* 29 (12): 2059–74.

Fjeldstad, O-H., and O. Therkildsen. 2008. "Mass Taxation and State-Society Relations in East Africa." In *Taxation and State-Building in Developing Countries: Capacity and Consent*, edited by D. Brautigam, O-H. Fjeldstad, and M. Moore, 114–34. Cambridge, UK: Cambridge University Press.

Fjeldstad, O-H., and B. Tungodden. 2003. "Fiscal Corruption: A Vice or a Virtue?" *World Development* 31 (8): 1459–67.

Franzsen, R., and W. McCluskey, eds. 2017. *Property Tax in Africa: Status, Challenges, and Prospects*. Cambridge, MA: Lincoln Institute for Land Policy.

Gaspar, V., L. Jaramillo, and M. P. Wingender. 2016. "Tax Capacity and Growth: Is There a Tipping Point?" IMF Working Paper WP/16/234, International Monetary Fund, Washington, DC.

Hardin, R. 1999. "Do We Want Trust in Government?" In *Democracy and Trust*, edited by M. E. Warren, 22–41. Cambridge, UK: Cambridge University Press.

Hassan, M., and W. Prichard. 2016. "The Political Economy of Domestic Tax Reform in Bangladesh: Political Settlements, Informal Institutions and the Negotiation of Reform." *Journal of Development Studies* 52 (12): 1704–21.

Hirvonen, K., G. Mascagni, and K. Roelen. 2018. "Linking Taxation and Social Protection: Evidence on Redistribution and Poverty Reduction in Ethiopia." *International Social Security Review* 71 (1): 3–24.

Isbell, T. 2017. "Tax Compliance: Africans Affirm Civic Duty but Lack Trust in Tax Department." Policy Paper No. 43, Afrobarometer, Accra, Ghana.

Jibao, S., and W. Prichard. 2015. "The Political Economy of Property Tax in Africa: Explaining Reform Outcomes in Sierra Leone." *African Affairs* 114 (456): 404–31.

Jibao, S., and W. Prichard. 2016. "Rebuilding Local Government Finances after Conflict: Lessons from a Reform Programme in Post-Conflict Sierra Leone." *Journal of Development Studies* 52 (12): 1759–75.

Kangave, J., S. Nakato, R. Waiswa, and P. Lumala Zzimbe. 2016. "Boosting Revenue Collection through Taxing High Net Worth Individuals: The Case of Uganda." Working Paper No. 45, International Centre for Tax and Development, Brighton, UK.

Kangave, J., S. Nakato, R. Waiswa, M. Nalukwago, and P. Lumala Zzimbe. 2018. "What Can We Learn from the Uganda Revenue Authority's Approach to Taxing High Net Worth Individuals?" Working Paper No. 72, International Centre for Tax and Development, Brighton, UK.

Khan, A., A. Khwaja, and B. Olken. 2016. "Tax Farming Redux: Experimental Evidence on Performance Pay for Tax Collectors." *Quarterly Journal of Economics* 131 (1): 219–71.

Kirchler, E., E. Hoelzl, and I. Wahl. 2008. "Enforced versus Voluntary Tax Compliance: The 'Slippery Slope' Framework." *Journal of Economic Psychology* 29 (2): 210–25.

Levi, M., and L. Stoker. 2000. "Political Trust and Trustworthiness." *Annual Review of Political Science* 3 (1): 475–507.

Lin, K. Z., L. F. Mills, F. Zhang, and Y. Li. 2018. "Do Political Connections Weaken Tax Enforcement Effectiveness?" *Contemporary Accounting Research* 35 (4): 1941–72.

Lustig, N. 2017. "Fiscal Policy, Income Redistribution and Poverty Reduction in Low and Middle Income Countries." Working Paper 448, Center for Global Development, Washington, DC.

Luttmer, E., and M. Singhal. 2014. "Tax Morale." *Journal of Economic Perspectives* 28 (4): 149–68.

McCulloch, N., and L-H. Piron. 2019. "Thinking and Working Politically: Learning from Practice." *Development Policy Review* 37 (S1): 1–15.

Miller, A., and O. Listhaug. 1990. "Political Parties and Confidence in Government: A Comparison of Norway, Sweden and the United States." *British Journal of Political Science* 20 (3): 357–86.

Mookherjee, D. 1998. "Incentive Reforms in Developing Country Bureaucracies: Lessons from Tax Administration." In *Annual World Bank Conference on Development Economics 1997,* edited by B. Pleskovic and J. E. Stiglitz, 103–25. Washington, DC: World Bank.

Moore, M. 2014. "Revenue Reform and State Building in Anglophone Africa." *World Development* 60: 99–112.

Moore, M. 2017. "The Political Economy of Long-Term Revenue Decline in Sri Lanka." Working Paper No. 65, International Centre for Tax and Development, Brighton, UK.

Moore, M., and W. Prichard. 2017. "How Can Governments of Low-Income Countries Collect More Tax Revenue?" Working Paper No. 70, International Centre for Tax and Development, Brighton, UK.

OECD (Organisation for Economic Co-operation and Development). 2019. "What Is Driving Tax Morale?" Public consultation document, OECD, Paris.

OECD (Organisation for Economic Co-operation and Development). 2020. *Government at a Glance: Latin America and the Caribbean 2020.* Paris: OECD Publishing.

Ortega, D., L. Ronconi, and P. Sanguinetti. 2016. "Reciprocity and Willingness to Pay Taxes: Evidence from a Survey Experiment in Latin America." *Economía* 16 (2): 55–87.

Paler, L., W. Prichard, R. Sanchez de la Sierra, and C. Samii. 2017. *Survey on Total Tax Burden in the DRC, Final Report.* Kinshasa: Department for International Development.

PCT (Platform for Collaboration on Tax). 2017. "Concept Note on the Medium-Term Revenue Strategy (MTRS). Platform for Collaboration on Tax." International Monetary Fund, Organisation for Economic Co-operation and Development, United Nations, and World Bank Group, Washington, DC.

Picciotto, S. 2007. "Constructing Compliance: Game Playing, Tax Law, and the Regulatory State." *Law and Policy* 29 (1): 11–30.

Piracha, M., and M. Moore. 2015. "Understanding Low-Level State Capacity: Property Tax Collection in Pakistan." Working Paper No. 33, International Centre for Tax and Development, Brighton, UK.

Pomeranz, D. 2015. "No Taxation without Information: Deterrence and Self-Enforcement in the Value Added Tax." *American Economic Review* 105 (8): 2539–69.

Prichard, W. 2010. "Taxation and State Building: Towards a Governance Focused Tax Reform Agenda." Working Paper No. 341, Institute of Development Studies, Brighton, UK.

Prichard, W. 2015. *Taxation, Responsiveness and Accountability in Sub-Saharan Africa: The Dynamics of Tax Bargaining.* Cambridge, UK: Cambridge University Press.

Prichard, W. 2016a. "Electoral Competitiveness, Tax Bargaining and Political Budget Cycles and Taxation in Developing Countries." *British Journal of Political Science* 48 (2): 427–57.

Prichard, W. 2016b. "What Have We Learned about Taxation, State Building, and Accountability?" Summary Brief No. 4, International Centre for Tax and Development, Brighton, UK.

Prichard, W. 2019. "Tax, Politics and the Social Contract in Africa." In *Encyclopedia of African Politics,* edited by M. Cheeseman. Oxford, UK: Oxford University Press.

Prichard, W. Forthcoming. "Unpacking Tax Morale: Distinguishing between Conditional and Unconditional Views of Tax Compliance." Working paper, Institute of Development Studies, Brighton, UK.

Prichard, W., A. Custers, R. Dom, S. Davenport, and M. Roscitt. 2019. "Innovations in Tax Compliance: Conceptual Framework." Policy Research Working Paper 9032, World Bank Group, Washington, DC.

Prichard, W., and M. Moore. 2018. "Tax Reform for Low-Income Countries: Five Ideas for Simplifying Tax Systems to Fit Local Realities." Summary Brief No. 17, International Centre for Tax and Development, Brighton, UK.

Raballand, G., C. Chalendard, A. Fernandes, A. Mattoo, and B. Rijkers. 2017. "Customs Reform and Performance Contracts: Early Results from Madagascar." Governance Notes No. 2, World Bank, Washington, DC.

Sælen, H., and S. Kallbekken. 2011. "A Choice Experiment on Fuel Taxation and Earmarking in Norway." *Ecological Economics* 70 (11): 2181–90.

Sanchez, O. 2006. "Tax Systems Reform in Latin America: Domestic and International Causes." *Review of International Political Economy* 13 (5): 772–801.

Scotchmer, S. 1987. "Audit Classes and Tax Enforcement Policy." *American Economic Review* 77 (2): 229–33.

Shapiro, M. D., and J. Slemrod. 2003. "Consumer Response to Tax Rebates." *American Economic Review* 93 (1): 381–96.

Slemrod, J. 2018. "Tax Compliance and Enforcement." Working Paper No. 24799, National Bureau of Economic Research, Cambridge, MA.

Timmons, J., and F. Garfias. 2015. "Revealed Corruption, Taxation, and Fiscal Accountability: Evidence from Brazil." *World Development* 70: 13–27.

Touchton, M., B. Wampler, and T. Peixoto. 2019. "Of Governance and Revenue: Participatory Institutions and Tax Compliance in Brazil." Policy Research Working Paper 8797, World Bank, Washington, DC.

van den Boogaard, V., W. Prichard, R. Beach, and F. Mohiuddin. Forthcoming. "Enabling Tax Bargaining: Supporting More Meaningful Tax Transparency and Taxpayer Engagement in Ghana and Sierra Leone." *Development Policy Review.*

van den Boogaard, V., W. Prichard, and S. Jibao. 2019. "Informal Taxation in Sierra Leone: Magnitudes, Perceptions and Implications." *African Affairs* 118 (471): 259–84.

World Bank. 2017. *World Development Report 2017: Governance and the Law.* Washington, DC: World Bank.

World Bank. 2019. *Doing Business 2019: Training for Reform.* Washington, DC: World Bank.

CHAPTER 2

Direct Taxes on Individuals and Households

Anna Custers, Roel Dom, and Wilson Prichard

The Tax Compliance Challenge

In wealthier member countries of the Organisation for Economic Co-operation and Development (OECD), direct taxes, primarily on personal income, are the backbone of revenue collection, while progressive rate structures for the personal income tax (PIT) are a key driver of progressivity in overall tax burdens. This system stands in stark contrast to those in lower-income countries where revenue from the PIT is far more limited, and there is mounting evidence of a striking lack of progressivity of direct taxes and other levies on individuals and households. This chapter provides an overview of the challenges associated with direct taxation and other direct fiscal burdens in lower-income countries. Subsequent chapters explore in greater detail specific aspects of that story, such as the taxation of so-called high-net-worth individuals (HNWIs).

Until the 1980s, the implementation of a broad-based, progressive PIT was the hallmark of international tax reform efforts (Bird 2013). Most countries adopted a PIT with high—often very high—marginal rates to ensure progressivity, although the effective rates were often much lower because of loopholes and exemptions (World Bank 1988). Many also had separate taxes on wealth, though often poorly enforced. In the late 1980s, attention shifted to the value added tax (VAT) and trade taxes, and PIT systems were gradually simplified and deemphasized as a central focus of reform efforts (Dom and Miller 2018).

The simplification of personal income taxes saw top marginal rates and structural progressivity decline significantly (figure 2.1). Evidence suggests that this may have reduced revenue in high-income countries, but the impact is less clear for low- and middle-income countries, where ineffective administration undermined revenue collection both before and after those reforms (Genschel and Seelkopf 2016; Peter, Buttrick, and Duncan 2010).

In recent years, the pendulum has begun to swing back toward strengthening direct taxes, and especially the PIT, amid increasing concerns about inequality and the ineffective taxation of high-net-worth individuals. This renewed emphasis reflects the fact that direct taxes—and the taxation of personal income, in particular—remain highly ineffective in much of the developing world, where PIT collection lags far behind levels found in OECD countries. Lower-income countries collect less than 3 percent of their gross domestic product (GDP) from personal income taxation, compared with 8 percent in OECD countries (figure 2.2). OECD countries also complement PIT with social security contributions (SSCs), which average about 10 percent of GDP. Low- and middle-income countries rely far less on SSCs, and low-income countries collect hardly any. Combined PIT and SSC revenue accounts for about 17 percent of total government revenue in lower-middle-income countries—a share that jumps to 40 percent in OECD countries. In all cases, these shares are smaller still in low-income countries.

Meanwhile, and perversely, there is growing evidence that although progressive taxes on personal income are frequently ineffective in low-income countries, other forms of direct taxation and especially informal fiscal burdens often impose substantial burdens on lower-income populations, in particular

FIGURE 2.1 **Evolution of Marginal Personal Income Tax Rates for Selected Countries, 1979–2002**

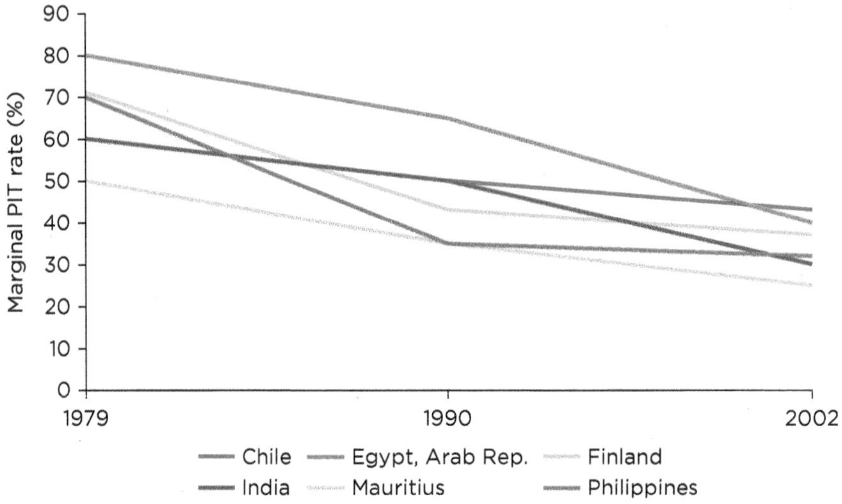

Source: Reynolds 2008.
Note: PIT = personal income tax.

Innovations in Tax Compliance

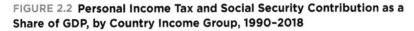

FIGURE 2.2 Personal Income Tax and Social Security Contribution as a Share of GDP, by Country Income Group, 1990–2018

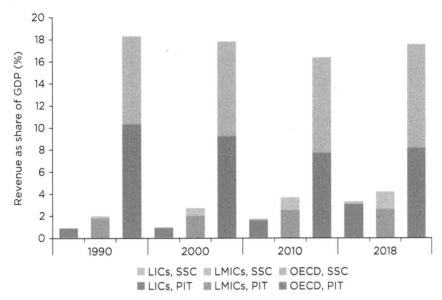

Source: Government Revenue Dataset of the International Centre for Tax and Development, United Nations University World Institute for Development Economics Research (UNU-WIDER), https://www.wider.unu.edu/project/government-revenue-dataset.
Note: LICs = low-income countries; LMICs = lower-middle-income countries; OECD = Organisation for Economic Co-operation and Development; PIT = personal income tax; SSC = social security contribution.

(Olken and Singhal 2011). This finding suggests that whereas in wealthier countries direct taxes are critical to revenue raising progressively, both revenue collection and progressivity are far more limited in low-income countries.

This chapter looks at the key barriers to more effective personal income taxation as well as other direct fiscal burdens on lower-income groups in lower-income countries. It examines not only how governments can collect more revenue, but also how direct taxes and other levies on individuals and households can be made fairer and more equitable. To do so, it explores the current progress in reform and the ways in which the conceptual framework developed in chapter 1 may inform future reform strategies. The discussion here then sets the stage for chapter 3, which goes into greater detail on the taxation of high-net-worth individuals because they present distinct tax challenges and possibilities, and chapter 5, which focuses on the taxation of small and medium enterprises (SMEs).

Undertaxation of the Rich

What explains low levels of PIT collection in low-income countries? Most accounts concentrate on narrow tax bases. Revenue administrations in many low- and middle-income countries often do not have an adequate handle on the population of taxpayers, resulting in low numbers of registered and active personal income taxpayers (Mayega et al. 2019). Estimates suggest that, on average, only 5 percent of the population of lower-income countries is registered for personal income taxation (versus 50 percent in high-income countries), covering only 15 percent of income (IMF 2011). This disparity often generates relatively vague calls to tax the "informal sector." However, such calls offer limited guidance for reformers. The critical question is then: Where are the largest gaps in PIT collection on which reformers should focus?

There is growing agreement that the most important challenge to improving PIT collection lies in broadening the base of relatively wealthy taxpayers, while also ensuring that all registered taxpayers are paying what they should. Across wealthier countries, the highest-income earners produce a large share of income tax revenue. This should be true as well in low-income countries characterized by high inequality and poverty, which places most taxpayers below the threshold for income taxation. Yet case studies point to widespread nonregistration and undertaxation of many high-income earners (Kangave, Byrne, and Karangwa 2020; Kangave et al. 2018).

Gaps in the taxation of wealthier taxpayers are also apparent in tax revenue data. In most low-income countries, most PIT revenue is produced by "pay as you earn" (PAYE) schemes, which withhold taxes on the income of workers, despite relatively small formal labor markets (Asiedu et al. 2017). Indeed, much of the formal employment in low-income countries subject to PAYE is in the public sector. Low PIT revenues are also driven by high minimum exemptions (thresholds) and tax expenditures. This finding reveals the severe undertaxation of nonwage income, including large informal sector operators, professional and consultancy incomes, capital gains, dividends, rental incomes, and commercial agricultural incomes (Prichard 2009).

The undertaxation of nonsalary income poses a particular challenge because the nonsalaried or self-employed economy is an important share of the economy of many countries and often is the dominant source of income for the relatively wealthy.[1] The self-employed include not only small street vendors, but also a wide range of wealthy individuals, including most professionals. Self-employed professionals such as doctors, lawyers, contractors, and consultants are a hard-to-tax group (Bahl 2004). Even though they often have high incomes, their activities are difficult to verify, particularly when they rely on cash transactions (Ogembo 2019). These self-employed professionals are likely one of the biggest compliance challenges as well as one of the largest threats to the equity of the tax system (Keen 2012).

Significant Tax Burdens on the Poor

Despite evidence that undertaxation of the relatively wealthy primarily accounts for weak PIT collection, many reform programs continue to focus on bringing those in the smaller informal sector—whether self-employed or informal workers—into the tax net.

Including these individuals, who are unquestionably large in number, in the tax net could have important short- and longer-term benefits. Exposure to the tax system may help to develop habits of tax compliance (Dunning et al. 2017), while potentially strengthening tax morale among larger taxpayers by demonstrating the universality of tax enforcement. Joining the formal tax net may also create space and incentives for expanding accountability. However, the revenue gain is likely to be modest because many of these individuals earn incomes below official thresholds for income taxation. For the earners above those thresholds, most incomes nonetheless remain low while presenting substantial challenges of enforcement because of limited bookkeeping and cash-based economies (Joshi, Prichard, and Heady 2014).

Although the policy discussion often centers on nonpayment of income taxes by smaller taxpayers, in at least some countries those taxpayers bear significant direct formal, but especially informal, burdens outside of the PIT (Olken and Singhal 2011; van den Boogaard and Santoro 2021). This is frequently true at the subnational level, where taxes, fees, and other levies on a variety of economic and other activities, often collected at flat rates, impose a disproportionate burden on the least well-off. It is also true of informal forms of revenue generation by state and nonstate actors involved in the provision of public goods (van den Boogaard and Santoro 2021). Easily overlooked are informal taxation by the state (such as through collection of bribes), demands for informal contributions to the construction and maintenance of public goods, and payments required by nonstate actors such as community associations.

A household survey in rural Sierra Leone found that less than 10 percent of the population paid any sort of tax to the central government, but most of the respondents did report various other types of payments to both local governments and nonstate actors (van den Boogaard, Prichard, and Jibao 2019). For the lowest quintile of taxpayers, these other payments approached 20 percent of household income, with similar results emerging from a parallel study in the Democratic Republic of Congo (Paler et al. 2017). These payments do not show up in national or international statistics, and they may not even be reflected in the government's budget. Yet they are highly prevalent and can represent a significant proportion of people's earnings in low-income countries.

Toward a More Nuanced Understanding

The combination of undercollection of income taxes on the rich and significant and less visible burdens on the poor means that the revenue-raising challenge becomes primarily about strengthening taxation of the relatively better-off rather than extending new burdens to those who already pay more than is often realized. This high-level picture points to a more nuanced understanding of several challenges in strengthening the direct taxation of individual taxpayers:

- The vast majority of PIT collection comes from salaried employees in the formal sector of the economy, but they often represent only a small share of the overall workforce.

- The largest revenue losses appear to be linked to the ineffective taxation of the relatively wealthy, including self-employed professionals. Effectively taxing nonsalary incomes has been particularly challenging.

- The relatively limited reach of the PIT net in most countries appears to be linked to poverty, which places most people below the income tax threshold. It also introduces challenges in taxing the employees of small and medium-size informal firms.

- Although most individuals fall outside of the income tax net, that does not mean they are not taxed at all. In some countries, other formal and informal fiscal burdens are significant.

In summary, the key challenge is to address weaknesses in income tax systems that allow the rich and the middle class to pay relatively little or no income tax.

Against this background, the challenge for tax authorities is developing strategies for different segments of taxpayers that reflect their distinctive needs and opportunities. The largest revenue potential lies in taxing higher-income taxpayers, and such a strategy will also expand equity and fairness. But doing so successfully presents technical challenges, and the political barriers are especially high. What follows is an overview of the key barriers to more effective direct taxation, followed by consideration of alternative approaches that have been deployed in seeking better outcomes.

Barriers to Reform

The basic challenge of levying personal income taxes applies across taxpayer types. Tax administrations must be able to (1) identify individual taxpayers to bring them into the tax net; (2) develop strategies for estimating their actual incomes and provide the appropriate services; and (3) enjoy adequate political backing to pursue collection, audits, and enforcement actions.

In recent decades, virtually all countries have moved toward systems of self-declaration for PIT, thereby moving away from systems of administrative assessment. However, in many countries significant subsets of taxpayers—including those with significant incomes—remain unregistered. Meanwhile, the incomes that are declared are often vastly understated, and there are significant political hurdles to improving administrative systems or pursuing enforcement.

Administration Challenges

Effective taxpayer registration is the cornerstone of any tax system—the platform on which all other functions of the administration are built. Yet many countries struggle to maintain complete and accurate tax registers and use effectively the data that are available. Their taxpayer registers appear to be plagued by two contradictory problems: tax registers fail to include many individuals with significant taxable incomes, but they are also overstuffed with large numbers of inactive taxpayers who are registered but do not file tax returns.

The failure to register large taxpayers is one of the most glaring tax administration weaknesses in many countries. Not only does it undermine revenue collection, but it also damages the fairness, equity, and legitimacy of the tax system. Yet registering taxpayers alone has proven to be an inadequate solution. Even when taxpayers are registered, nonfiling is a major problem in many countries, but especially in lower-income countries (figure 2.3). In Uganda, the revenue authority quadrupled the number of registered taxpayers, but the new number represents only 5.5 percent of people of working age and, more important, less than half of these registered individuals are *active* taxpayers—that is, they are

Innovations in Tax Compliance

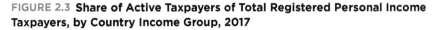

FIGURE 2.3 Share of Active Taxpayers of Total Registered Personal Income Taxpayers, by Country Income Group, 2017

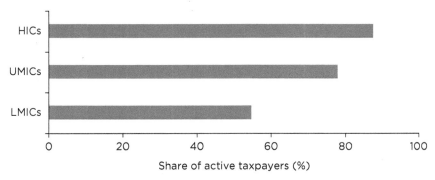

Share of active taxpayers (%)

Source: International Monetary Fund, Revenue Administration Fiscal Information Tool (RA-FIT), http://data.rafit.org.
Note: No data available for low-income countries. HICs = high-income countries; LMICs = lower-middle-income countries; UMICs = upper-middle-income countries.

filing returns (Mayega et al. 2019). In India, only one in six taxpayers file, while in Pakistan this share falls to only one in 100 (Chattopadhyay and Das-Gupta 2002; Waris 2013).

Nonfiling may have many causes. For example, it may reflect inaccuracies in the registry. Uganda's register suffers from serious inaccuracies, such as duplicates and wrong or missing information, but the country is not alone. Recent Tax Administration Diagnostic Assessment Tool (TADAT) assessments show similar problems in countries such as Guatemala and Jordan (Ansón et al. 2017; Rozner et al. 2016).[2]

A related problem involves nil-filers—that is, taxpayers who submit returns but declare zero income. Despite being a well-known phenomenon to tax administrators, it is largely ignored in the tax literature. Emerging evidence suggests that evasion plays a relatively small role. Instead, what seems to be more important is the interaction between aggressive recruitment campaigns by the revenue authorities and taxpayers' response to a complex and often confusing tax system (Mascagni et al., forthcoming; Santoro and Mdluli 2019).

Data Challenges

To assess the possibility of avoidance and evasion, governments need adequate data and the capacity to evaluate the income that taxpayers declare. Doing so is a data-intensive task, and the taxation of formal sector employees is relatively successful because it relies on parallel reporting of income by employers (Saez 2010).

For individuals outside of the formal sector—that is, most individuals in most low- and middle-income countries—and for nonlabor income, the third-party data needed to verify incomes are not easily available. This scarcity of data often reflects legal limits on access to third-party data and ineffective sharing of data within governments arising from poor coordination, institutional rivalries, or political resistance (in part because effective digitalization may undermine opportunities for corruption).

Yet even where data access and sharing are effective, challenges of data management and quality can mean that the available data are not fully exploited to maximize tax enforcement (Mascagni, Dom, and Santoro 2021). Lower-level staff often lack the skills to properly maintain databases, while senior staff neither have the time nor view it as a priority. All too often, systems are administered by hand or in rudimentary electronic formats.

In addition, low information technology (IT) literacy among taxpayers leads to simple mistakes in tax returns or registration forms. Taxpayers enter their tax identification (ID) numbers as amounts, or vice versa, or miss a zero somewhere. Without quality checks, these data have to be (re)coded, often manually, before they can be exploited, which leaves a significant margin for errors (Mascagni, Mukama, and Santoro 2019).

Political Challenges

Finally, efforts to improve taxpayer identification and income verification, and to subsequently pursue audits and enforcement, are often severely undermined by political resistance. History is littered with examples of unsuccessful attempts to introduce a personal income tax, even a temporary one. Moreover, once such a tax is introduced, expanding the taxation of personal income and raising significant revenue from it are often a lengthy process (Aidt and Jensen 2009).

Introducing and enforcing a lasting PIT that produces significant revenue are difficult. Mobilization against income taxation is often productive because the individual costs are high and clearly visible, whereas the benefits are diffuse. Successful implementation has generally been underpinned by a clear bargain with taxpayers (Brautigam, Fjeldstad, and Moore 2008). In Europe, the expansion of personal income taxation went hand in hand with the rollout of the welfare state during the interwar period (Besley and Persson 2013), whereas in South Africa elite groups accepted expanded direct taxation as the price to pay to sustain and defend minority rule (Lieberman 2003). Yet even when introduced, tax design and implementation reflect political interests (Easter 2008). In many countries such as India, policy makers keep taxation thresholds high, effectively exempting large swaths of the population (Piketty and Qian 2009).

Variations by Taxpayer Income Level and Type

Beyond these commonalities, however, the technical and political challenges that arise vary significantly across different subsets of individual taxpayers.

High-Net-Worth Individuals

For high-net-worth individuals (HNWIs), discussed at greater length in chapter 3, the technical challenges extend beyond the domestic sphere, while the political challenges revolve around the unique political power and connections of small groups of elites.

The wealthiest taxpayers around the world often secure some or most of their income from nonwage sources, which can be hard to identify or to value. This factor further complicates the use of withholding taxes. Moreover, tax systems are often riddled with provisions that further reduce the size of the tax base, particularly in the upper-middle and upper classes (Goode 1993; World Bank 1988). Exemptions and loopholes are easier to exploit by those who have the resources to consult tax professionals. This exploitation can occur domestically, but the wealthy also often hold significant parts of their wealth and the income that flows from it offshore, where it is difficult for domestic tax administrations to access (Alstadsæter, Johannesen, and Zucman 2018; Zucman 2014, 2015). Consequently, these sources of income are barely taxed, especially in lower-income countries (Mascagni, Monkam, and Nell 2016; Piketty and Saez 2007).

Yet, although there are certainly technical barriers to more effective income taxation of HNWIs, governments also have failed to use many of the tools available to them. Reforms to improve the taxation of HNWIs have often proven difficult, especially when economic and political elites are aligned, but case studies show that it can be done (Fairfield 2013). The Global Forum on Transparency and Exchange of Information for Tax Purposes has made important strides in this regard, but major challenges persist, as further discussed in chapters 3 and 4.

Nonsalaried or Self-Employed Earners

For the broader base of relatively high-income taxpayers with significant nonsalary sources of income—from capital gains, rental, or professional sources, in particular—challenges to improved outcomes have arisen from the limitations of existing investments in enforcement, facilitation, and trust.

Even when included in the tax net, self-employed professionals have more opportunities than salaried workers to minimize their reported incomes (Kleven et al. 2011). They are also more likely to exploit these opportunities (Bhat 2017; le Maire and Schjerning 2013; Saez 2010) and underreport their incomes (Engström and Holmlund 2009; Hurst, Li, and Pugsley 2014), although there is variation by occupation (Schuetze 2002). Moreover, it is difficult to subject self-employment income, which is often cash-based, to schemes such as PAYE tax withholding.

Although opportunity is one factor, research suggests that the attitudes of the self-employed are unlike those of other taxpayers toward taxation; they express less favorable views on taxes and the tax authorities (Kogler and Kirchler 2020). Survey evidence indicates that the self-employed tend to have lower tax morale than other taxpayers (Hug and Spörri 2011; Torgler 2004). It is therefore not surprising to find evidence of higher tax evasion among the self-employed (Chetty, Friedman, and Saez 2013).

The evidence furthermore suggests that although professionals are generally highly educated and often more aware of their tax obligations and rights, their relationship with the revenue administration is often difficult (Gatt and Owen 2018; Kogler and Kirchler 2020). Professionals complain that revenue administrations do not understand the nature of their work and, as a consequence, apply tax rules in arbitrary and inconsistent ways. Revenue administrations are said to prefer to cultivate relationships with larger companies and HNWIs (they offer more potential for reaching revenue targets) and to focus only on larger self-employed professionals, undermining perceptions of fairness (Ogembo 2019).

Moreover, although it is often assumed that this is an issue only for lower-income taxpayers, research suggests that some higher-income taxpayers, and particularly less-experienced self-employed, may also have significant knowledge gaps (Kangave et al. 2016; Ogembo 2019). Complying with all tax obligations and keeping reliable books of accounts are difficult for some well-educated self-employed professionals (Ogembo 2019; Tadesse and Taube 1996).

Yet self-employed professionals do not have to be among the "hard to tax" in an administrative sense. They are relatively easily identified because they often have signs on their doors or do business with government. Verifying their incomes and enforcing compliance are more difficult (Bird and Wallace 2004). Self-employed professionals can easily switch to cash and can take advantage of the various loopholes in the tax system to reduce their taxable income, such as retaining earnings in the firm, transfers to assisting spouses, pension contributions, and classification of personal income as capital income (le Maire and Schjerning 2013).

Employees of Small and Medium Enterprises
For smaller taxpayers employed by small and medium enterprises, often in the informal sector, the administrative challenges are also quite distinct, rooted in managing large numbers of small taxpayers—and the tax collectors that pursue them—and in navigating a particular set of political questions and challenges.

The income of individuals working for SMEs in low- and middle-income countries is often (partly) untaxed either because the firm is not registered or, if it is registered, it may not fully report on all its employees or the full income paid to their employees (Ulyssea 2018). The biggest challenge for tax administrations in attempting to tax the income of employees of unregistered firms is likely identifying those firms.

Dealing with partial reporting may be even more complex. The envelope wages and cash payments that complement official salaries are notoriously difficult to track, even in high-income economies (Williams and Padmore 2013). Moreover, the evidence is mixed on the effectiveness of hard enforcement responses to tackle this problem. Instead, softer approaches such as fostering a culture of compliance by promoting the benefits of formal work and tax fairness appear more effective (Williams and Lansky 2013).

Even if SME employees are taxed, the revenue gain may not be substantial, and the administrative cost of enforcement is likely to be high. Coupled with the importance of small traders and workers during elections—because of their numbers and organizational capacity—this factor can complicate the tax bargaining process (Gatt and Owen 2018; Prichard 2015; Tendler 2002). Chapter 5 offers a more detailed discussion of the challenges related to bringing SMEs into the tax net.

Smaller Taxpayers
Finally, for smaller taxpayers, often poorer individuals, reforms may not be about increasing taxation but rather about limiting more extractive and regressive fiscal burdens, both formal and informal, which presents entirely different technical and political challenges.

Options for increasing extraction from these taxpayers seem limited. In fact, in many cases these taxpayers may already be paying too much rather than too little. Meanwhile, enforcement is complicated by difficulties in identifying and tracking taxpayers and by the limited availability of third-party information to establish their income, which is usually limited. As a result, the collection of these payments often involves significant negotiation and corruption and lacks transparency, while uneven administration of taxes across different activities leads to horizontal inequalities between taxpayers who have similar incomes but are engaged in different activities. Moreover, some of these payments never reach state coffers because they are lost to corruption.

When nonstate actors, such as customary authorities or rebel groups, collect such taxes reform efforts are further complicated, not least when such actors are more effective service providers than the government and consequently more trusted by the population (Paler et al. 2017; van den Boogaard, Prichard, and Jibao 2019).

Therefore, the most important tasks in relation to smaller taxpayers may well be simplifying compliance, reducing informality, and increasing equity and service provision, while also reducing the overall payment burden, particularly for the poorest (Moore, Prichard, and Fjeldstad 2018a). Revenue maximization is unlikely to be the primary objective. Improving administration of the system and the social contract between these taxpayers and the state is likely to be more important.

Reform Progress—and Future Options

The revenue potential of PIT remains extremely large in lower-income countries, as figure 2.2 illustrates. Yet despite the challenges of strengthening the taxation of individual taxpayers, most countries have seen gradual progress, while a few success stories point to the potential for much larger improvements. Their experiences suggest that major improvements are possible where political commitment and suitable technical interventions are combined with efforts to strengthen trust and to build a new, more durable social contract (box 2.1).

That said, because of the heterogeneity among individual taxpayers, the appropriate combinations of investments in enforcement, facilitation, and trust in individual contexts are likely to be diverse. Improving compliance among self-employed professionals will require strategies different from those needed to encourage the formalization of small traders or the negotiation of a broad-based tax bargain with organized labor. What follows considers various options related to enforcement, facilitation, and trust.

Enforcement
Improving Data Access, Sharing, and Management
At its core, effective personal income taxation depends on the effective collection and deployment of data to identify taxpayers and verify their tax liabilities. Efforts to strengthen income tax collection have frequently followed a standard template. It puts in place more sophisticated IT systems to improve data collection and management and then, especially for small taxpayers, couples this improvement with drives to bring large numbers of new taxpayers into the tax net. However, the results have often been disappointing as IT systems struggle to get off the ground or are underused once implemented, and as tax administrations struggle to use the new data and expanded tax registers effectively (Mayega et al. 2019).

For lower-income countries, in particular, a strong argument could be made for adopting more-targeted approaches to reform, identifying where the specific challenges are in relation to data access, sharing, and management and where

BOX 2.1

Personal Income Tax Reform: Success Stories

Poland

During its transition period, Poland struggled to restructure its tax system. Initial attempts at enforcing income taxation among public sector workers were heavily resisted by popular protests. Yet in 1992 the government managed to successfully introduce a personal income tax (PIT) that quickly became a significant part of the state's revenue base. Within two years, the PIT contributed around 25 percent of total government revenue.

This success followed a revenue bargain that offered something tangible to workers in exchange for their compliance. Not only did the government redistribute the tax burden; it also invited workers into the policy-making process and guaranteed a basic level of social welfare.

South Africa

The importance of bargaining for successful income taxation is perhaps most clearly, but crudely, illustrated by South Africa. The effectiveness of South Africa's income tax system stands out in the region. It has been traced back to the apartheid regime, which collected income taxes (overwhelmingly from the wealthy white minority it represented) more effectively than virtually any other low- to middle-income country, and almost on par with many Organisation for Economic Co-operation and Development countries. Compliance with high taxation of income was tolerated because the elites understood that it was the price they had to pay to sustain and defend minority rule.

Lagos, Nigeria

In Lagos, Nigeria's commercial capital, a series of PIT reforms have increased taxpayers' quasi-voluntary compliance, which has facilitated PIT collection to an unprecedented level. To gain support for income tax reform, the state first had to earn taxpayers' trust. Enforcement actions were prioritized only for large pay-as-you-earn businesses. Elsewhere, the government focused on visibly linking tax collection to service delivery and tax sensitization through a proactive approach of reaching out to and bargaining with both formal and informal associations of self-employed professionals and traders. Lagos State initiated a shift in state-society relations that resulted in significantly higher compliance.

Sources: Easter (2008); Gatt and Owen (2018); Lieberman (2003).

immediate progress can be achieved. This approach guards against making large investments in more sophisticated systems when the most important barriers may lie elsewhere.

Especially critical is determining whether the data-related challenges lie in limited legal access to data, a limited capacity in practice to access and share data, or an inability to use existing data effectively.

Legal access to data. In some contexts, tax administrations face sharp constraints on their legal ability to access data across government or from nongovernment third parties, thereby limiting their options in improving enforcement. Here the starting point is likely to lie in understanding why those limitations exist, whether they might be changed, and whether improved legal access to data would in fact lead to better outcomes.

Limited capacity to access and share data. An alternative possibility in many contexts is that more data are legally accessible than can actually be accessed and shared across government or beyond. Here the critical question is why legally permitted data sharing is not happening—whether because of lack of capacity, ineffective systems, institutional rivalries, or political barriers—and how progress may be made.

Inability to use data effectively. Finally, governments may have more than adequate access to data, but they fail to use it systematically to identify taxpayers and audit their tax declarations. In these cases, the focus is likely to be on how to improve the use of data, which is often related to lack of skills and constraints on IT tools.

Targeted Enforcement

Most countries have figured out how to collect taxes from large segments of their population by enlisting employers as collectors. In both high-income and low- to middle-income countries, firms remit about 80 percent of total tax revenue (Slemrod and Velayudhan 2018). For personal income taxation, PAYE systems force firms to withhold taxes from the income of their employees. However, taxing nonsalary income has proven to be significantly more difficult.

Chapter 3 on HNWIs highlights the technical and, most important, political challenges shaping enforcement strategies for wealthy elites. Other segments, such as self-employed professionals and small taxpayers, require quite distinct strategies.

Self-employed professionals. Among the most overlooked groups of potential taxpayers—albeit with significant potential for improving compliance—are relatively wealthy professionals.

Evidence on possible effective strategies for these groups closely follows the logic of traditional compliance models. Mostly from higher-income countries, it suggests that audit and penalty rates are both reliable deterrents to noncompliance (Ali, Cecil, and Knoblett 2001; Beer et al. 2020). Tightening enforcement by increasing the audit rates of the self-employed and allocating more time for auditors to process such returns are therefore likely to be an effective strategy. But whether such a strategy is also efficient largely depends on the cost of administration. Management, human resource, and budget constraints can be an obstacle to scaling up enforcement measures for large groups of taxpayers. Auditing self-employed professionals also generally takes much longer than auditing other taxpayers (Romanov 2003). Yet the revenue gains are often well worth it (Erard and Ho 2004).

Another way to boost cost-effectiveness is by making the tax administrator's job easier. Transition economies in Europe have generally moved to simplified or special tax regimes for the self-employed (Bird and Wallace 2004). Some countries apply a turnover tax instead of an income tax. Other countries have put in place presumptive taxes. Developing appropriate indicators for the tax liabilities of different occupations can be a challenge (Bahl 2004). Nevertheless, presumptive taxes and simplified regimes—if well thought out—could be useful tools for taxing the self-employed (box 2.2).

Presumptive Taxes: A Good Option for Taxing Professionals?

Presumptive taxes have typically been reserved for farmers and small and medium enterprises (SMEs) in many low- and middle-income countries. Yet a recent paper argues that they may also be a useful solution for the taxation of self-employed professionals if they are well designed (Ogembo 2019).

In presumptive tax regimes, the desired base of a tax is not measured directly but approximated indirectly by indicators that are more easily captured. This is usually done to simplify taxation, both for the taxpayer and for the administration. Presumptive taxes can also enhance horizontal equity and enlarge the revenue base if they manage to draw into the tax net taxpayers who otherwise would not have complied. However, if not properly designed—that is, if the indicators do not track the desired base well—they could lead to vertical inequities because taxpayers may end up paying the same amount of tax despite significantly different levels of real income. Because self-employed professionals may also find it easy to manipulate a turnover-based threshold, it is important to look at issues that could drive bunching at the threshold and to provide incentives for graduating out of the presumptive group once businesses grow too big.

Although self-employed professionals are part of the hard-to-tax (HTT) group, presumptive taxes widely used to tax other HTTs, such as SMEs and farmers, often explicitly exclude the self-employed. In part, this exclusion stems from a belief that presumptive taxes are not suitable for self-employed professionals because they tend to be highly educated and are therefore assumed to be financially literate enough to keep proper accounts and comply with general income tax rules and regulations.

Yet recent research finds that the self-employed and SMEs often face similar issues. In fact, many self-employed professionals see themselves as SMEs. According to Ogembo (2020), many Kenyan dentists and lawyers lack the knowledge and accounting expertise necessary to comply with their obligations. This lack particularly hinders younger professionals, who cannot afford professional accounting services. Presumptive taxes, if well designed and if the sector is involved in the design process, can help not only with this group's tax compliance but also with addressing the common complaint that administrations do not understand the nature of self-employed businesses.

Finally, showing that the self-employed are taxed is important in itself for ensuring quasi-voluntary compliance among other taxpayer segments. Presumptive taxes can address widely held public perceptions of horizontal inequity. Many believe that the self-employed enjoy countless opportunities to escape taxation, while those in salaried positions bear the full burden. Bringing the self-employed into the tax net is therefore necessary to ensure the voluntary compliance of others. To that end, presumptive taxes can help. Over time, the first-best option would be to move to an equilibrium of informed taxpayers and effective audits. Until then, a combination of second-best alternatives may be used.

Smaller taxpayers. A quite different and more varied set of questions arises about strategies for taxing smaller taxpayers, many of whom are either self-employed or employed by small firms, often in the informal sector. These taxpayers present special challenges, especially when it comes to enforcement. Meanwhile, the potential revenue is often modest due to low income. As important, such individuals may face significant formal and informal fiscal burdens outside of PIT, calling into question claims that they face limited "tax" burdens and further complicating the question of whether taxing such small taxpayers should be a priority for governments.

Targeted enforcement measures such as door-to-door or private collection can improve revenue mobilization. But such measures are also expensive, and the available evidence suggests that such heavy-handed enforcement can negatively affect trust and undermine state–citizen relations. This finding reflects, in part, the fact that such collection is vulnerable to collusion, corruption, and possibly harassment of the weakest taxpayers (Iversen et al. 2006; Khan, Khwaja, and Olken 2016). Moreover, as described in chapter 5, large-scale campaigns to register new taxpayers and broaden the tax base can often backfire by diverting resources from more important priorities and creating bloated tax registers that governments are unable to track and update over time (Demirgüç-Kunt et al. 2018; Moore 2020).

Enforcement efforts among smaller taxpayers are likely instead to closely overlap with the taxation of small firms (see chapter 5) and thus are characterized by two key features. The first is a more targeted approach to the registration of taxpayers that focuses on setting thresholds high enough to reduce the burden on the poorest and avoid collection costs that exceed the revenue actually collected. The second is an emphasis on rules-based enforcement and creating positive inducements to compliance through facilitation and trust-building rather than relying on heavy-handed enforcement among groups that generate relatively limited revenue.

Tax Nudges

Another emerging trend in enforcing income tax compliance in many low- and middle-income countries is the use of so-called tax nudges. Rooted in social psychology and behavioral economics, "nudging" techniques aim to bring about desirable changes in the behavior of individuals by influencing their choices. This process consists of altering their perceptions of the costs and benefits of the outcomes linked with the choices they have (Thaler and Sunstein 2008).

Information interventions, such as sending a message, are usually deployed to push or nudge an individual toward the desired outcome. In one of the best-known examples, the United Kingdom's tax administration mailed letters to over 200,000 taxpayers to influence the occurrence and timing of their income tax payments by reminding them of penalties for late payments (Hallsworth et al. 2017). This low-cost approach is being replicated elsewhere in Europe, Latin America, Asia, and increasingly across Africa (BIT and DJP 2019; Hernandez et al. 2017, 2019; Luts and Van Roy 2019; Mascagni, Nell, and Monkam 2017; Pomeranz 2015).

However, questions remain about whether one-off messages are enough to shock taxpayers into a new compliance equilibrium, whether sustained messaging is necessary to ensure the sustainability of the effect, and whether even sustained messaging may have diminishing impacts over time (Kettle et al. 2016; Manoli and Turner 2014). Anecdotal evidence suggests that some of the tax administrations that were early supporters of this approach have been overloading taxpayers with text messages, emails, and letters, possibly leading to messaging fatigue among taxpayers, who then cease to be influenced by them.

Although tax nudges have proven their effectiveness in the short term, their long-term effectiveness is likely to depend on the structural changes that underpin them. For example, telling taxpayers that their money is used for public goods is unlikely to lead to sustained improvements in tax morale if taxpayers do not see material improvements in actual service delivery outcomes.

Facilitation

Simplifying Compliance

Because of the enforcement challenges presented by personal income taxation, facilitating compliance is likely to be particularly important across different types of taxpayers, beginning with simplification. The importance of simplifying income tax systems in low- and middle-income countries to facilitate compliance is widely recognized (IFC, MIGA, and World Bank 2009; Prichard and Moore 2018). The implicit cost of complying with income tax obligations is often high (Blumenthal and Slemrod 1992; Chattopadhyay and Das-Gupta 2002). Small businesses, in particular, often cannot meet the required accounting standards or pay for external professional support (Terkper 2003).

Moreover, complicated tax systems, especially when they require many face-to-face encounters between taxpayers and tax collectors, give rise to opportunities for collusion, harassment, or corruption (Chattopadhyay and Das-Gupta 2002). This is true not only for the self-employed, but perhaps even more so for the many low-income taxpayers, since, as discussed, they often face a wide range of petty or informal payments (Paler et al. 2017).

It thus comes as no surprise that simplifying compliance and improving user friendliness have been a top priority of many tax administration reforms (Fjeldstad and Moore 2008). Although such reforms initially adopted a technical focus on reducing compliance costs, primarily through the introduction of new information and communication technology (ICT) systems, they have evolved to include building taxpayer trust by expanding transparency and promoting taxpayer education.

E-services

Investments in ICT, and especially e-services, continue to figure prominently in reform programs to facilitate tax compliance by individuals. According to OECD, there has been a shift within tax administrations to increase options for self-service (OECD 2019a). In many higher-income countries, most individuals can now file their tax returns (often prepopulated) online, and almost everyone pays their taxes electronically.

In addition, many administrations are experimenting with the use of advanced technologies to further enhance taxpayers' customer experience. Contact between taxpayers and tax administrations is also rapidly being digitalized. The introduction of artificial intelligence (AI)-powered chatbots is reducing the need for direct interactions between taxpayers and tax officials. Low- and middle-income and emerging countries are following and sometimes leading the way (OECD 2019a). For example, in India the e-Sahyog project provides an online mechanism to resolve mistakes in the income tax returns of those whose returns are selected for review without the need to visit the tax office. In Brazil, the My Income Tax App allows taxpayers to complete and file their PIT returns via mobile devices.

Although the adoption of new technologies holds great potential, the actual translation of new IT investments into improved performance has not always materialized. Evidence on the impact of e-systems on compliance costs and the behavior of taxpayers is thin, and the results are mixed (Okunogbe and Pouliquen 2018). In part, this finding reflects the fact that, for certain taxpayers, switching to e-systems may entail a significant learning curve, which could render these services inaccessible to them (Yilmaz and Coolidge 2013). To use these services, taxpayers must have a basic level of IT literacy as well as internet access, which requires a reliable source of electricity. Where these preconditions are not met, further digitalization—while perhaps cost-effective from the tax administration's perspective—risks leaving behind large swaths of the population.

Moreover, research shows that perceptions play a crucial role in the decision of taxpayers to adopt these new technologies (Carter et al. 2011; Gallant, Culnan, and McLoughlin 2007; Fjeldstad et al. 2020; Ibrahim 2013). This finding highlights the need to complement the rollout of these technologies with information and taxpayer education.

Taxpayer Education

Over the past decade, the potential role of well-designed taxpayer education programs in facilitating compliance, as well as their (often unrealized) potential to play a broader role in increasing trust and tax morale, have received particular attention. Similar to—and overlapping with—small firms, lower-income taxpayers may face significant challenges in understanding what is required and how to navigate tax payments. Their limited understanding of the tax system may also make them more vulnerable to informal payments and illegal demands from unscrupulous public officials.

In response, many low- and middle-income countries are rolling out tax education programs designed to help taxpayers understand how to pay their taxes, as well as the details of tax systems more broadly. There is now a wide range of taxpayer outreach and education activities across countries. Nigeria developed a tax-based soap opera called "Binding Duty." Bangladesh celebrates National Income Tax Day. And the Kenya Revenue Authority is working with schools to mainstream tax education into the education curriculum (OECD and FIIAPP 2015).

Government taxpayer education and outreach programs are generally aimed at explaining to taxpayers why they pay taxes and encouraging them to do so, often by appealing to state-building narratives. Such education programs are valuable, but it is essential that they move beyond the frequent emphasis on *why* taxpayers should pay taxes and instead move toward an emphasis on *who* pays taxes, *how* to pay taxes, and *what* taxpayers receive in return. Surveys indicate that taxpayers are searching for the latter information, which is critical to strengthening perceptions of fairness, equity, reciprocity, and accountability (van den Boogaard et al. forthcoming). Indeed, at its best, taxpayer education not only can instruct taxpayers how to pay taxes, but also can engage them in dialogue about how revenues are used, the quality of administration, and broader accountability (van den Boogaard et al., forthcoming). In practice, however, taxpayer education programs have generally been more limited in scope.

In that spirit, recent research has yielded new insights into the kinds of taxpayer education programs that may be most successful in targeting the broad base of taxpayers and supporting improvements not only in knowledge about how to pay but also in broader trust in tax systems. The available evidence confirms that taxpayer outreach and education programs can improve tax morale, but to be effective these programs must be tailored to specific taxpayer segments in line with an overall compliance strategy (Fjeldstad and Heggstad 2012). Successful initiatives have often been underpinned by partnerships with outside actors that reach large parts of the population, such as schools, civil society, or business organizations (OECD and FIIAPP 2015). Religious organizations have been particularly effective partners because they are countrywide and have a high degree of legitimacy (Fjeldstad and Heggstad 2012). These kinds of partnerships will increase the reach of taxpayer education programs, but they can be equally important in increasing taxpayer trust (van den Boogaard et al., forthcoming).

Yet the case for taxpayer education programs is often hard to make because administrations have limited time and financial and human resources, and it is challenging to establish a direct link with improvements in compliance or public support for reform. High-level political support can help. In Rwanda, the president himself gives out annual taxpayer awards, while Turkey's minister of finance spoke directly to taxpayers on YouTube (OECD and FIIAPP 2015). Meanwhile, rigorous evaluation, while rare, is possible (Chetty, Friedman, and Saez 2013). Evidence from Rwanda suggests that taxpayer education improves knowledge and compliance behavior (box 2.3). Moreover, technology increasingly presents opportunities to communicate with taxpayers on a large scale and at low cost (Kira 2017).

Trust
Fairness and Equity
Just as facilitation is likely to be critical to encouraging quasi-voluntary compliance, so too is there an opportunity for more sustained investments in building trust with taxpayers. The relevance of tax morale in shaping compliance behavior has been researched overwhelmingly in relation to individual taxpayers not subject to PAYE tax withholding, and it is likely to be broader and more powerful for individuals than for business taxpayers (Kamleitner, Korunka, and Kirchler 2012; OECD 2019b; Yücedoğru and Hasseldine 2016). In turn, that research leaves little doubt that improvements in trust are likely to drive both improvements in tax compliance and a more supportive political environment for needed reforms (Leonardo and Martinez-Vazquez 2016). In practice, however, government efforts to build such trust have often been limited to small-scale interventions, such as sending letters to taxpayers that emphasize the connections between revenue and services or various kinds of public education and outreach campaigns pursuing a similar purpose. More intense efforts to build trust thus seem to be needed.

BOX 2.3

Teach to Comply? Evidence from a Taxpayer Education Program in Rwanda

Increasingly, tax administrations in low- and middle-income countries are putting in place taxpayer education initiatives. The Rwanda Revenue Authority (RRA) routinely organizes training sessions for new taxpayers—individuals or firms that recently registered for a tax identification number (TIN).

The RRA's training program introduces new taxpayers to the basics of paying taxes. As opposed to other taxpayer outreach programs that focus on *why* it is important to pay taxes, Rwanda's program focuses on *how* to pay taxes. During a half-day class, officials from the RRA's Taxpayer Services Department walk taxpayers through the various taxes and explain how to file tax returns, what the deadlines are, and which services are available to them.

Little is known about the effects of these programs, especially in low- and middle-income countries. A recent research paper therefore set out to evaluate the effectiveness of Rwanda's initiative (Mascagni, Santoro, and Mukama 2019). By linking survey data with attendance lists and administrative tax return data, the researchers were able to assess the impact of the taxpayer education campaign on the knowledge, perceptions, and compliance of about 1,000 newly registered taxpayers.

The results are encouraging. Taxpayer education drastically increases taxpayers' understanding of the tax system. Their perceptions of the complexity of the tax system also improve markedly. This is important not only to help taxpayers comply with their obligations but also to make them less vulnerable to harassment and coercion. But, most important, taxpayers who benefited from the training are also much more likely to file tax returns.

These findings show that "soft" approaches to compliance can yield significant improvements. Moreover, there is evidence to suggest that this effect persists over multiple years, indicating that one-off training can push taxpayers into a new compliance equilibrium, which is especially important in light of the massive number of nonfilers in low- and middle-income countries.

A starting point for such trust-building appears to lie in improving the basic fairness of tax systems. Although discussions of building tax morale often center on improving the quality of public spending, improvements in fairness may be equally important (Kogler, Muehlbacher, and Kirchler 2015). Such improvements are also much more directly under the control of tax administrations, which may be pursuing reform and seeking to build quasi-voluntary compliance. Survey evidence indicates that perceived corruption in tax authorities remains a significant barrier to improving quasi-voluntary compliance (Aiko and Logan 2014; Fjeldstad 2005). In fact, some studies suggest that the self-employed are particularly sensitive to grand corruption scandals, perceptions of government waste, and what they see as preferential treatment of larger taxpayers (Ogembo 2020).

Addressing corruption, collusion, and harassment—especially of vulnerable taxpayers—should therefore be a priority. Technology can reduce the opportunities for discretion and collusion by lessening the need for face-to-face interactions between officials and taxpayers (Awasthi and Bayraktar 2014). Yet when pushing for technology reform, especially when attempting to address corruption, it is important that reformers understand the underlying political context. Evidence shows that corruption is often part of a broader set of informal institutions used by individuals, including taxpayers, to pursue strategic gains at the margins and therefore could make them resistant to adopting technological fixes (Hassan and Prichard 2016).

Equally critical is improving the equity of tax burdens borne by taxpayers at different points in the income distribution. Evidence suggests that compliance by individual taxpayers is closely linked to their perceptions of equity, which are, in turn, influenced by their perceptions of compliance by others, including firms (Fjeldstad and Heggstad 2011). Considerable efforts have gone into designing and implementing progressive PIT systems in lower-income countries to ensure that better-off groups pay more in taxes as a share of their incomes. Yet, in practice, most countries fall far short of this goal, and PIT progressivity has been steadily declining since the 1980s (Gerber et al. 2018). This finding reflects, above all, the weakness of PIT enforcement among the best-off, revealing, in turn, politicization, weak enforcement, and the fact that PIT is levied almost exclusively on formal sector employees in most low-income countries, thereby largely missing the most important sources of income for the richest, such as capital gains, rental income, and professional incomes (Bird and Zolt 2014; Moore, Prichard, and Fjeldstad 2018b). It likewise reveals the often overlooked but significant burdens on lower-income groups.

In the context of such significant and widely recognized inequities, convincing taxpayers to comply voluntarily with tax demands and support expanded taxation more broadly is likely to remain difficult. This problem points to the importance of a subset of key priorities to expanding equity—and, as a result, trust, tax morale, and political support for reform. First, redouble efforts to strengthen taxation of the best-off. As discussed in more detail in the next chapter, there is growing evidence that even the governments of low-income countries have the tools needed to identify the wealthiest taxpayers if those governments have the political will to improve outcomes (Kangave et al. 2016). Second, focus on strengthening horizontal equity between formal sector employees and those who are self-employed by strengthening collection among targeted middle-income groups, including professionals (Ogembo 2019). Third, try harder to better manage the burdens of lower-income groups through measures such as simplification. Ultimately, such efforts may be most successful when pursued in parallel by, for example, pairing pushes to strengthen compliance with efforts to improve horizontal and vertical equity.

Reciprocity and Accountability

Whereas tax administrations have some measure of control in seeking to expand the fairness and equity of tax systems, they have limited direct control in trying to foster reciprocity and accountability. Nevertheless, what taxpayers receive in return for the taxes they pay is one of the most intuitive aspects of the social contract. Evidence overwhelmingly shows that where taxes are translated into valued public goods, tax morale tends to be significantly higher (Ali, Fjeldstad, and Sjursen 2013; Ortega, Ronconi, and Sanguinetti 2016). By contrast, when taxpayers are frustrated by the way their government spends their taxes and cannot legitimately hold the government accountable, they may end up viewing tax evasion as the only tool they have to do so (Ogembo 2020).

Successful efforts to strengthen collection of direct taxes are therefore likely to depend on the government's ability to demonstrate that taxes are used for taxpayers' benefit. Taxes must, then, be spent on public services that taxpayers value; taxpayers must be aware of those links; and, ideally, taxpayers must feel they have a voice in shaping those decisions. Yet revenue authorities do not have much control over how tax revenue will be spent or over the extent and nature of public input into such decisions. These decisions rest with other parts of the government. A key message, then, is that successfully reforming income taxation is likely to require cross-government collaboration in communicating—and demonstrating—to taxpayers the real benefits of expanded compliance.

However, tax administrations can also have a role as advocates for improved reciprocity and accountability around taxation, including exploring specific strategies under their control for strengthening these efforts. These may include increasing transparency, expanding taxpayer education and outreach, or engaging more actively with civil society actors to strengthen public understanding and engagement (Prichard 2015). Although tax administrations are often perceived as being relatively corrupt organizations, they often have a strong interest in improving the responsiveness of public spending to encourage quasi-voluntary tax compliance, thereby making their jobs significantly easier. In that sense, tax administrations in many cases may be natural allies of those pushing for greater clarity about and transparency in the links between expanded revenue and improvements in public spending outcomes.

As for their own services, revenue administrations are increasingly trying to understand—and act on—taxpayer preferences because they realize that this is a significant factor in shaping compliance attitudes. Many have set up processes to include the input of various stakeholders in the design of their services (OECD 2019a). And although taxpayer education initiatives have little direct influence on spending decisions, they highlight how tax revenues are used and are quickly becoming core parts of the outreach programs of tax administrations (OECD and FIIAPP 2015; Prichard et al., forthcoming). Some evidence suggests that these efforts to increase the visibility of the links between tax and expenditures can be as effective as enforcement strategies in improving compliance (Mascagni, Nell, and Monkam 2017). However, even though transparency may be necessary, it is not sufficient. It must be underpinned by actual improvements in public services.

Conclusion

Direct taxation of individuals in lower-income countries (where PIT collections represent a much smaller share of GDP than in OECD countries) is characterized by high levels of inequality. In those countries, PIT is collected overwhelmingly from salaried employees, often in the public service, because of the role employers play as tax collectors via income withholding. By contrast, taxation of the nonwage income sources critical to the upper and upper-middle class—such as capital gains, rental income, and the income of self-employed professionals—is particularly weak. The result is evidence of severe—often dramatic—undertaxation of the wealthy. Meanwhile, although lower-income individuals may fall below the threshold to pay PIT, they often do bear a range of other, less visible burdens. Emerging evidence thus makes clear that the key tax reform challenge is not simply increasing collection of direct taxes, but also shifting taxation in a more equitable direction by strengthening taxation of the rich and rationalizing the often fragmented, opaque, but still significant burdens of payments on the poor.

Country experience shows that targeted approaches that address segments of taxpayers and specific impediments to tax administration can yield significant gains, despite well-documented challenges. Reform design and implementation are key. A broad, poorly defined effort risks leading to generic and intrusive reforms, including large-scale institutional changes, new IT systems, and intensive capacity building, but without yielding commensurate improvements in outcomes. Research suggests that such ambitious reforms may be difficult politically while often not adequately focused on the most important technical constraints to tax administration.

More targeted, lower-profile, sequenced efforts may be necessary and could, for example, begin by investing in cleaning up taxpayer registries or better collecting and analyzing third-party data. Such an effort might also entail specific investments in strengthening audit capacity or the introduction of simplified presumptive tax regimes for professionals or other hard-to-tax groups. Tax nudges, while limited in their long-term impact, have nonetheless demonstrated their potential to yield enhanced revenue at low cost in the short term. International efforts, such as the Global Forum, to improve the ability of tax administrations to access data on wealth held abroad by their citizens are also likely to be important and offer the potential for immediate improvements in outcomes, even in countries with relatively limited technical capacity.

Meanwhile, there is growing evidence that accessing the relevant data, breaking down institutional barriers to sharing and using it effectively, and expanding audit capacity are political rather than solely technical challenges. The challenge of rationalizing burdens on lower-income groups is similarly political. Simplifying subnational taxation, for example, is technically straightforward and could yield immediate benefits. Because of the political nature of such measures, efforts to proactively build political support for reform among the broad base of taxpayers who would stand to benefit from expanded equity and revenue mobilization are likely to be important.

Part of such a strategy may lie in expanding the increasingly widespread efforts to facilitate compliance through, among other things, taxpayer education and new digital tools such as e-filing, automated customer service, and electronic and bank-based payment systems. Such facilitation measures may not only lower barriers to compliance but, where well designed, also foster expanded trust in tax systems and reduce opportunities for corruption and harassment. Future research could study these kinds of facilitation reforms more deeply to gauge their effectiveness and tease out key factors determining implementation success.

In the long term, however, the success of these efforts will almost certainly depend on achieving concrete improvements in outcomes for taxpayers. This is where trust comes in. Tax administrations themselves can play a significant role by seeking to expand fairness and equity in tax administration. This effort, in particular, is likely to place a greater emphasis on taxing the most well-off, increasing horizontal equity among middle-income taxpayers, and rationalizing burdens on lower-income groups, often at the subnational level. In general, governments in lower-income countries already have the tools to begin to address these challenges. That said, because the tax literature has only recently begun to emphasize the importance of informal fiscal burdens, there is significant scope for further research into effective ways to best reduce the overall tax burden of the poor.

The larger challenge is establishing stronger links among revenues, services, and accountability. To some extent, tax authorities can contribute to a sense of fairness and accountability by bringing more of a customer service orientation to their own interactions with taxpayers. More broadly, ensuring visible links between service delivery and increased taxation has almost always been part of political strategies to encourage quasi-voluntary compliance. Success on this front will require cooperation across government beyond revenue agencies alone. Tax administrations can also play a role as advocates for strengthening these links and, by expanding transparency and engagement, in ways that can empower taxpayers.

At its core, the challenge of strengthening direct taxation appears to be centrally about strengthening the social contract. Lower- and middle-income taxpayers are unlikely to support greater tax burdens or to voluntarily comply if the wealthy go untaxed. And taxpayers in general are unlikely to become more compliant or offer the political support needed for more effective enforcement in the absence of a belief that revenues will be used productively. Thus the most convincing strategy for improving outcomes appears to lie in combining efforts to strengthen taxation of the better-off with efforts to demonstrate the public benefits of taxation more clearly, both with a view toward mobilizing broader-based, sustainable political support for more effective direct taxation.

Notes

1. The International Labour Organization (ILO) puts the share of self-employed at 80 percent of workers in low-income countries (ILOSTAT database, "Self-employed, total [% of total employment] [modeled ILO estimate]—low income," https://data.worldbank.org/indicator/SL.EMP.SELF.ZS?locations=XM).
2. For more information, see the TADAT website, https://www.tadat.org/.

References

Aidt, T., and P. Jensen. 2009. "The Taxman Tools Up: An Event History Study of the Introduction of the Personal Income Tax." *Journal of Public Economics* 93 (1–2): 160–75.

Aiko, R., and C. Logan. 2014. "Africa's Willing Taxpayers Thwarted by Opaque Tax Systems, Corruption." Policy Paper No. 7, Afrobarometer, Accra, Ghana.

Ali, M. M., H. W. Cecil, and J. A. Knoblett. 2001. "The Effects of Tax Rates and Enforcement Policies on Taxpayer Compliance: A Study of Self-Employed Taxpayers." *Atlantic Economic Journal* 29 (2): 186–202.

Ali, M., O-H. Fjeldstad, and I. Sjursen. 2013. "To Pay or Not to Pay? Citizens' Attitudes toward Taxation in Kenya, Tanzania, Uganda, and South Africa." *World Development* 64: 828–42.

Alstadsæter, A., N. Johannesen, and G. Zucman. 2018. "Who Owns the Wealth in Tax Havens? Macro Evidence and Implications for Global Inequality." *Journal of Public Economics* 162: 89–100.

Ansón, A., M. Calijuri, M. Gallagher, U. Lautenbacher, and J. F. Redondo. 2017. "Informe de Evaluacion del Desempeno TADAT." International Monetary Fund, Washington, DC.

Asiedu, E., B. Chuqiao, D. Pavelesku, R. Sato, and T. Tanaka. 2017. "Income Tax Collection and Noncompliance in Ghana." Ghana Policy Brief, World Bank, Washington, DC.

Awasthi, R., and N. Bayraktar. 2014. "Can Tax Simplification Help Lower Tax Corruption?" Policy Research Working Paper 6988, World Bank, Washington, DC.

Bahl, R. 2004. "Reaching the Hardest to Tax: Consequences and Possibilities." In *Taxing the Hard-to-Tax: Lessons from Theory and Practice*, edited by James Alm, Jorge Martinez-Vazquez, and Sally Wallace, 337–54. Bingley, UK: Emerald Group Publishing.

Beer, S., M. Kasper, E. Kirchler, and B. Erard. 2020. "Do Audits Deter or Provoke Future Tax Noncompliance? Evidence on Self-Employed Taxpayers." *CESifo Economic Studies* 66 (3): 248–64.

Besley, T., and T. Persson. 2013. "Taxation and Development." In *Handbook of Public Economics: Volume 5*, edited by Alan J. Auerbach, Raj Chetty, Martin Feldstein, and Emmanuel Saez, 51–100. New York: Elsevier.

Bhat, V. N. 2017. "Attitudes toward Tax Evasion and the Choice of Self-Employment." In *Applied Behavioural Economics Research and Trends*, edited by Rodica Ianole, 39–53. Hershey, PA: IGI Global.

Bird, R. M. 2013. "Foreign Advice and Tax Policy in Developing Countries." International Center for Public Policy Working Paper No. 13-07, Andrew Young School of Policy Studies, Georgia State University, Atlanta.

Bird, R. M., and S. Wallace. 2004. "Is It Really So Hard to Tax the Hard-to-Tax? The Context and Role of Presumptive Taxes." In *Taxing the Hard-to-Tax: Lessons from Theory and Practice*, edited by J. Alm, J. Martinez-Vazquez, and S. Wallace, 121–58. Bingley, UK: Emerald Group Publishing.

Bird, R., and E. Zolt. 2014. "Redistribution via Taxation: The Limited Role of the Personal Income Tax in Developing Countries." *Annals of Economics and Finance* 15 (2): 625–83.

BIT (Behavioural Insights Team) and DJP (Indonesian Directorate General of Taxes). 2019. "Encouraging Earlier Tax Returns in Indonesia." Project report, BIT, London; DJP, Jakarta.

Blumenthal, M., and J. Slemrod. 1992. "The Compliance Cost of the U.S. Individual Income Tax System: A Second Look after Tax Reform." *National Tax Journal* 45 (2): 185–202.

Brautigam, D., O-H. Fjeldstad, and M. Moore, eds. 2008. *Taxation and State-Building in Developing Countries: Capacity and Consent*. Cambridge, UK: Cambridge University Press.

Carter, L., L. C. Shaupp, J. Hobbs, and R. Campbell. 2011. "The Role of Security and Trust in the Adoption of Online Tax Filing." *Transforming Government: People, Process and Policy* 5 (4): 303–18.

Chattopadhyay, S., and A. Das-Gupta. 2002. "The Personal Income Tax in India: Compliance Costs and Compliance Behaviour of Taxpayers." Project of the Study Team on Compliance Costs, National Institute of Public Finance and Policy (NIPFP), New Delhi.

Chetty, R., J. N. Friedman, and E. Saez. 2013. "Using Differences in Knowledge across Neighborhoods to Uncover the Impacts of the EITC on Earnings." Working Paper No. 18232, National Bureau of Economic Research, Cambridge, MA.

Demirgüç-Kunt, A., L. Klapper, D. Singer, S. Ansar, and J. Hess. 2018. "The Unbanked." In *The Global Findex Database 2017: Measuring Financial Inclusion and the Fintech Revolution*, 35–41. Washington, DC: World Bank.

Dom, R., and M. Miller. 2018. "Reforming Tax Systems in the Developing World: What Can We Learn from the Past?" Overseas Development Institute, London.

Dunning, T., F. Monestier, R. Piñeiro, F. Rosenblatt, and G. Tuñón. 2017. "Is Paying Taxes Habit Forming? Theory and Evidence from Uruguay." Working paper, University of California, Berkeley.

Easter, G. 2008. "Capacity, Consent and Tax Collection in Post-Communist States." In *Taxation and State-Building in Developing Countries: Capacity and Consent*, edited by Deborah Brautigam, Odd-Helge Fjeldstad, and Mick Moore, 64–88. Cambridge, UK: Cambridge University Press.

Engström, P., and B. Holmlund. 2009. "Tax Evasion and Self-Employment in a High-Tax Country: Evidence from Sweden." *Applied Economics* 41 (19): 2419–30.

Erard, B., and C-C. Ho. 2004. "Mapping the US Tax Compliance Continuum." *Contributions to Economic Analysis* 268: 167–86.

Fairfield, T. 2013. "Going Where the Money Is: Strategies for Taxing Economic Elites in Unequal Democracies." *World Development* 47: 42–57.

Fjeldstad, O-H. 2005. "Corruption in Tax Administration: Lessons from Institutional Reforms in Uganda." Working Paper No. 2005:10, Chr. Michelsen Institute, Bergen, Norway.

Fjeldstad, O-H., and K. K. Heggstad. 2011. "The Tax Systems in Mozambique, Tanzania and Zambia: Capacity and Constraints." Report No. 2011:3, Chr. Michelsen Institute, Bergen, Norway.

Fjeldstad, O-H., and K. K. Heggstad. 2012. "Building Taxpayer Culture in Mozambique, Tanzania, and Zambia: Achievements, Challenges and Policy Recommendations." Report No. 2012:1, Chr. Michelsen Institute, Bergen, Norway.

Fjeldstad, O-H., C. Kagoma, E. Mdee, I. H. Sjursen, and V. Somville. 2020. "The Customer Is King: Evidence on VAT Compliance in Tanzania." *World Development* 128: 104841.

Fjeldstad, O-H., and M. Moore. 2008. "Tax Reform and State-Building in a Globalised World." In *Taxation and State-Building in Developing Countries: Capacity and Consent*, edited by D. Brautigam, O-H. Fjeldstad, and M. Moore, 235–60. Cambridge, UK: Cambridge University Press.

Gallant, L. M., M. J. Culnan, and P. McLoughlin. 2007. "Why People E-file (or Don't E-file) Their Income Taxes." In *Proceedings of the 40th Annual Hawaii International Conference on System Sciences—2007* 1: 107b.

Gatt, L., and O. Owen. 2018. "Direct Taxation and State–Society Relations in Lagos, Nigeria." *Development and Change* 49 (5): 1195–222.

Genschel, P., and L. Seelkopf. 2016. "Did They Learn to Tax? Taxation Trends Outside the OECD." *Review of International Political Economy* 23 (2): 216–244.

Gerber, C., A. Klemm, L. Liu, and V. Mylonas. 2018. "Income Tax Progressivity: Trends and Implications." IMF Working Paper WP/18/246, International Monetary Fund, Washington, DC.

Goode, R. 1993. "Tax Advice to Developing Countries: An Historical Survey." *World Development* 21 (1): 37–53.

Hallsworth, M., J. A. List, R. D. Metcalfe, and I. Vlaey. 2017. "The Behavioralist as Tax Collector: Using Natural Field Experiments to Enhance Tax Compliance." *Journal of Public Economics* 148: 14–31.

Hassan, M., and W. Prichard. 2016. "The Political Economy of Domestic Tax Reform in Bangladesh: Political Settlements, Informal Institutions and the Negotiation of Reform." *Journal of Development Studies* 52 (12): 1704–21.

Hernandez, M., J. Jamison, E. Korczyc, N. Mazar, and R. Sormani. 2017. *Applying Behavioral Insights to Improve Tax Collection: Experimental Evidence from Poland.* Washington, DC: World Bank.

Hernandez, M., J. Karver, M. Negre, and J. Perng. 2019. *Promoting Tax Compliance in Kosovo with Behavioral Insights.* Washington, DC: World Bank.

Hug, S., and F. Spörri. 2011. "Referendums, Trust, and Tax Evasion." *European Journal of Political Economy* 27 (1): 120–31.

Hurst, E., G. Li, and B. Pugsley. 2014. "Are Household Surveys Like Tax Forms? Evidence from Income Underreporting of the Self-Employed." *Review of Economics and Statistics* 96 (1): 19–33.

Ibrahim, I. B. 2013. "Electronic Filing of Personal Income Tax Returns in Malaysia: Determinants and Compliance Costs." PhD diss., Curtin Business School, School of Economics and Finance, Curtin University, Perth, Australia.

IFC (International Finance Corporation), MIGA (Multilateral Investment Guarantee Agency), and World Bank. 2009. "A Handbook for Tax Simplification." Report No. 58815, World Bank, Washington, DC.

IMF (International Monetary Fund). 2011. "Revenue Mobilization in Developing Countries." Policy paper, IMF, Washington, DC.

Iversen, V., O-H. Fjeldstad, G. Bahiigwa, F. Ellis, and R. James. 2006. "Private Tax Collection—Remnant of the Past or a Way Forward? Evidence from Rural Uganda." *Public Administration and Development* 26 (4): 317–28.

Joshi, A., W. Prichard, and C. Heady. 2014. "Taxing the Informal Economy: The Current State of Knowledge and Agendas for Future Research." *Journal of Development Studies* 50 (10): 1325–47.

Kamleitner, B., C. Korunka, and E. Kirchler. 2012. "Tax Compliance of Small Business Owners: A Literature Review and Conceptual Framework." *International Journal of Entrepreneurial Behaviour and Research* 18 (3): 330–51.

Kangave, J., K. Byrne, and J. Karangwa. 2020. "Tax Compliance of Wealthy Individuals in Rwanda." Working Paper No. 109, Institute of Development Studies, Brighton, UK.

Kangave, J., S. Nakato, R. Waiswa, and P. Lumala Zzimbe. 2016. "Boosting Revenue Collection through Taxing High Net Worth Individuals: The Case of Uganda." Working Paper No. 45, International Centre for Tax and Development, Brighton, UK.

Kangave, J., S. Nakato, R. Waiswa, M. Nalukwago, and P. Lumala Zzimbe. 2018. "What Can We Learn from the Uganda Revenue Authority's Approach to Taxing High Net Worth Individuals?" Working Paper No. 72, International Centre for Tax and Development, Brighton, UK.

Keen, M. 2012. "Tax and Development—Again." Working Paper No. 12/220, International Monetary Fund, Washington, DC.

Kettle, S., M. Hernandez, S. Ruda, and M. Sanders. 2016. "Behavioral Interventions in Tax Compliance: Evidence from Guatemala." Policy Research Working Paper 7690, World Bank, Washington, DC.

Khan, A., A. Khwaja, and B. Olken. 2016. "Tax Farming Redux: Experimental Evidence on Performance Pay for Tax Collectors." *Quarterly Journal of Economics* 131 (1): 219–71.

Kira, A. R. 2017. "An Evaluation of Governments' Initiatives in Enhancing Small Taxpayers' Voluntary Tax Compliance in Developing Countries." *International Journal of Academic Research in Accounting, Finance, and Management Sciences* 7 (1): 253–67.

Kleven, H., M. Knudsen, C. Kreiner, S. Pedersen, and E. Saez. 2011. "Unwilling or Unable to Cheat? Evidence from a Tax Audit Experiment in Denmark." *Econometrica* 79 (3): 651–92.

Kogler, C., and E. Kirchler. 2020. "Taxpayers' Subjective Concepts of Taxes, Tax Evasion, and Tax Avoidance." In *Ethics and Taxation*, edited by Robert F. van Brederode, 191–205. Singapore: Springer.

Kogler, C., S. Muehlbacher, and E. Kirchler. 2015. "Testing the 'Slippery Slope Framework' among Self-Employed Taxpayers." *Economics of Governance* 16 (2): 125–42.

le Maire, D., and B. Schjerning. 2013. "Tax Bunching, Income Shifting and Self-Employment." *Journal of Public Economics* 107: 1–18.

Leonardo, G., and J. Martinez-Vazquez. 2016. "Politicians, Bureaucrats, and Tax Morale: What Shapes Tax Compliance Attitudes?" International Center for Public Policy Working Paper, Andrew Young School of Policy Studies, Georgia State University, Atlanta.

Lieberman, E. 2003. *Race and Regionalism in the Politics of Taxation in Brazil and South Africa*. Cambridge, MA: Cambridge University Press.

Luts, M., and M. Van Roy. 2019. "Nudging in the Context of Taxation: How the Belgian FPS Finance Uses Behavioural Insights to Encourage Taxpayers to Pay Faster." IOTA Papers, Intra-European Organisation of Tax Administrations, Budapest, Hungary.

Manoli, D. S., and N. Turner. 2014. "Nudges and Learning: Evidence from Informational Interventions for Low-Income Taxpayers." Working Paper No. 20178, National Bureau of Economic Research, Cambridge, MA.

Mascagni, G., R. Dom, and F. Santoro. 2021. "The VAT in Practice: Equity, Enforcement and Complexity." Working Paper No. 117, International Centre for Tax and Development, Brighton, UK.

Mascagni, G., N. Monkam, and C. Nell. 2016. "Unlocking the Potential of Administrative Data in Africa: Tax Compliance and Progressivity in Rwanda." Working Paper No. 56, International Centre for Tax and Development, Brighton, UK.

Mascagni, G., D. Mukama, and F. Santoro. 2019. "An Analysis of Discrepancies in Taxpayers' VAT Declarations in Rwanda." Working Paper No. 92, International Centre for Tax and Development, Brighton, UK.

Mascagni, G., C. Nell, and N. Monkam. 2017. "One Size Does Not Fit All: A Field Experiment on the Drivers of Tax Compliance and Delivery Methods in Rwanda." Working Paper No. 58, International Centre for Tax and Development, Brighton, UK.

Mascagni, G., F. Santoro, and D. Mukama. 2019. "Teach to Comply? Evidence from a Taxpayer Education Programme in Rwanda." Working Paper No. 91, International Centre for Tax and Development, Brighton, UK.

Mascagni, G., F. Santoro, D. Mukama, J. Karangwa, and N. Hakizimana. Forthcoming. "Active Ghosts: Nil-Filing in Rwanda." Working paper, Institute of Development Studies, Brighton, UK.

Mayega, J., R. Ssuuna, M. Mubajje, M. I. Nalukwago, and L. Muwonge. 2019. "How Clean Is Our Taxpayer Register? Data Management in the Uganda Revenue Authority." African Tax Administration Paper No. 12, International Centre for Tax and Development, Brighton, UK.

Moore, M. 2020. "What Is Wrong with African Tax Administration?" Working Paper No. 111, International Centre for Tax and Development, Brighton, UK.

Moore, M., W. Prichard, and O-H. Fjeldstad. 2018a. "Small Taxes and Large Burdens: Informal and Subnational Revenues." In *Taxing Africa: Coercion, Reform and Development*, 147–78. London: Zed Books.

Moore, M., W. Prichard, and O-H. Fjeldstad. 2018b. *Taxing Africa: Coercion, Reform and Development*. London: Zed Books.

OECD (Organisation for Economic Co-operation and Development). 2019a. *Tax Administration 2019: Comparative Information on OECD and Other Advanced and Emerging Economies*. Paris: OECD Publishing.

OECD (Organisation for Economic Co-operation and Development). 2019b. "What Is Driving Tax Morale?" Public consultation document, OECD, Paris.

OECD (Organisation for Economic Co-operation and Development) and FIIAPP (Ibero-American Foundation for Administration and Public Policies). 2015. *Building Tax Culture, Compliance and Citizenship: A Global Source Book on Taxpayer Education*. Paris: OECD Publishing.

Ogembo, D. 2019. "Are Presumptive Taxes a Good Option for Taxing Self-Employed Professionals in Low- and Middle-Income Countries?" *Journal of Tax Administration* 5 (2): 26–57.

Ogembo, D. 2020. "Taxation of Self-Employed Professionals in Africa: Three Lessons from a Kenyan Case Study." African Tax Administration Paper No. 17, International Centre for Tax and Development, Brighton, UK.

Okunogbe, O. M., and V. M. J. Pouliquen. 2018. "Technology, Taxation, and Corruption: Evidence from the Introduction of Electronic Tax Filing." Policy Research Working Paper 8452, World Bank, Washington, DC.

Olken, B. M., and M. Singhal. 2011. "Informal Taxation." *American Economic Journal: Applied Economics* 3: 1–28.

Ortega, D., L. Ronconi, and P. Sanguinetti. 2016. "Reciprocity and Willingness to Pay Taxes: Evidence from a Survey Experiment in Latin America." *Economía* 16 (2): 55–87.

Paler, L., W. Prichard, R. Sanchez de la Sierra, and C. Samii. 2017. "Survey on Total Tax Burden in the DRC, Final Report." Study for the Department for International Development (UK), Kinshasa, Democratic Republic of Congo.

Peter, K. S., S. Buttrick, and D. Duncan. 2010. "Global Reform of Personal Income Taxation, 1981–2005: Evidence from 189 Countries." *National Tax Journal* 63 (3): 447–78.

Piketty, T., and N. Qian. 2009. "Income Inequality and Progressive Income Taxation in China and India, 1986–2015." *American Economic Journal: Applied Economics* 1 (2): 53–63.

Piketty, T., and E. Saez. 2007. "How Progressive Is the U.S. Federal Tax System? A Historical and International Perspective." *Journal of Economic Perspectives* 21 (1): 3–24.

Pomeranz, D. 2015. "No Taxation without Information: Deterrence and Self-Enforcement in the Value Added Tax." *American Economic Review* 105 (8): 2539–69.

Prichard, W. 2009. "Taxation and Development in Ghana: Finance, Equity and Accountability." Tax Justice Country Report Series, Tax Justice Network, London.

Prichard, W. 2015. *Taxation, Responsiveness and Accountability in Sub-Saharan Africa: The Dynamics of Tax Bargaining.* Cambridge, UK: Cambridge University Press.

Prichard, W., R. Beach, F. Mohiuddin, and V. van den Boogaard. Forthcoming. "The Micro-Links between Taxation and Accountability Initiatives." Working Paper, International Centre for Tax and Development, Brighton, UK.

Prichard, W., and M. Moore. 2018. "Tax Reform for Low-Income Countries: Five Ideas for Simplifying Tax Systems to Fit Local Realities." Summary Brief No. 17, International Centre for Tax and Development, Brighton, UK.

Reynolds, A. 2008. "Marginal Tax Rates." In *The Concise Encyclopedia of Economics,* Library of Economics and Liberty (Econlib). https://www.econlib.org/library/Enc/MarginalTaxRates.html.

Romanov, D. 2003. "Costs and Benefits of Marginal Reallocation of Tax Agency Resources in Pursuit of the Hard-to-Tax." Paper presented at Conference on the Hard-to-Tax, International Studies Program, Andrew Young School of Policy Studies, Atlanta.

Rozner, S., S. Hester, R. Ettrige, and M. Bardawil. 2016. "Performance Assessment Report: Hashemite Kingdom of Jordan." Tax Administration Diagnostic Assessment Tool (TADAT) Assessment, TADAT Secretariat.

Saez, E. 2010. "Do Taxpayers Bunch at Kink Points?" *American Economic Journal: Economic Policy* 2 (3): 180–212.

Santoro, F., and W. Mdluli. 2019. "Nil-Filing in Eswatini: Should the Revenue Administration Be Concerned?" African Tax Administration Paper No. 6, International Centre for Tax and Development, Brighton, UK.

Schuetze, H. J. 2002. "Profiles of Tax Non-Compliance among the Self-Employed in Canada: 1969–1992." *Canadian Public Policy* 28 (2): 219–38.

Slemrod, J., and T. Velayudhan. 2018. "Do Firms Remit at Least 85% of Tax Everywhere? New Evidence from India." *Journal of Tax Administration* 4 (1): 24–37.

Tadesse, H., and G. Taube. 1996. "Presumptive Taxation in Sub-Saharan Africa: Experiences and Prospects." Working Paper No. 65/5, International Monetary Fund, Washington, DC.

Tendler, J. 2002. "Small Firms, the Informal Sector, and the Devil's Deal." *IDS Bulletin* 33 (3).

Terkper, S. 2003. "Managing Small and Medium-Size Taxpayers in Developing Economies." *Tax Notes International* 29 (2): 211–34.

Thaler, R. H., and C. R. Sunstein. 2008. *Nudge: Improving Decisions about Health, Wealth, and Happiness.* New Haven, CT: Yale University Press.

Torgler, B. 2004. "Tax Morale in Asian Countries." *Journal of Asian Economics* 15 (2): 237–66.

Ulyssea, G. 2018. "Firms, Informality, and Development: Theory and Evidence from Brazil." *American Economic Review* 108 (8): 2015–47.

van den Boogaard, V., W. Prichard, R. Beach, and F. Mohiuddin. Forthcoming. "Enabling Tax Bargaining: Supporting More Meaningful Tax Transparency and Taxpayer Engagement in Ghana and Sierra Leone." *Development Policy Review.*

van den Boogaard, V., W. Prichard, and S. Jibao. 2019. "Informal Taxation in Sierra Leone: Magnitudes, Perceptions and Implications." *African Affairs* 118 (471): 259–84.

van den Boogaard, V., and F. Santoro. 2021. "Explaining Informal Taxation and Revenue Generation: Evidence from South-Central Somalia." Working Paper No. 118, International Centre for Tax and Development, Brighton, UK.

Waris, A. 2013. "Growing Tax Evasion a Serious Threat: Only 1.2m Pakistanis File Tax Returns, Which Is Even Less than 1%." *Daily Times Pakistan,* December 29, 2013.

Williams, C. C., and M. A. Lansky. 2013. "Informal Employment in Developed and Developing Economies: Perspectives and Policy Responses." *International Labour Review* 152 (3–4): 355–80.

Williams, C. C., and J. Padmore. 2013. " 'Envelope Wages' in the European Union." *International Labour Review* 152 (3–4): 411–30.

World Bank. 1988. *World Development Report 1988.* New York: Oxford University Press for the World Bank.

Yilmaz, F., and J. Coolidge. 2013. "Can E-filing Reduce Tax Compliance Costs in Developing Countries?" Policy Research Working Paper 6647, World Bank, Washington, DC.

Yücedoğru, R., and J. Hasseldine. 2016. "Understanding Tax Morale of SMEs: A Qualitative Study." *eJournal of Tax Research* 14 (3): 531–66.

Zucman, G. 2014. "Taxing across Borders: Tracking Personal Wealth and Corporate Profits." *Journal of Economic Perspectives* 28 (4): 121–48.

Zucman, G. 2015. *The Hidden Wealth of Nations: The Scourge of Tax Havens.* Chicago: University of Chicago Press.

CHAPTER 3

Taxing High-Net-Worth Individuals

Wilson Prichard, Roel Dom, and Anna Custers

The Tax Compliance Challenge

The largest gap in tax compliance in most low- and middle-income countries is in taxes on income and wealth—the latter most prominently through property taxes. In Organisation for Economic Co-operation and Development (OECD) countries, taxes on personal income amount to about 8 percent of the gross domestic product (GDP), and social security contributions account for about 10 percent of GDP on average. By contrast, in low- and lower-middle-income countries taxes on personal income, including social security contributions, average only about 3.5 percent of GDP (see figure 2.2 in chapter 2).

Across countries, taxes on wealth are more limited, though here, too, lower-income countries raise significantly less revenue. The most important source of wealth taxation across countries is property taxes, which are the foundation of local government finances in almost all OECD countries, generally amounting to 1–2 percent of GDP and sometimes more. In low-income and lower-middle-income countries, property taxes are severely underexploited, with more fragmented data suggesting that in many countries they amount to only 0.1–0.2 percent of GDP and rarely more than 1 percent of GDP in even the most successful cases (see figure 6.1 in chapter 6). Wealthier countries also frequently collect taxes on inheritance and related transfers of wealth, though revenues are generally limited.

The COVID-19 pandemic has seen a growing consensus about the importance of strengthening taxation of the wealthy. In lower-income countries, such a step generally requires both broadening the base among wealthy taxpayers, some of whom are not registered at all, and improving compliance among the relatively wealthy, higher-income earners. Central to this challenge is improving taxation of the income from diverse nonlabor sources, including property, and devising new strategies for taxing wealth held and earned offshore. Meanwhile, worldwide there has been renewed interest in strengthening broader taxes on wealth, with some middle-income countries passing new legislation. For low-income countries, broad-based taxes on wealth are unlikely to have the highest priority because of the immediate opportunities to strengthen enforcement of the existing taxes on income and property, although those efforts may also lay the foundation for broader taxation of wealth in the future.

High-net-worth individuals (HNWIs) are typically defined as those with wealth exceeding US$1 million, excluding a person's main residence (OECD 2009). HNWIs include both high-wealth and high-income individuals. Generally, taxes on HNWIs can target diverse bases: stocks of wealth (such as real and other property), flows (income, savings, and consumption), and hybrids (capital gains and asset transfers). This chapter discusses most of these, focusing on the challenges of taxing the diverse incomes and property of wealthier individuals.

Small numbers of wealthy taxpayers should, in theory, account for a very large share of all income tax revenue, reflecting their ownership of a large share of total income. In the United States, for example, the top 1 percent of taxpayers contributes an estimated 37 percent of all income tax revenue, despite avoidance and evasion via international tax havens (Tanzi 2018). This share would likely be even higher in most low- and middle-income countries if income taxes were well enforced owing to high inequality and the fact that most citizens fall below the threshold for income taxation.

Comparable numbers are not available for property taxes, but the vast wealth of HNWIs—making up about 35 percent of the declared total wealth in OECD countries (New World Wealth 2018)—would be expected to translate into a large share of property tax payments. Again, this may be even truer in low- and middle-income countries, where property taxes are concentrated in larger cities and in more formal settlements, and where there is evidence that the wealthy are more heavily invested in real estate (Battle 2014).

Tax Revenue Losses from HNWIs

Income Taxes

Although the wealthy should provide the bulk of income tax revenue, in practice they seem the most able to avoid and evade legally required income taxes. Across most low- and middle-income countries, most personal income tax revenue is produced by withholding taxes on salaries. Yet the wealthiest taxpayers around the world secure most of their income from nonwage sources, mostly from professional services, investment income, capital gains (often on real estate), and rental income. These sources of income are often barely taxed, particularly in lower-income countries. The effective tax rate for the top 1 percent in the United States is estimated at 24 percent—at the lower end of the OECD spectrum—while for

Rwanda's top decile, it can be as low as 0.7 percent (Mascagni, Monkam, and Nell 2016; Piketty and Saez 2007).

Weak income tax collection is driven predominantly by weak domestic tax systems. However, this problem is exacerbated by the lack of transparency in the international tax system. According to the lower-bound estimate produced by Alstadsæter, Johannesen, and Zucman (2018), the equivalent of 10 percent of world GDP is held as financial wealth in offshore tax havens outside the reach of national tax authorities. This estimate excludes other nonfinancial sources of wealth. The overall wealth held offshore is thus almost certainly somewhat higher—and possibly substantially higher, which is reflected in other estimates (see review in Alstadsæter, Johannesen, and Zucman 2018). As illustrated in figure 3.1, the authors find that this average masks much regional heterogeneity. However, differences across income levels are much more modest. In lower-income countries, about as much financial wealth, as a share of GDP, is held offshore as in richer countries. Critically, they also find that that offshore wealth is dominated by HNWIs, who they estimate often hold 30–40 percent of their total wealth offshore—and sometimes more. This finding is consistent with evidence elsewhere: in Colombia the rich were found to be much more likely to hide their wealth offshore, with over 40 percent of the top 0.01 percent hiding on average one-third of their wealth (Londoño-Vélez and Ávila-Mahecha 2021).

FIGURE 3.1 **Offshore Wealth as a Share of GDP, by Region and Country Income Group, 2007**

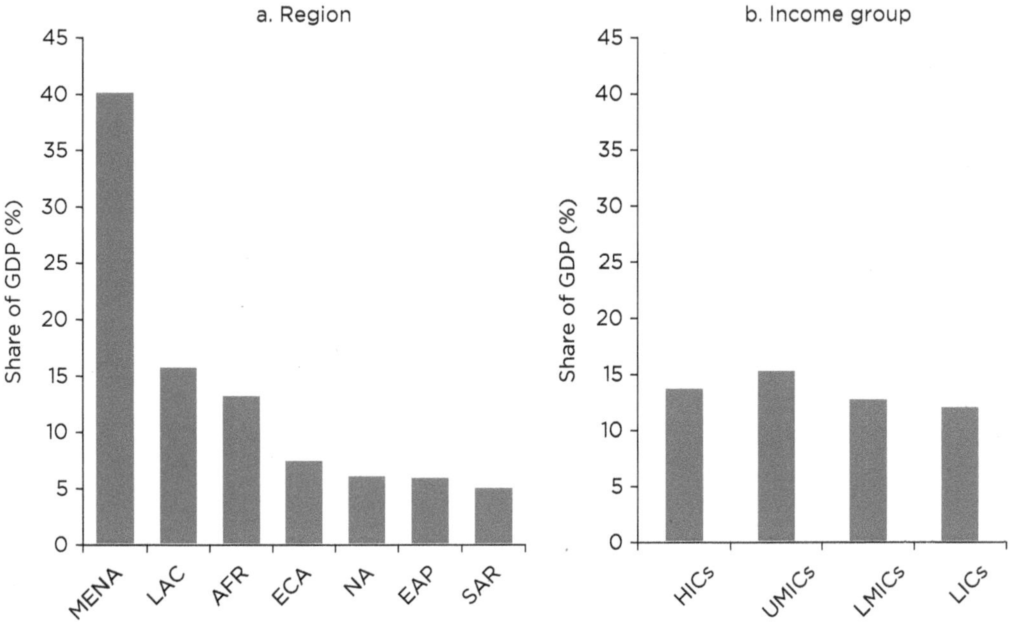

Source: Alstadsæter, Johannesen, and Zucman 2018, table A.3.
Note: AFR = Africa; EAP = East Asia and Pacific; ECA = Europe and Central Asia; LAC = Latin America and the Caribbean; MENA = Middle East and North Africa; NA = North America; SAR = South Asia. HICs = high-income countries; LICs = low-income countries; LMICs = lower-middle-income countries; UMICs = upper-middle-income countries.

Property Taxes

Meanwhile, the weakness of property taxes is a growing concern amid booming real estate markets and investments in many low- and middle-income countries. Data suggest that capital cities, particularly in many of these countries, have been home to some of the most rapidly appreciating real estate values in the world, with some prices rivaling those in the most expensive cities in OECD countries. This situation appears to have been driven, in part, by HNWIs reinvesting their wealth in real estate, which has been viewed as a stable, lightly taxed, and relatively opaque destination for (often undeclared) wealth. Against this background, the impetus for stronger taxation of property—and especially speculative real estate investments—is growing as a way for governments to capture some of the gains from urban property booms, increase affordability in urban areas, and reduce opacity in real estate markets (Goodfellow 2017b).

Wealth Taxes

Despite renewed interest, the taxation of net wealth remains very limited in most countries. The term *wealth tax* refers to the taxation of an individual's net worth—that is, assets minus liabilities. The assets can include, among other things, cash, shares, jewelry, property, or art. Property taxes are also a form of wealth tax. Taxes can be levied as well on the transfer of wealth, such as through an inheritance tax.

French economist Thomas Piketty resuscitated the notion of using wealth taxes to raise revenue and curb inequality (Piketty 2014). However, even though estimates suggest that a wealth tax can raise around 1 percent of GDP in revenue (Saez and Zucman 2019), few countries have one, although inheritance taxes are common (Drometer et al. 2018). In fact, many countries have abolished their wealth taxes. In 1990, 12 OECD countries taxed wealth, but only four still did so in 2017 (OECD 2018). Technical challenges are a partial explanation. Putting a value on assets such as art or privately held businesses is challenging. Meanwhile, the wealthy have become adept at sheltering and hiding wealth from taxation, often by holding it offshore.

The Broader Cost of Tax Inequity: A Weaker Social Contract

The weakness of taxes on the wealthy not only affects revenue but also risks undermining broader trust in the tax system and weakening the social contract. Taxpayers are less likely to trust the tax system if they do not feel that everyone pays their "fair share." The most egregious, and apparently widely understood, example of tax inequity is the ability of the wealthy to avoid paying taxes.

This inequity may have consequences for the tax system more broadly:

- It is likely to undermine the willingness of other taxpayers to comply with their tax obligations "quasi-voluntarily."[1]

- Insofar as inequity undermines trust in tax authorities, it likely undermines governments' ability to mobilize broader popular support for tax reform.

- When some wealthy taxpayers can effectively "opt out" of paying taxes, popular advocacy aimed at demanding reciprocity and accountability for tax payments is undermined, thereby weakening the social contract (Prichard 2015).

Ultimately, recognition of the importance of building trust and the social contract suggests that there may be substantial value in redirecting reform efforts toward taxing the wealthy. In recent decades, taxes on personal income and property have received relatively less attention than strengthening the value added tax (VAT). The emphasis on the VAT reflects a pragmatic calculus: the likely revenue gains from VAT reform appear likely to outweigh those from income and property taxes because of the high technical and political barriers to strengthening the latter. But there is a growing sense that such an approach may be short-sighted. Taxing the wealthy more effectively is critical not only to increasing revenue, but also to building trust in the tax system, thereby unlocking more sustained political support for taxation and the achievement of longer-term gains.

Barriers to Reform

Technical and Capacity Challenges to Tax Enforcement

The weakness of taxes on the wealthy is rooted, in part, in the technical, legal, and capacity challenges that limit income tax enforcement. Effective enforcement depends on the ability of tax authorities to access information on taxpayers' income. Access is relatively straightforward in the case of wages because essentially all countries require firms to withhold taxes from salary payments. Firms, in turn, have reasonable incentives to do so relatively honestly to reduce their taxable profits.

The trouble arises for nonwage payments. How can governments establish the amounts of private payments for professional services or rental payments? Meanwhile, taxes on capital gains require detailed information on the purchase and sale prices of assets, which is frequently not readily available, particularly when assets are held overseas. As a result, capital gains taxes are likely to be the most systematically undercollected of all the major taxes in low- and middle-income countries, although consistent data are not available.

In OECD countries, governments seek to close the enforcement gap through access to third-party data such as bank accounts, credit cards, stock exchanges, and land registries. Such data can then provide the basis for effective audits, both by informing the risk-based assessment of files for audit and by providing the information needed to assess liabilities. The success of third-party information matching has been much more uneven in middle-income countries. Costa Rica, for example, hardly uses any third-party information, whereas in India the tax administration has access to only a limited number of outside sources of information (OECD 2017).

Few low-income countries have systematic access to such third-party data, and their audit capacity is also often sharply limited. The third-party information that is available is usually held within the tax administration because information sharing across government institutions is often difficult. Moreover, even when data are available, the potential of data cross-checking is not always fully exploited (Mascagni, Mukama, and Santoro 2019). Although recent reforms to international tax rules should, in principle, provide governments with access to information on the assets of taxpayers held abroad, in practice concerns persist that the hurdles to accessing and using such information will remain formidable for lower-income countries. These issues will require continued monitoring and support in the years ahead.

Property taxes should offer a far less daunting enforcement challenge because property is both visible and immovable, but complex and dysfunctional laws have often complicated improved outcomes (see chapter 6 for more detail). The central technical barrier to more effective property taxation lies in the need to assess the value of taxable property and then to update that value regularly. Many countries use relatively complex criteria for valuing properties—most often, assessment of "market value" or "rental value" based on expert assessments, despite frequently inactive and opaque property markets. Yet they often employ few professional valuation officers to do so (Mohiuddin and Ohemeng, forthcoming). The result is that new properties fail to be valued in a timely manner, while older property valuations can get wildly out of date—sometimes not reassessed for decades—and thus erode the level of tax revenue and equity across properties.

Meanwhile, reliance on often difficult-to-assess "market values" is ripe for both collusion and corruption—collusion when valuation officers accept bribes to reduce assessed values, and corruption when they threaten to inflate valuations to extract payments (Khan, Khwaja, and Olken 2016). Finally, property tax systems in many countries are also affected by large loopholes, including for primary residences, government-owned property, and, in some cases, exemptions for certain kinds of new developments (Franzsen and McCluskey 2017; Piracha and Moore 2015).

Obstacles to Quasi-Voluntary Compliance

The weakness of the taxes levied on HNWIs—especially income taxes—appears to reflect a lack of both trust and quasi-voluntary compliance among potential taxpayers. Although the evidence is limited, what is available suggests that HNWIs differ from the wider population in terms of their norms, values, and appetite for risk. They also have greater access to tax advisers and wealth managers who design and help implement tax minimization strategies. This access is likely to have consequences for trust and thus for tax compliance. A higher tolerance for risk, for example, may lead them to explore more aggressive tax planning strategies or to be less sensitive to enforcement (Gangl and Torgler 2020).

At the level of fairness, although some wealthy taxpayers generally pay far less than they should under the law, many privately express concerns that greater cooperation with tax authorities could result in harassment by tax collectors seeking to meet revenue targets—and audits are often reported to be highly antagonistic.

As for equity, the weak taxation of the wealthy is a concern for most taxpayers, but the wealthy themselves appear to worry about being singled out for enforcement while others fail to pay. To the extent that the wealthy identify with and liken themselves to their wealthy peers, this social reference point may give rise to perceptions of horizontal and vertical inequalities *among* the wealthy, even as they may be severely undertaxed relative to most taxpayers.

And finally, like other taxpayers the wealthy worry that their tax payments will not translate into effective services and broader improvements in accountability. This worry may be especially pertinent in low- and middle-income countries, where governments may simply not have the capacity to provide benefits. Research has suggested that some wealthy taxpayers may be unwilling to pay taxes—particularly local property taxes—because they often consume private alternatives to public schools, health care, and other government services (Jibao and Prichard 2015). However, as further described in this chapter, recent evidence indicates that strengthening the visible links between tax payments and services can make a difference.

Political Constraints

Above all, the weakness of income taxes reflects the absence of political will to support reform. Although there are certainly technical barriers to more effective income taxation, governments have failed to use many of the tools available to them. Most obviously, many governments have failed to take advantage of even rudimentary data sharing across government agencies to detect avoidance and evasion.

Failures to Use Available Data and Build Capacity

In a recent study in Uganda, a simple comparison of data from corporate taxes, customs declarations, and income tax declarations revealed that many of the country's large importers and business owners were not paying any income taxes (box 3.1). Likewise, many individuals identified by the popular media as the country's wealthiest people did not appear on the tax rolls. This information was readily available, and political pressure seems to be the only compelling explanation for ignoring it (Kangave et al. 2016). Yet anecdotal evidence suggests that weak or no data sharing is common in many countries.

In the same vein, international leaks in recent years have revealed significant wealth held offshore by residents of low- and middle-income countries, but most governments have taken little action against them. In turn, it is well known that accessing third-party data, whether from within or beyond government, can greatly improve enforcement, and yet many low- and middle-income countries make little use of such data or even legally limit such use (Best 2014; Kleven et al. 2011). Government information on assets (such as property, houses, and cars) and business registrations can quickly point to potential avoidance and evasion, but they are frequently not pursued. Access to private third-party data, most notably from bank accounts, can be hugely valuable, but many low- and middle-income countries continue to restrict access to such information.

Meanwhile, investments in building audit capacity have remained limited despite strong evidence of significant returns from additional capacity (Kleven et al. 2011). At the same time, as Indonesia's experience with the establishment of a tax office for HNWIs has revealed, a higher audit capacity may lead to mixed compliance effects and does not always produce additional income tax revenue. In Indonesia, the higher audit threat led to a sizable increase in reported taxable income by HNWIs, but it did not increase the income tax paid, and it reduced the reported net wealth, suggesting that wealthy taxpayers find other ways to avoid taxation when monitoring increases (Chan et al., forthcoming). More creative options—such as a greater reliance on withholding taxes—have been employed in limited ways but offer promising avenues to explore.

Taxing High-Net-Worth Individuals: Lessons from Uganda

Wealthy individuals in Uganda pay little personal income tax (PIT). Only 5 percent of the directors of the top tax-paying companies remitted income tax in 2013. Similarly, in a sample of 60 lawyers, less than a third paid income tax in 2012. Meanwhile, although some Ugandans paid about US$180,000 in customs duties in 2014, none paid personal income tax. Finally, most politicians with stakes in commercial enterprises did not comply with personal income tax between 2011 and 2014.

The challenge to taxing these high-net-worth individuals (HNWIs) in Uganda was not so much lack of appropriate legislation; instead, the information available was not being fully exploited. Data held by the Uganda Revenue Authority (URA) were not used because no systems were in place to cross-check databases, in part because departments operated in silos or competed against each other to achieve their revenue targets. Information sharing across government institutions was equally limited because of procedural differences or institutional rivalries.

In 2015, the URA established an HNWI unit. Missing a precise methodology, the unit drew up a list of HNWIs simply based on common knowledge and on information that was readily available within URA data systems. Supported by senior management, the unit then arranged meetings with the HNWIs to talk about their tax affairs. These meetings served two purposes: educating the taxpayers and signaling that the URA was looking into their tax compliance.

Subsequently, the HNWI unit created a register of wealthy individuals of whom more than 65 percent filed tax returns. Tax revenue from HNWIs increased from US$390,000 in 2015 to US$5.5 million in 2016. Moreover, the URA observed a significant improvement in the attitudes of HNWIs toward paying their taxes, suggesting a boost in tax morale. Over time, however, compliance with the personal income tax has not been sustained. Hampered by weak enforcement capacity, the unit found that by 2020 the share of HNWIs submitting a PIT return was lower than shortly after the unit was established. Compliance with the value added tax and rental income remained relatively stable.

As a result, URA's collection from HNWIs still almost certainly represents only a tiny fraction of the revenue plausibly available from improving the taxation of wealthy individuals. But several lessons can be learned from Uganda's experience:

- Identifying HNWIs is possible, even if it is not a comprehensive list because of the difficulties in identifying offshore wealth.
- Picking low-hanging fruit in the information environment can be enough to get started.
- HNWIs are often publicly known, but because of their economic and political influence, high-level political and administrative support is needed to enforce their tax compliance.
- Especially initially, careful relationship management and appropriate communication are more important than enforcement.

Sources: Kangave et al. (2018); Kangave et al. (forthcoming).

An Exception to the Rule: South Africa

Perhaps the best evidence of the political roots of weak income tax enforcement is provided by the primary exception to this pattern: South Africa. Whereas most middle-income countries have limited collection of personal income taxes, South Africa has long been an exception, with personal income tax collection exceeding 10 percent of GDP by the end of the 1990s—and remaining more than 8 percent of GDP before and after.

The technical features of the tax base in South Africa offer little to explain this exceptional performance relative to that of other middle-income countries. Instead, it has been attributed to South Africa's unique politics. During the period of white rule under apartheid (1948–94), there was largely a consensus among the wealthy in favor of taxation—that is, wealthier white South Africans were willing to accept significant income taxes as the "price" of sustaining white rule (Lieberman 2003).

South Africa's experience reveals how persistent tax systems can be. In the postapartheid period, those institutions of tax collection have largely persisted amid a strong popular politics of taxation—that is, broad support for redistributive taxation to reduce historical inequalities. The key message is that effective income tax systems can be put in place, but that is likely to depend on either an elite consensus or broad popular support for taxation (Prichard 2019).

Political Barriers to Property Taxation

Political logic has similarly hindered the enforcement of property taxes in low- and middle-income countries, even though property—a major source of wealth in many countries—appears ideally suited to tax enforcement even in low-capacity environments (see chapter 6 for more details).

The clearest illustration of the political barriers to effective property taxation is the extent of countries' collection arrears. Among African countries, arrears range from 25 percent in Zambia to 80 percent in Niger (Franzsen and McCluskey 2017). In Latin America, Castro and Scartascini (2015) report compliance of only about 40 percent among billed properties. Where tax arrears have been identified, enforcement should be straightforward. Properties are immovable, and thus identifying owners, or at least tenants, is generally simple. And yet arrears frequently persist, uncollected.

Meanwhile, although the persistent failure to build more effective property valuation systems is often attributed to technical challenges, it is difficult not to trace these to deeper political roots. Lack of valuation capacity and problems with complex models of valuation have been evident for decades, but governments have generally failed to act. In some countries, explicit gaps in existing laws appear to benefit those with political and economic power—such as partially or fully exempting unequally distributed rural land from taxation or long delays in placing new developments on the property tax rolls (Piracha and Moore 2015).

Political Forces against Reform

The absence of political support for taxing the wealthy reflects competing political pressures (Fairfield 2013). On the one hand, the absence of reform is unsurprising. HNWIs are likely to wield extensive political influence—and indeed, in some cases, hold political office. Efforts to tax powerful, politically connected individuals face powerful interests resistant to reform, while also threatening to disrupt patronage networks important to political leaders. For example, the notion that wealthy individuals are particularly well placed to mobilize against expanded taxation is illustrated by the dispute in the United States over the inheritance tax or so-called death tax (Graetz 2016).

On the other hand, one would expect a large majority of taxpayers to strongly support more effective tax enforcement among the wealthy. Although taxpayers may not support what they view as punitive taxes on the rich, it seems reasonable to believe that most taxpayers are likely to support enforcement of existing laws, particularly when it could expand investment in public services. The empirical message appears to be that, in almost all cases, the potential political gains from catering to the majority of taxpayers have failed to offset the costs of confronting more powerful vested interests.

Reform Progress—and Future Options

It is useful to consider recent reform priorities, and possible future reform directions, through the lens of these diverse barriers to progress. This section thus begins with more traditional interventions targeting enforcement and simplification before turning to issues related to trust—such as quasi-voluntary compliance and the compilation of political support for reform.

Enforcement

Efforts to strengthen the taxation of HNWIs have focused primarily on strengthening enforcement, improving data collection, implementing more effective information technology (IT) systems, and ramping up audits. The push for improved information collection and management is at the core of all these efforts, which recently are highlighting the critical role of data sharing within government and access to third-party data in strengthening enforcement.

Enforcing Wealth Taxes

In recent decades, many observers have argued that the advantages of taxing wealth over focusing on personal income tax may be limited. They point out that wealth taxes would be costly to collect and would raise significantly less revenue than predicted because of avoidance and evasion. Many countries have similarly focused on inheritance taxes or other taxes on transfers of wealth based on the view that it is easier to tax wealth when it is moved after a death or at any other point. This reasoning was the basis for the United Kingdom's Capital Transfer Tax introduced in the 1970s but abolished in the 1980s.

Yet experiences in Colombia and Europe reveal that wealth taxes can work if well designed. In Colombia, compliance with wealth taxes improved when coupled with stronger enforcement. The higher probability of detection triggered by the Panama Papers leak improved wealth tax collection through disclosures (Londoño-Vélez and Ávila-Mahecha 2021). Meanwhile, the wealth tax in Norway, Spain, and Switzerland raises between 0.5 and 3.7 percent of total tax revenue (Drometer et al. 2018). In Denmark, efforts by the wealthy to avoid and evade the wealth tax in place until 1997 were sizable, but they were less than what is generally (theoretically) assumed (Jakobsen et al. 2020). In response to the further expansion of wealth inequality stemming from the COVID-19 pandemic, many countries, now armed with tools to identify wealth held offshore through the automatic exchange of information for tax purposes and aided by the new limits on anonymous shell corporations, are reconsidering the potential merits of wealth taxes.

Domestic Data Sharing and Audit Capacity

The administrative challenges encountered in data sharing and audits arise at both the institutional and individual levels within and beyond tax agencies. Legal reform is often needed to grant tax authorities greater access to third-party data. Laws that allow data sharing across government agencies are a starting point. But the actual sharing of data has often lagged far behind what is permitted by law. To solve this problem, reformers have often tended to rely on the development of sophisticated IT systems to automate the process. And yet, as explored in greater detail in chapter 7, such systems have not always been successful.

In lower-income countries, in particular, strengthening specific and strategic areas of data sharing using simpler and even manual methods may prove to be more effective solutions at lower cost, at least in the short term. For example, the customs department could simply share a spreadsheet with the taxpayer identification numbers of the largest importers in a given year to cross-reference against databases of individual and corporate taxpayers. Similar exchanges of basic data could be applied across different tax types, with the business registrar, or with other data sources. Slightly more sophisticated but still achievable would be efforts to understand the network of relationships that a HNWI has built, including family members and key business relationships, thereby helping to piece together the transactions in which they are involved. Such an effort could, in turn, serve as the foundation for simplified identification of audits, with systems of risk-based audit to be upgraded over time.

Even where data have been accessed, many countries urgently need an expanded audit capacity—and a greater willingness and ability to prosecute noncompliance. This need for audit capacity is expanding with the prospect of access to new data, and a variety of international programs have begun to target capacity building in this area. A key barrier to the effort is the surprising dearth of research into which modalities are most effective for building—and sustaining—new audit capacity. Anecdotal evidence suggests that capacity building has tended to remain relatively fragmented and theoretical, even while tax agencies have pushed for more coordinated and applied training and support. Empowering local authorities to coordinate capacity-building support to fit their needs is an important but imperfectly implemented principle (Fjeldstad 2014; Moore et al. 2015).

Capacity building for tax enforcement that targets HNWIs faces a unique additional challenge: government staff often enjoy significant and lucrative job prospects with large accounting firms. Therefore, tax agencies must have plans for retaining skilled staff. Meanwhile, barriers to prosecution for tax evasion sometimes lie beyond tax authorities—that is, with the courts—thereby requiring broader legal reforms (Hassan and Prichard 2016).

Simplifying Property Tax Administration

Difficulties in enforcing property taxes share similar characteristics and are often characterized by significant neglect. Frequent commitments have been made to strengthening property valuation and improving enforcement of arrears—all supported by often-fragmented efforts to introduce new IT systems. However, success has often been fleeting, primarily amid large-scale failures to produce complete, up-to-date property registers and valuations. Despite these failures, some reform programs continue to push the same agenda of capacity upgrading, in some cases by shifting administration of property taxes from subnational to national governments (Goodfellow 2017a). Finally, at its root the enforcement problem is often political rather than technical, as most clearly illustrated by large unenforced arrears—for property taxes, in particular.

Yet, as with income tax enforcement, an alternative narrative around simplification has gained traction. This alternative view holds that in many contexts expert-driven, market-based valuation of properties is too onerous, complex, and subjective, and thus prone to both delays and collusion or corruption. Further complicating property tax administration are complex institutional arrangements in which land registries, valuation departments, and tax authorities rarely cooperate. Against this background, a growing chorus of reformers have called for simplified systems of property identification, simplified but still progressive valuation, and simplified links between valuation and tax collection to make property tax systems more enforceable given local capacity constraints (Franzsen and McCluskey 2017; Zebong, Fish, and Prichard 2017). More concrete options are discussed in greater detail in chapter 6.

International Exchange of Information

Recently, the focus has shifted to accessing third-party data on wealth held internationally, primarily through the OECD-led agreement on Automatic Exchange of Information (AEOI) for tax purposes.[2] Since 2014, this agreement has had substantial potential to curb tax evasion undertaken by stashing wealth abroad, but low- and middle-income countries must not only sign on to the agreement but also be able to use the data effectively, implement data management safeguards sufficient to satisfy other members, and collect adequate data domestically to meet reciprocity requirements for participation.

In practice, these requirements have so far served as a major hurdle to participation by low-income countries (Collin 2020), which have yet to participate in the AEOI agreement (table 3.1). Many of them worry that they may struggle to put in place systems adequate enough to fully participate in the AEOI, or else they lack information about how or whether to participate. Advocates have argued for greater outreach and support, as well as for simplifying the participation process—including through lower thresholds for participation, nonreciprocal provision of data to lower-income countries, "pairing" with wealthy partners in implementing new processes, or the provision of simplified data where full participation is not possible (Knobel 2017).

Another option for countries seeking to strengthen taxation of wealth held overseas is multilateral cooperation between (regional) tax authorities. Such cooperation can facilitate information flows and the recovery of foreign tax claims, as illustrated in the success of the OECD and Council of Europe's Convention on Mutual Administrative Assistance in Tax Matters.

TABLE 3.1 Number of Countries Participating in Automatic Exchange of Information Agreement, by Region and Country Income Group, 2021

Region		Country income group	
East Asia and Pacific	16	High-income	71
Europe and Central Asia	45	Upper-middle-income	26
Latin America and the Caribbean	24	Lower-middle-income	6
Middle East and North Africa	8	Low-income	0
North America	2		
South Asia	3		
Sub-Saharan Africa	5		
Total	**103**		**103**

Source: OECD 2021.
Note: Regions follow the World Bank regional definitions (under which North America comprises Bermuda, Canada, and the United States). All country income categories use World Bank–defined classifications.

Indeed, the clout of regional initiatives such as the Inter-American Center of Tax Administrations or the African Tax Administration Forum seems to be growing.

Although bilateral tax treaties often include information exchange clauses, evidence is mounting that many treaties unnecessarily limit the taxing powers of low- and middle-income countries. For example, tax treaties may stipulate a maximum rate at which a country can tax dividends (Hearson and Kangave 2016). There is, however, a growing push for countries to renegotiate those tax treaties. The OECD or United Nations (UN) model conventions could serve as a starting point. For many lower-income countries, the UN Model Double Taxation Convention may be more appropriate because it includes more source taxation rights (also see chapter 4).

Tax Amnesties and Voluntary Disclosure

For countries seeking to encourage taxpayers to declare wealth held offshore, one option is reliance on tax amnesties—time-limited government offers that allow taxpayers to pay a defined amount in exchange for forgiveness of a past tax liability, including interest and penalties (Le Borgne and Baer 2008). Amnesties are often seen as a way to raise additional revenue in the short term while expanding the tax base in the medium term by bringing hidden wealth and income into the tax net.

However, successful amnesties are the exception rather than the rule (Alm, Martinez-Vazquez, and Wallace 2009; Le Borgne and Baer 2008). Success depends on a delicate balance between encouraging declarations, avoiding undermining the rule of law, and offering credible incentives along with a credible threat of enforcement. Poorly designed amnesties may actually result in a revenue loss either by undermining perceptions of fairness and tax morale or by counterintuitively creating incentives for the wealthy to move wealth offshore in the expectation of future amnesty programs.

An alternative to amnesty programs is voluntary disclosure programs, and their results have been promising (OECD 2015). Whereas amnesty programs typically include relief from tax liabilities and penalties, voluntary disclosure programs insist on payment of tax liabilities, but they agree to partly or fully waive the severest penalties and the possibility of prosecution. The key difference is that amnesty programs leave beneficiaries better off than individuals who have been consistently compliant, whereas voluntary disclosure programs create no such benefit. Voluntary disclosure programs are therefore less likely to undermine perceptions of fairness, although they create weaker incentives for disclosure.

Although still scarce, rigorous research on the effectiveness of tax amnesties and voluntary disclosure programs in low- and middle-income countries is growing (Langenmayr 2017). A recent paper examines the effect of a 2019 voluntary disclosure program in Colombia (Londoño-Vélez and Ávila-Mahecha 2021). A key feature of Colombia's program was that, in exchange for paying a penalty of 10 percent of the value of the disclosed wealth, all evaded income and wealth taxes from past years were waived. However, disclosers did have to start paying income and wealth taxes upon disclosure. The program was accompanied by broader enforcement measures such as the criminalization of tax evasion. It produced disclosures worth more than 1.7 percent of GDP, raised 0.2 percent of GDP in penalty revenues, and substantially increased tax revenue, nearly doubling the effective tax rate on the rich. Moreover, the improvements in compliance persisted over time (Londoño-Vélez and Ávila-Mahecha 2021). Further research in this area, especially on the impact of tax amnesties and voluntary disclosure on HNWIs' disclosures, would help to inform policy discussions.

Facilitation

Alongside enforcement reforms, most tax authorities have invested significantly in facilitating tax compliance by the relatively wealthy. Among the first such initiatives was the creation of large taxpayer units across the world. These agencies, while designed to improve enforcement through greater capacity and data sharing, were equally intended to offer a single point of contact and service for the most valuable taxpayers (Baer, Benon, and Toro 2002—also see box 3.1 for a description of Uganda's "VIP tax unit"). Some tax authorities—among others, in Brazil, Indonesia, Romania, and South Africa (TJN 2018)—also have special liaisons to deal with HNWIs, in part owing to the political complexity of taxing these individuals and reportedly to address their concerns about privacy and harassment.

The introduction of new IT systems has also implicitly sought to facilitate payments primarily by the wealthy. A central component of many IT systems has been the introduction of online self-assessment for income tax purposes—a service that in most low- and middle-income countries is relevant to only a small segment of the population. Meanwhile, the ability to make tax payments at banks was initially most relevant to a handful of larger taxpayers before being rolled out (to varying degrees) to larger groups of taxpayers and tax types.

Although these reforms seem broadly desirable, they raise a question about the right balance between special treatment for the wealthy and equity for all taxpayers. The wealthiest taxpayers are disproportionately important for national revenue, while improving broader public perceptions about their compliance may be critical to broader trust in tax systems. HNWIs also harbor plausible concerns about their privacy and potential harassment when paying taxes. At the same time, to the extent they have powerful political allies, taxing them may prove sensitive for tax officials as well. The tax affairs of HNWIs are also likely to be substantially more complex than the affairs of other taxpayers. For all these reasons, specialized units to facilitate their compliance may be justifiable (OECD 2009).

On the other hand, these specialized units may risk further alienating rank-and-file taxpayers who may already suspect that the wealthy enjoy preferential treatment. At a minimum, it thus seems essential that efforts be made to progressively expand facilitation measures (such as online filing and third-party payments) to the broader base of taxpayers. In short, absent a meaningful impact on revenue, the creation of special structures to cater to wealthy taxpayers may exacerbate a lack of popular trust in the equity of the tax system.

Trust: Improving Quasi-Voluntary Compliance

Alongside efforts to facilitate tax compliance by the relatively wealthy, some evidence now indicates that investments in trust may expand quasi-voluntary compliance among HNWIs.

Building Trust by Showing Public Benefits

In Rwanda, short message service (SMS) messages linking income tax payments to services led to a significant increase in declared income (Mascagni, Nell, and Monkam 2017). OECD countries have seen similar outcomes (Bott et al. 2017; Hallsworth et al. 2017), but such studies in low- and middle-income countries have reported somewhat mixed results overall (Castro and Scartascini 2015; Weigel 2018).

One reason for these mixed results could be that taxpayers in low-income countries may lack confidence in the ability of governments to deliver meaningful and valuable improvements in service quality. Although this is true for all taxpayers, it may be particularly important when considering HNWIs because of their ability to secure access to comparatively high-quality goods and services through private providers. In other words, the tax–benefit link may, in at least some cases, be less important for rich taxpayers because of their access to outside options, making them less willing to comply with taxes.

HNWIs are not likely able to opt out of the social contract entirely, however. For example, they probably value public goods such as roads and airports. Reflecting that logic, the Colombian government was able to introduce a surtax on the income of the wealthy by explicitly linking it to popular investments in security, along with the creation of additional oversight mechanisms. Survey experiments in Mexico suggest the potential broader effectiveness of such strategies (Flores-Macías 2012, 2016).

Although these studies show connections between trust and quasi-voluntary compliance, they do point out challenges for operationalization on a larger scale. SMS messages linking taxes to services have an effect, but it may be eroded over time if not paired with actual and visible improvements in services. Meanwhile, the model of Colombian security taxes is potentially risky on a larger scale:

governments cannot afford to create a system in which the wealthy are paying taxes primarily to fund services heavily valued by the wealthy. A key motivation for stronger personal income taxes is to support redistribution and to signal to taxpayers more broadly that the tax system is equitable. The type of bargain established in Colombia may undermine that goal if expanded too far.

Overall, linking revenues more clearly to improved spending and government performance is likely to be a critical component of trust-building to expand quasi-voluntary tax compliance. That said, in seeking to strengthen compliance among HNWIs it appears important to recognize their concerns and priorities, but also to approach those concerns carefully to ensure that broad-based, sustainable benefits remain the priority.

Building Trust by Strengthening Fairness, Equity, and Accountability

Considerable scope remains to continue to focus on fairness, equity, and accountability, while more rigorously assessing the demand for reform in these areas and its impacts on compliance by HNWIs:

- *Regarding fairness,* despite a lack of systematic data on harassment of wealthy taxpayers by tax collectors, anecdotal evidence suggests that in some countries subsets of wealthy taxpayers are targeted by revenue-seeking tax collectors—or by retributive governments (Hassan and Prichard 2016). In these contexts, it is easy to imagine that stronger appeals processes and large taxpayer units could help, but more information is sorely needed.

- *Regarding equity,* low- and middle-income countries are characterized by highly uneven tax enforcement among the wealthy, with some paying significant income and property taxes and others little or none.[3]

- *Expansion of accountability* to larger taxpayers, even through simple steps such as greater consultation, could have value. Many governments have pursued such a strategy with larger businesses (Moore 2014). However, such strategies must be balanced with the need for equitable engagement with taxpayers more broadly.

Building Political Support for Reform

Notwithstanding the reform options described so far, there is little doubt that the key to more effective income taxation of HNWIs lies in building the necessary political support. The central questions facing reformers are (1) whose support is needed, and (2) how can that support be achieved?

Building on case study evidence from Latin America, Fairfield (2013) distinguishes broadly between two mechanisms: mobilizing popular support and tempering elite antagonism. These strategies are, of course, not mutually exclusive, although they likely imply slightly different approaches.

Mobilizing popular support. The first mechanism focuses on building broad-based popular support for taxation of the wealthy, thus generating a political payoff for reformist governments. In principle, most taxpayers stand to benefit from more effective taxation of the wealthy and therefore are a natural constituency for reform. Fairfield (2013) documents two strategies used by Latin American governments to mobilize this support:

- *Legitimating appeals (vertical equity)*. By appealing to widely held norms and beliefs, reformists can mobilize popular support, thereby putting pressure on politicians. This strategy is more likely to succeed when the issues are highly salient. Common techniques include linking tax reform to vertical and horizontal equity.

- *Linking tax reform to popular benefits*. Whereas legitimating appeals strategies draws on inherent legitimacy, linking tax reform to popular benefits invokes legitimacy from the benefits financed by the tax. This link can be established in discourse, which can be made more credible by including the tax and benefits in a single reform package, making benefits contingent on the tax, or earmarking the revenues.

However, outside of some leftist governments in Latin America, such efforts to mobilize popular support for taxing the wealthy appear to have been relatively rare. One explanation is that even in democracies elites wield sufficient political power that such broader popular appeals are unlikely to succeed without expanded elite buy-in (Slater 2010). Another possibility is that such appeals could succeed, but in practice, taxpayers so deeply distrust taxation that mobilizing positive support for taxation, even of the rich, is extremely difficult (Ascher 1989).

Insofar as the latter is true, the challenge for potentially reformist governments lies in understanding the root causes of popular distrust of stronger tax enforcement and finding ways to then build greater trust and political support. A survey of US respondents revealed that preferences for redistribution and wealth taxation can be shifted. Informing respondents that property tax only affects the very rich significantly increased support for it (Kuziemko et al. 2015).

Tempering elite antagonism or enlisting elite support. The alternative mechanism tempers elite antagonism or seeks support among the wealthy either by targeting a subset of supportive taxpayers or by building a mutual interest in expanded tax collection. Related reform strategies observed by Fairfield (2013) include:

- *Attenuating impact*. The smaller the impact of a reform on HNWIs' wealth, the less likely they are to oppose it. Several strategies can be pursued to achieve a reform. It can be phased in, introduced gradually over time, or introduced for a certain period.

- *Obfuscating incidence*. Strategies that obfuscate tax incidence aim to reduce HNWIs' awareness of their tax burden. One commonly used technique is burden sharing, which exploits the difference between the legal incidence (who pays the tax) and the economic incidence (who bears the cost).

- *Compensating HNWIs*. This strategy provides compensation to HNWIs to convince them to accept a tax reform. This compensation can take many forms such as subsidies or spending that directly benefits HNWIs or support for specific reforms elites advocate in other areas. However, the better organized HNWIs are, the more exclusive the compensation must be. If they are fragmented, then compensating a few key groups can suffice.

- *Linking to universal benefits*. This strategy aims to attenuate HNWI resistance by linking tax reform to public goods from which they stand to benefit, such as new investments to expand economic opportunities (Schneider 2012) or strengthen security (Flores-Macías 2012, 2016).

- *Legitimating appeals (horizontal equity).* Examples of reforms that improve horizontal equity include eliminating sector-specific benefits and broadening the base to include, for example, nonwage incomes. Leveling the playing field among HNWIs can generate support from those who did not enjoy the benefits or were already included in the tax net. This scenario creates a potentially virtuous circle: the more incremental progress a government makes in bringing wealthy individuals into the tax net, the larger the constituency for further reform—especially if success is paired with efforts to expand taxpayer trust.[4]

In the abstract, this mechanism has significant appeal: by and large, the most successful experiences of expanding personal income taxes in low- and middle-income countries have been rooted in such elite bargains (Prichard 2019). Yet these bargains may only be politically feasible when the right window of opportunity opens up. Historically, such bargains have often been the product of external circumstances or immediate threats (Lieberman 2003; Slater 2010). The COVID-19 crisis seems to offer such momentum. Various time-limited "solidarity" surcharges have been added to the personal income tax for the well-off.

Building the Social Contract

Successful efforts to expand taxation of the wealthy also have the potential to strengthen broader social contracts and contribute to virtuous circles of improved revenue and outcomes. Income and property taxes have long been central to research on the processes of tax bargaining and state-building. They are highly visible to taxpayers, and thus, all else being equal, they appear more likely to spur popular mobilization and demands for public services and accountability. Property taxes particularly could be linked explicitly to local services. Yet despite growing policy interest in linking tax reform to accountability and state-building, the taxes most likely to spur such gains have sometimes received only muted support.

A key finding from research on tax bargaining is that taxpayers are significantly less able to make reciprocal demands on governments when taxpayer interests—and thus collective action—are divided. This division is likely where taxes on the wealthy are ineffective—that is, wealthy taxpayers are more likely to use their political capital to seek to escape taxation than to join with other taxpayers in demanding reciprocity. The long-term public costs of weak taxation of elites may thus be substantial, and the ongoing role of both international and domestic tax havens in facilitating tax evasion may have economic and governance consequences (Prichard 2015).

Meanwhile, efforts to expand taxation of the wealthy may be an especially effective way to spur broader state-building. The collection of income taxes—and to a lesser extent property taxes—gives somewhat unique priority to cross-government collaboration in gathering and sharing data. This finding has the potential to spur improvements in administrative competence across agencies, while the data themselves can become valuable input for policy making elsewhere in government (Gavin et al. 2013; Pieterse, Kreuser, and Gavin 2016). Meanwhile, property taxes may serve as a key impetus for building often weak local state structures and engaging citizens directly with local authorities.

Conclusion

Bringing wealthy and relatively high-income individuals into the tax net may be the single most meaningful way for governments to improve tax collection as a whole. The extent of offshoring of wealth by HNWIs, coupled with other forms of evasion, represents an enormous loss of public revenue. In addition to the revenue motivation, there is a strong case that lack of equity in taxation undermines the social contract. A sense that the wealthiest in society do not pay their fair share can undermine voluntary compliance among other taxpayer groups and weaken support for tax reform more generally. By increasing efforts to tax the wealthy, governments may be able to build broad-based trust in the system, ultimately generating even greater revenue gains over time.

Although most personal income tax revenue is collected via tax withholding from wage employees, HNWIs derive most of their income from nonwage sources, which tend to be taxed ineffectively. To cite a few examples, income from professional services and capital gains tend to be taxed very little if at all in lower-income countries, and the vast offshore holdings of the wealthiest lie outside the national tax net. There is also low-hanging fruit for reformers in the realm of property taxation. Many HNWIs have invested heavily in rapidly appreciating real estate, but property taxation tends to be extremely weak in lower-income countries.

A key challenge lies in identifying the most significant technical barriers to reform. Verifying nonwage income is not a straightforward matter. Assessing capital gains taxes is particularly problematic because of the detailed data required and the lack of access to, or lack of effective sharing of, third-party information (such as from bank accounts and stock exchanges) in many countries. Although real estate holdings are more visible, property valuation can be a technically difficult process that is also vulnerable to collusion and corruption. Further research on the most effective means of building and maintaining expanded audit capabilities would be welcome, as would more work to understand the results of initiatives such as tax amnesties and voluntary disclosure programs. Lack of administrative capacity is frequently cited as a major barrier to reform, but rather than continuing to push for capacity building, reformers may wish to consider whether the complexity of the tax system is itself part of the problem. In that case, simplification of some aspects may be helpful.

Yet despite the variety of technical barriers, the genuinely binding constraints on reform efforts tend to be political. Indeed, seemingly technical challenges may reflect underlying political or institutional resistance. For example, even where third-party data are available, governments often choose not to share or use them effectively. Similarly, governments often fail to exploit other relatively simple opportunities for improving tax collection, such as enhancing audit capacity, increasing the use of withholding taxes, implementing better methods for property valuation, or pursuing collection of property tax arrears.

Similar to other groups of taxpayers, among HNWIs improvements in voluntary compliance and broader support for reform are likely dependent on combining enforcement and facilitation measures with new investments in fairness, equity, reciprocity, and accountability. Some investments are likely to aim at assuring wealthy taxpayers that they will be treated fairly and confidentially by tax officials and at offering evidence that expanded tax enforcement will apply to a broad range of HNWIs and not just a select few who are targeted. At the same time, more research is needed on the types of measures that could improve tax morale and voluntary compliance among HNWIs.

Meanwhile, like other taxpayers, the wealthy may harbor doubts that their tax payments will be used productively by the government. Drawing a line between tax payments and public services may help. But a delicate balancing act may be required. The wealthy are often relatively less dependent than other groups on public services such as education and health care, and therefore they may feel less compelled to fund them. However, increasing the rhetorical emphasis on public services they may find more personally relevant, such as security, may run counter to the goal of securing broad public buy-in among the general population.

More broadly, successful reform is likely to require careful analysis of the political economy environment to understand what it will take to mobilize the support needed for reform, not only among the wealthy but also among a broader base of taxpayers, all the while attenuating HNWI resistance. Effective reform strategies are likely to reflect country-specific objectives, constraints, and opportunities. A reform coalition in one context may be characterized by a technocratic and state-led push. Other options could be constructing political support among wealthy taxpayers (an elite bargain) or appealing to the broader base of taxpayers. Among the broader base there likely is, in principle, substantial support for strengthening taxation of the affluent, but perhaps a lack of trust that it will be done fairly or yield broader benefits. Where significant political support exists or can be fostered, it may be possible to immediately expand the sharing and use of available data as well as enforcement efforts.

Where political support is lacking, tax administrations may instead adopt a more incremental strategy, focusing on the building blocks of future improvements and investing in offering citizens evidence of concrete benefits. It may also mean adopting more targeted goals by focusing on a subset of high-income taxpayers, or higher-value properties, and emphasizing more cooperative approaches to compliance when more aggressive enforcement is not politically feasible. That said, national governments often cannot address the challenges posed by HNWIs alone. International partners have an important role to play in revisiting tax treaties that may unreasonably constrain the tax collecting powers of low- and middle-income countries, and in collaborating on ways to implement international data-sharing and cooperation agreements.

Notes

1. As further discussed in chapter 1, this study distinguishes between "enforced compliance" (resulting from the state's enforcement power) and "voluntary" or "quasi-voluntary" compliance (driven by values, social norms, *and* levels of trust in the fairness, equity, reciprocity, and accountability of tax systems). Both enforcement power and high levels of trust help to ensure the highest overall tax compliance.
2. For more information, see OECD (2016).
3. See, for example, Kangave, Byrne, and Karangwa (2020).
4. Research has documented such a dynamic in relation to larger firms (Prichard 2015).

References

Alm, J., J. Martinez-Vazquez, and S. Wallace. 2009. "Do Tax Amnesties Work? The Revenue Effects of Tax Amnesties during the Transition in the Russian Federation." *Economic Analysis and Policy* 39 (2): 235–53.

Alstadsæter, A., N. Johannesen, and G. Zucman. 2018. "Who Owns the Wealth in Tax Havens? Macro Evidence and Implications for Global Inequality." *Journal of Public Economics* 162: 89–100.

Ascher, W. 1989. "Risk, Politics, and Tax Reform: Lessons from Some Latin American Experiences." In *Tax Reform in Developing Countries*, edited by M. Gillis, 417–72. Durham, NC: Duke University Press.

Baer, K., O. Benon, and J. Toro. 2002. "Improving Large Taxpayers' Compliance: A Review of Country Experience." Occasional Paper No. 125, International Monetary Fund, Washington, DC.

Battle, L. 2014. "Where (and Why) the Super-Rich Are Investing in Real Estate." *Financial Times*, January 17, 2014.

Best, M. 2014. "The Role of Firms in Workers' Earnings Responses to Taxes: Evidence from Pakistan." Working paper, London School of Economics.

Bott, K. M., A. W. Cappelen, E. Ø. Sørensen, and B. Tungodden. 2017. "You've Got Mail: A Randomised Field Experiment on Tax Evasion." Discussion Paper No. 10/2017, NHH Department of Economics, Bergen, Norway.

Castro, L., and C. Scartascini. 2015. "Tax Compliance and Enforcement in the Pampas: Evidence from a Field Experiment." *Journal of Economic Behavior and Organization* 116: 65–82.

Chan, H. F., K. Gangl, M. W. Supriyadi, and B. Torgler. Forthcoming. "The Effects of Increased Monitoring on High Wealth Individuals: Evidence from a Quasi-Natural Experiment in Indonesia." Working paper, Andrew Young School of Policy Studies, Georgia State University, Atlanta.

Collin, M. 2020. "Can Developing Countries Rein In Offshore Wealth?" Future Development blog post, October 9, 2020, Brookings Institution, Washington, DC. https://www.brookings.edu/blog/future-development/2020/10/09/can-developing-countries-rein-in-offshore-wealth/.

Drometer, M., M. Frank, M. Hofbauer Pérez, C. Rhode, S. Schworm, and T. Stitteneder. 2018. "Wealth and Inheritance Taxation: An Overview and Country Comparison." *Ifo DICE Report* 16 (2): 45–54.

Fairfield, T. 2013. "Going Where the Money Is: Strategies for Taxing Economic Elites in Unequal Democracies." *World Development* 47: 42–57.

Fjeldstad, O-H. 2014. "Tax and Development: Donor Support to Strengthen Tax Systems in Developing Countries." *Public Administration and Development* 34 (3): 182–93.

Flores-Macías, G. 2012. "Financing Security through Elite Taxation: The Case of Colombia's 'Democratic Security Taxes.'" *Studies in Comparative International Development* 49 (4): 477–500.

Flores-Macías, G. 2016. "Building Support for Taxation in Developing Countries: Experimental Evidence from Mexico." Working Paper No. 51, International Centre for Tax and Development, Brighton, UK.

Franzsen, R., and W. McCluskey, eds. 2017. *Property Tax in Africa: Status, Challenges, and Prospects.* Cambridge, MA: Lincoln Institute for Land Policy.

Gangl, K., and B. Torgler. 2020. "How to Achieve Tax Compliance by the Wealthy: A Review of the Literature and Agenda for Policy." *Social Issues and Policy Review* 14 (1): 108–51.

Gavin, E., D. Breytenbach, R. Carolissen, and M. Leolo. 2013. "The Roles of Tax Administration Data in the Production of Official Statistics in South Africa." *Proceedings, 59th ISI World Statistics Congress, Hong Kong, August 25–30*, 1483–88.

Goodfellow, T. 2017a. "Central-Local Government Roles and Relationships in Property Taxation." Summary Brief No. 12, International Centre for Tax and Development, Brighton, UK.

Goodfellow, T. 2017b. "Taxing Property in a Neo-Developmental State: The Politics of Urban Land Value Capture in Rwanda and Ethiopia." *African Affairs* 116 (465): 549–72.

Graetz, M. J. 2016. "'Death Tax' Politics." *Boston College Law Review* 57 (3): 801–14.

Hallsworth, M., J. A. List, R. D. Metcalfe, and I. Vlaey. 2017. "The Behavioralist as Tax Collector: Using Natural Field Experiments to Enhance Tax Compliance." *Journal of Public Economics* 148: 14–31.

Hassan, M., and W. Prichard. 2016. "The Political Economy of Domestic Tax Reform in Bangladesh: Political Settlements, Informal Institutions and the Negotiation of Reform." *Journal of Development Studies* 52 (12): 1704–21.

Hearson, M., and J. Kangave. 2016. "A Review of Uganda's Tax Treaties and Recommendations for Action." Working Paper No. 50, International Centre for Tax and Development, Brighton, UK.

Jakobsen, K., K. Jakobsen, H. Kleven, and G. Zucman. 2020. "Wealth Taxation and Wealth Accumulation: Theory and Evidence from Denmark." *Quarterly Journal of Economics* 135 (1): 329–88.

Jibao, S., and W. Prichard. 2015. "The Political Economy of Property Tax in Africa: Explaining Reform Outcomes in Sierra Leone." *African Affairs* 114 (456): 404–31.

Kangave, J., K. Byrne, and J. Karangwa. 2020. "Tax Compliance of Wealthy Individuals in Rwanda." Working Paper No. 109, International Centre for Tax and Development, Brighton, UK.

Kangave, J., S. Nakato, R. Waiswa, and P. Lumala Zzimbe. 2016. "Boosting Revenue Collection through Taxing High Net Worth Individuals: The Case of Uganda." Working Paper No. 45, International Centre for Tax and Development, Brighton, UK.

Kangave, J., S. Nakato, R. Waiswa, M. Nalukwago, and P. Lumala Zzimbe. 2018. "What Can We Learn from the Uganda Revenue Authority's Approach to Taxing High Net Worth Individuals?" Working Paper No. 72, International Centre for Tax and Development, Brighton, UK.

Kangave, J., S. Nakato, R. Waiswa, M. Nalukwago, and P. Lumala Zzimbe. Forthcoming. "Taxing High Net Worth Individuals: A Case Study of the Uganda Revenue Authority's Approach." Adapted from Working Papers Nos. 45 and 72, International Centre for Tax and Development, Brighton, UK.

Khan, A., A. Khwaja, and B. Olken. 2016. "Tax Farming Redux: Experimental Evidence on Performance Pay for Tax Collectors." *Quarterly Journal of Economics* 131 (1): 219–71.

Kleven, H., M. Knudsen, C. Kreiner, S. Pedersen, and E. Saez. 2011. "Unwilling or Unable to Cheat? Evidence from a Tax Audit Experiment in Denmark." *Econometrica* 79 (3): 651–92.

Knobel, A. 2017. "Findings of the 2nd TJN Survey on Automatic Exchange of Information (AEOI): Sanctions against Financial Centres, AEOI Statistics and the Use of Information beyond Tax Purposes." Policy paper, Tax Justice Network, London.

Kuziemko, I., M. Norton, E. Saez, and S. Stantcheva. 2015. "How Elastic Are Preferences for Redistribution? Evidence from Randomized Survey Experiments." *American Economic Review* 105 (4): 1478–1508.

Langenmayr, D. 2017. "Voluntary Disclosure of Evaded Taxes: Increasing Revenue, or Increasing Incentives to Evade?" *Journal of Public Economics* 151: 110–25.

Le Borgne, E., and K. Baer. 2008. *Tax Amnesties: Theory, Trends, and Some Alternatives*. Washington, DC: International Monetary Fund.

Lieberman, E. 2003. *Race and Regionalism in the Politics of Taxation in Brazil and South Africa*. Cambridge, MA: Cambridge University Press.

Londoño-Vélez, J., and J. Ávila-Mahecha. 2021. "Enforcing Wealth Taxes in the Developing World: Quasi-Experimental Evidence from Colombia." *American Economic Review: Insights* 3 (2): 131–48.

Mascagni, G., N. Monkam, and C. Nell. 2016. "Unlocking the Potential of Administrative Data in Africa: Tax Compliance and Progressivity in Rwanda." Working Paper No. 56, International Centre for Tax and Development, Brighton, UK.

Mascagni, G., D. Mukama, and F. Santoro. 2019. "An Analysis of Discrepancies in Taxpayers' VAT Declarations in Rwanda." Working Paper No. 92, International Centre for Tax and Development, Brighton, UK.

Mascagni, G., C. Nell, and N. Monkam. 2017. "One Size Does Not Fit All: A Field Experiment on the Drivers of Tax Compliance and Delivery Methods in Rwanda." Working Paper No. 58, International Centre for Tax and Development, Brighton, UK.

Mohiuddin, F., and F. L. K. Ohemeng. Forthcoming. "The Enigma of Central and Local Governments Relationship and the Impact on Property Tax Administration in Ghana." Research project, International Centre for Tax and Development, Brighton, UK.

Moore, M. 2014. "Revenue Reform and State Building in Anglophone Africa." *World Development* 60: 99–112.

Moore, M., O-H. Fjeldstad, J. Isaksen, O. Lundstøl, R. McCluskey, and W. Prichard. 2015. "Building Tax Capacity in Developing Countries." Policy Briefing No. 96, Institute of Development Studies, Brighton, UK.

New World Wealth. 2018. "United Kingdom 2018 Wealth Report." Johannesburg: AfrAsia Bank.

OECD (Organisation for Economic Co-operation and Development). 2009. *Engaging with High Net Worth Individuals on Tax Compliance*. Paris: OECD.

OECD (Organisation for Economic Co-operation and Development). 2015. *Update on Voluntary Disclosure Programmes: A Pathway to Tax Compliance*. Paris: OECD.

OECD (Organisation for Economic Co-operation and Development). 2016. *Automatic Exchange of Financial Account Information: Background Information Brief*. Paris: OECD.

OECD (Organisation for Economic Co-operation and Development). 2017. *Tax Administration 2017: Comparative Information of OECD and Other Advanced and Emerging Economies*. Paris: OECD.

OECD (Organisation for Economic Co-operation and Development). 2018. *The Role and Design of Net Wealth Taxes in the OECD*. OECD Tax Policy Studies No. 26. Paris: OECD.

OECD (Organisation for Economic Co-operation and Development). 2021. "Automatic Exchange of Information (AEOI): Status of Commitments."

Global Forum on Transparency and Exchange of Information for Tax Purposes, OECD, Paris. https://www.oecd.org/tax/transparency/AEOI-commitments.pdf.

Pieterse, D., F. Kreuser, and E. Gavin. 2016. "Introduction to the South African Revenue Service and National Treasury Firm-Level Panel." Working Paper No. 2016/42, United Nations University World Institute for Development Economics Research (UNU-WIDER), Helsinki.

Piketty, T. 2014. *Capital in the Twenty-First Century*. Cambridge, MA: Belknap Press of Harvard University.

Piketty, T., and E. Saez. 2007. "How Progressive Is the U.S. Federal Tax System? A Historical and International Perspective." *Journal of Economic Perspectives* 21 (1): 3–24.

Piracha, M., and M. Moore. 2015. "Understanding Low-Level State Capacity: Property Tax Collection in Pakistan." Working Paper No. 33, International Centre for Tax and Development, Brighton, UK.

Prichard, W. 2015. *Taxation, Responsiveness and Accountability in Sub-Saharan Africa: The Dynamics of Tax Bargaining*. Cambridge, UK: Cambridge University Press.

Prichard, W. 2019. "Tax, Politics, and the Social Contract in Africa." In *Oxford Research Encyclopedia of Politics*. Oxford, UK: Oxford University Press. doi:10.1093/acrefore/9780190228637.013.853.

Saez, E., and G. Zucman. 2019. "How Would a Progressive Wealth Tax Work? Evidence from the Economics Literature." Working paper, University of California, Berkeley.

Schneider, A. 2012. *State-Building and Tax Regimes in Central America*. Cambridge, UK: Cambridge University Press.

Slater, D. 2010. *Ordering Power: Contentious Politics and Authoritarian Leviathans in Southeast Asia*. Cambridge, UK: Cambridge University Press.

Tanzi, A. 2018. "Top 3% of U.S. Taxpayers Paid Majority of Income Tax in 2016." Bloomberg, October 16, 2018.

TJN (Tax Justice Network). 2018. "Key Financial Secrecy Indicator 11: Tax Administration Capacity." In *Financial Secrecy Index 2018*. London: TJN.

Weigel, J. 2018. "Building State and Citizen: How Tax Collection in Congo Engenders Citizen Engagement with the State." Harvard University, Cambridge, MA.

Zebong, N., P. Fish, and W. Prichard. 2017. "Valuation for Property Tax Purposes." Summary Brief No. 10, International Centre for Tax and Development, Brighton, UK.

CHAPTER 4

Taxing Corporate Income

Roel Dom and Wilson Prichard

The Tax Compliance Challenge

The challenges of taxing large corporate taxpayers, and especially multinationals, have attracted increasing attention over the last decade because many larger firms do not appear to be paying their fair share (ICRICT 2015; IMF 2021). This perception not only undermines revenue collection, but also may lead to unfair competition across firms and greater tax burdens on other taxpayers. Moreover, perceptions of unfair taxation of corporate actors may negatively affect the tax morale of other taxpayers and reduce their political support for broader tax reforms.

The taxation of larger corporate taxpayers is of particular concern to low- and middle-income countries where revenue from corporate income taxes is almost as high, as a share of the gross domestic product (GDP), as in high-income countries. Because of their lower levels of revenue collection overall, however, in low- and middle-income countries corporate income taxes make up a significantly larger share of total revenue. Meanwhile, lower-income countries may be particularly vulnerable to international tax avoidance and evasion because of the challenges they face in enforcing international rules. Lower-income countries have also been most likely to experience revenue losses stemming from tax incentives and exemptions (Andersen, Kett, and von Uexkull 2018).

The growing global concern about corporate income taxation has also been driven by concerns that the rise of the digital economy could, if not addressed proactively, facilitate expanded avoidance and evasion via the international tax system. The assets and activities of digital firms are especially amenable to profit shifting by moving intangible assets and services—and key activities more broadly—to low-tax jurisdictions. This practice has prompted major global initiatives to revise the existing rules to deal more effectively with this changing economic reality. However, such revisions may not take into account the unique needs and priorities of lower-income countries.

This chapter reviews the income taxation of large corporate taxpayers, highlighting the challenges and barriers to reform. It discusses key reforms and reflects on what the conceptual framework developed in this report implies for thinking about future reforms. The term *large corporate taxpayers* refers to those firms, incorporated and partnerships alike, that have a significant economic size in terms of assets, turnover, or employees. They generally include but are not limited to multinational firms as well as large domestic firms, which may or may not exploit the international tax system to lower their tax burdens. The chapter refrains from defining a specific size threshold, recognizing that countries may use different criteria and thresholds to identify large taxpayers (IMF 2002; IOTA 2008).

A Revenue Paradox

Superficially, corporate income taxation (CIT) does not appear to be in an immediate state of crisis. Across countries, revenue collected from CIT has been relatively stable over time. Since the 2008–09 global financial crisis, corporate income taxes have remained steady as a share of GDP and even increased for low-income countries (see figure 4.1).

However, these aggregate figures paint an overly optimistic picture, as most evidence suggests that CIT collection is declining in effectiveness relative to its potential over time. This finding reflects the fact that CIT revenue has remained flat despite significant increases in corporate profits over the same period. Since at least the 1980s, the profitability of firms, especially multinationals, has been growing both in absolute terms and as a share of GDP in many higher-income countries (McKinsey 2015; Tørsløv, Wier, and Zucman 2018).[1] This finding implies that if effective rates of corporate taxation had remained unchanged, one would expect to see large increases in corporate tax revenue in line with increases in profitability. Although such data are not available for lower-income countries, a similar pattern appears likely. Higher levels of corporate profitability in low-income countries relative to Organisation for Economic Co-operation and Development (OECD) countries would predict still higher levels of corporate tax revenue (Tørsløv, Wier, and Zucman 2018).

The stagnation in corporate income tax revenue reflects declines in the effective tax rates on corporate income (Abbas and Klemm 2013; Markle and Shackelford 2009). Tax competition, profit shifting, tax exemptions, and limited administrative capacity have all reduced effective levels of corporate income taxation, especially in lower-income countries.

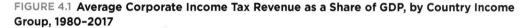

FIGURE 4.1 **Average Corporate Income Tax Revenue as a Share of GDP, by Country Income Group, 1980–2017**

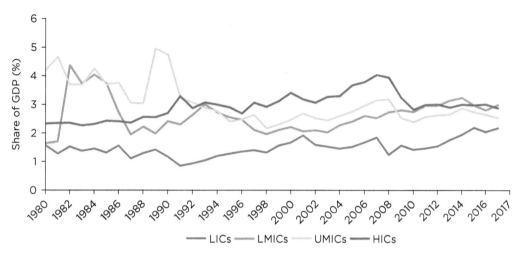

Source: United Nations University World Institute for Development Economics Research (UNU-WIDER), Government Revenue Dataset of the International Centre for Tax and Development, https://www.wider.unu.edu /project/government-revenue-dataset.
Note: GDP = gross domestic product; HICs = high-income countries; LICs = low-income countries; LMICs = lower-middle-income countries; UMICs = upper-middle-income countries.

International Tax Competition

Globalization has placed long-term downward pressure on statutory corporate tax rates around the world. Increased capital and financial mobility have allowed firms to seek out locations that minimize production costs and maximize profits. To the extent that taxes increase production costs and lower profits, governments find it in their interest to lower corporate tax burdens to attract and retain investment as well as profits at home (Keen and Konrad 2013). For both lower- and higher-income countries, the tax competition between countries now seems a well-established fact (Devereux, Lockwood, and Redoano 2008; Keen and Mansour 2010). As a result, statutory tax rates have been in decline since the 1980s (figure 4.2), which runs the risk of a race to the bottom and undermines tax revenue. The precise extent of the revenue forgone because of international tax competition is difficult to estimate, but it may well be much more than that from international tax avoidance.

Not only have statutory rates declined, but the effective rates of taxation—the actual tax burdens faced by corporate taxpayers—have also fallen over the last two decades for both multinational and domestic firms (Dyreng et al. 2017; Markle and Shackelford 2009). Effective rates of corporate income taxation vary across firms and in part depend on the aggressiveness of corporate tax planning strategies (Cooper and Nguyen 2020). Although the evidence on the importance of firm size is more mixed, especially among larger firms, effective tax rates are often found to be the highest for small firms, especially in lower-income countries (Carreras, Dachapalli, and Mascagni 2017; Mascagni and Mengistu 2019; Muller and Kolk 2015). Thus, although all firms can theoretically benefit from

FIGURE 4.2 **Average Statutory Corporate Income Tax Rate, 1979–2017**

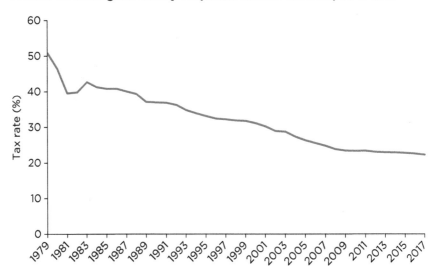

Source: K. Habu, Centre for Business Taxation Tax Database 2017, Oxford University Research Archive, https://ora.ox.ac.uk/.
Note: The graph presents the average statutory tax rate for a sample of 48 countries between 1979 and 2017. For some countries, data were not available for the earlier years. The following countries composed the sample: Argentina, Australia, Austria, Belgium, Bosnia and Herzegovina, Brazil, Bulgaria, Canada, Chile, China, Croatia, Czech Republic, Denmark, Estonia, Finland, France, Germany, Greece, Hungary, Iceland, India, Indonesia, Ireland, Israel, Italy, Japan, the Republic of Korea, Luxembourg, Mexico, Netherlands, New Zealand, Norway, Poland, Portugal, Romania, Russian Federation, Saudi Arabia, Serbia, Slovak Republic, Slovenia, South Africa, Spain, Sweden, Switzerland, Turkey, Ukraine, United Kingdom, and United States.

tax planning, in practice, it is likely to be more accessible for larger firms, giving them a competitive advantage over smaller businesses.

Tax Incentives
The extent to which companies can lower their effective tax rates further depends on the availability of tax planning opportunities. Domestically, such opportunities often reside in legal loopholes and tax incentives such as tax holidays, exemptions, or tax credits. Countries continue to rely on such tax incentives to attract and retain businesses. More than half of lower-income countries have introduced new tax incentives or increased the generosity of existing ones since 2009 (Andersen, Kett, and von Uexkull 2018). Evidence on the usefulness of tax incentives in attracting investment is mixed. Although a recent survey of multinational corporation (MNC) executives in low- and middle-income countries found that tax incentives generally do not drive investment decisions (World Bank 2018), empirical evidence suggests that in some cases they do (Chaurey 2017). The current consensus is that tax incentives can be effective if well designed and targeted, but that is frequently not true in practice (James 2014; PCT 2015).

Tax exemptions invariably generate costs such as revenue losses, administrative costs, market distortions, or higher risks of rent-seeking. Countries are increasingly reporting on the revenue losses, or tax expenditures, associated with tax incentives, but the quality of these reports is often weak (Kassim and

Mansour 2018). Moreover, cross-country comparisons can be misleading because definitions, methodologies, and exemptions vary (Dom and McCulloch 2019; Villela, Lemgruber, and Jorratt 2010). Many studies include all exemptions, with figures often dominated by relatively uncontroversial exemptions from value added tax (VAT) and customs duties for basic consumer goods (Oppong and James 2016). Of interest here, however, are investment incentives. Estimates of their size are more limited, but they can reach up to 2 percent of GDP (TJN-A and AAI 2012; Trigueros 2014).

Of perhaps as much concern is the process around them. Tax incentives continue to be subject to significant discretion and poor oversight, thereby reducing their efficacy and increasing the scope for corruption and abuse, especially in lower-income countries (Li 2006). Many countries need to improve transparency and properly establish the costs and benefits of tax incentives (Kronfol and Steenbergen 2020). However, achieving such transparency has proven stubbornly difficult. Calls to improve reporting have been heard for several decades, but with limited success, and superficial improvements in reporting often fail to address key areas of concern.

Profit Shifting

Weaknesses in the international tax system can also be exploited by firms, especially MNCs, to reduce their tax burdens. Profits are shifted to low-tax jurisdictions using a variety of aggressive tax planning strategies. As a result, multinational companies often face the lowest effective tax rates (Egger, Eggert, and Winner 2010). The impact of international profit shifting on revenue and competitiveness is difficult to estimate precisely because of the secretive nature of the practice. But the available evidence suggests the impact on revenue is sizable, which, in turn, suggests that these practices also offer international firms a significant competitive advantage.

Some early efforts appear, in retrospect, to have overestimated the likely scale of tax losses from tax avoidance. Recent and more refined analyses by Crivelli, de Mooij, and Keen (2016) and Tørsløv, Wier, and Zucman (2018) suggest total global losses of somewhere between US$200 billion (0.4 percent of GDP) and US$600 billion (1.1 percent of GDP). These numbers are significant in simple revenue terms, despite the lower estimates being intentionally conservative (Tørsløv, Wier, and Zucman 2018). Even more striking are other comparisons. These revenue losses represent roughly 10 percent of global corporate tax revenue, while offshore profits represent about 40 percent of the total profits of MNCs (Tørsløv, Wier, and Zucman 2018). These profits are, in turn, likely to increase overall income inequality because the owners of capital who benefit from this reduced taxation tend to be comparatively wealthy (Tørsløv, Wier, and Zucman 2018).

Meanwhile, the challenges in international tax enforcement appear to be most acute in lower-income countries. The best estimates of corporate tax revenue losses consistently point to somewhat higher losses (as a share of GDP) in lower-income countries as follows:

- An International Monetary Fund (IMF) study estimates average losses of 1.3 percent of GDP in low- and middle-income countries, compared with 1.0 percent in OECD countries (Crivelli, de Mooij, and Keen 2016).

- A study by Cobham and Janský (2017), using a similar methodology but more complete data, estimates similar global losses overall, but puts losses in low-income and lower-middle-income countries at almost 2 percent of GDP on average, compared with less than 1 percent of GDP for OECD countries.

- Estimates by Tørsløv, Wier, and Zucman (2018) focus less explicitly on lower-income countries but point to roughly similar levels of revenue loss across income levels.

These patterns are consistent with intuition: effective implementation of existing international tax rules requires significant administrative capacity, thereby raising the bar for lower-income countries.

Effective Tax Administration

Finally, equally critical to the challenges of international tax competition, tax exemptions, and profit shifting are the domestic challenges of building effective tax administrations. Especially in lower-income countries, poor corporate compliance is likely to be driven less by international evasion and more by the mundane domestic drivers of noncompliance: underreporting of profits, overreporting of costs, weak administrative capacity, corruption, and politicization (Moore, Prichard, and Fjeldstad 2018). Absent a robust tax administration relatively free from corruption and politicization, more successful corporate tax collection will remain a challenge.

Moreover, ensuring the effective administration of corporate taxpayers is crucial well beyond the corporate income tax. In India, firms remit about 85 percent of all tax revenue to the government, and similar patterns seem to hold in other countries (Slemrod and Velayudhan 2018). Firms not only pay the government the direct taxes due on their own incomes, but also act as remitters for sales or excise taxes or as withholding agents for salary incomes.

Barriers to Reform

In seeking to strengthen the taxation of large corporations, tax administrations face serious information asymmetries. At its most basic, all tax enforcement involves some form of verifying incomes, assets, and transactions. Because of the private nature of this information, information asymmetries between the taxpayer and the administration are one of the most important hurdles reformers must overcome. In taxing corporate income, this challenge is compounded by the nature of international tax rules, limited local administrative capacity, and politics.

International Tax Rules

International tax rules can create significant scope for aggressive tax planning strategies that exploit gaps and mismatches in tax rules to artificially shift profits to locations with no or low tax rates and no or little economic activity. While relevant to all countries, this challenge is especially acute in lower-income countries because (1) they are typically more dependent on revenue from corporate income taxes than higher-income countries (Crivelli, de Mooij, and Keen 2016); and (2) estimates of revenue lost from base erosion and profit shifting are at least as high if not higher for lower-income countries than for rich countries (Reynolds and Wier 2016). Recent international reforms designed to combat international tax avoidance, culminating in proposals for a global minimum tax on the largest multinational enterprises, are therefore welcome. Yet concerns remain about whether recent achievements address all challenges, especially those of lower-income countries.

The OECD/G20-led Base Erosion and Profit Shifting (BEPS) Project has been at the center of recent progress and represents one of the most ambitious reforms of the international tax system in recent memory (OECD 2013a, 2019a). The project was launched by the G20 following the global financial crisis of 2008–09 with the aim of setting up a new international framework to limit tax avoidance by multinational enterprises. In 2015, a 15-point BEPS Action Plan endorsed by the G20 set out a variety of measures, including new minimum standards, revision of existing standards, and common approaches to facilitating the convergence of national practices and guidance drawing on best practices (OECD 2017). The OECD-based Inclusive Framework has continued to lead the finalization, refinement, and implementation of the measures proposed under the BEPS Action Plan. The effort is widely acknowledged as one of the most comprehensive efforts to reform the international tax system.

Although the BEPS Action Plan has much potential, it may not fully address some core concerns of lower-income countries. Implementation of many of its proposals, such as Action 4 on interest deductibility, is relatively straightforward and should deliver some immediate gains. Yet in other areas there are important questions about whether reforms have addressed the core needs of lower-income countries. For example, they have failed to reduce, or have even increased, the complexity of international rules—complexity that has long made it extraordinarily difficult for many low-income countries to implement and enforce international rules effectively (Moore, Prichard, and Fjeldstad 2018). However, some of these concerns are being addressed through toolkits developed by the Platform for Collaboration on Tax (OECD/G20 2014).

These concerns are on view in the "arm's-length" principle under which transactions between related parties are to be priced as if they were between independent entities. This principle remains the bedrock of international rules, but its implementation presents lower-income countries with particularly big challenges because they frequently lack access to adequate data on "comparables" and adequate capacity to scrutinize and challenge MNCs' profit-shifting strategies (Durst 2019). Many lower-income countries and their supporters have called for more formulary approaches to allocating profits across countries, but those calls have been largely rejected by wealthier states (ATAF 2021). The expansion of the digital economy has only intensified this problem: pricing digital transactions—like other intangibles—is particularly complex, and digital firms are raising challenging questions about whether and how firms should pay taxes in countries in which they sell goods and services but may not have a significant physical presence (ATAF 2020).

These problems are compounded by lopsided tax treaties that often are not adequately implemented. Alongside the general challenges posed by international tax rules and reform processes, many low-income countries apparently continue to lose meaningful tax revenue thanks to tax treaties that can be easily abused to enable avoidance, such as through treaty shopping (see box 4.1), or that unnecessarily limit local taxing rights. Despite some examples of good negotiating practices, the tax treaty networks of most low-income countries are not fit for their purpose, having been built up over half a century on the basis of short-term political priorities, weak negotiating capacity, and an absence of checks and balances on the treaty-making process (Hearson 2018b). Research continues to produce mixed conclusions on the impact of tax treaties on investment flows while pointing to significant revenue losses.

BOX 4.1
Tax Treaties

Tax treaties allocate taxing rights between countries. Intended to avoid double taxation and facilitate cross-border investment, they clarify the balance between two principles of tax jurisdiction: (1) the *principle of source,* which entitles a country to tax income earned within its borders; and (2) the *principle of residence,* which entitles a country to tax income earned by one of its residents. In practice, tax treaties generally restrict source taxation by limiting the rate and scope of withholding taxes and by providing certain exemptions.

The balance between source and resident taxation matters, particularly when the investment flows between two countries are uneven. Source taxation favors capital-importing countries (often lower-income countries), while resident taxation benefits capital-exporting countries (often higher-income countries). Empirical evidence shows that tax treaties concluded between higher-income countries and lower-income countries have become more restrictive over time regarding the taxing rights of lower-income countries (Hearson 2016).

By clearly demarcating taxing rights, tax treaties alleviate concerns about double taxation of cross-border investment and are therefore expected to support investment. However, the evidence on tax treaties' impact on investment is inconclusive at best, especially for lower-income countries (Beer and Loeprick 2018; IMF 2014). To minimize their tax burden, firms take advantage of tax treaty networks to route their investments through countries that have favorable treaties—so-called treaty shopping. In practice, then, tax treaties lower the effective tax rate, but they may fail to grow the tax base and therefore often result in significant revenue losses, especially in lower-income countries.

Steps are being taken to address treaty shopping. Some lower-income countries are proactively reviewing their policies toward tax treaties (Hearson and Kangave 2016). Meanwhile, the Organisation for Economic Co-operation and Development's Multilateral Instrument (MLI) is lessening the opportunity for tax avoidance by multinational enterprises through tax treaty abuse. It offers concrete ways in which governments can close the gaps in international tax rules by transposing results from the OECD/G20 BEPS Project into bilateral tax treaties worldwide, and also implements agreed-on minimum standards to counter treaty abuse and to improve dispute resolution mechanisms (OECD 2020a). However, many lower-income countries have not yet signed onto or ratified the MLI.

Limited Local Administrative Capacity

Problems with international tax treaties are often compounded by the domestic tax code. A good example is offshore indirect transfers of assets—that is, the indirect interest and the asset in question are located in two different countries.[2] Attention here has rightly focused on certain clauses often absent from treaties that are needed to tax an offshore transfer, but that focus has also obscured the fact that many countries lack the power in their domestic law to benefit from those clauses in the first place. Even with reform and simplification of international rules, effective enforcement will still require that new policies be adopted locally along with the development of significant administrative capacity and expertise (PCT 2020). Neither should be taken for granted.

Although international tax rules and treaties pose significant challenges, improved outcomes are likely to depend most critically on building stronger domestic systems. Recent studies have highlighted the challenges facing low-income countries in trying to administer the existing international rules (GIZ 2018). Meanwhile, other studies suggest that if raising revenue is the only objective, then countries might do better to focus on the domestic taxation of firms rather than international taxation (Forstater 2018).

A host of administrative and policy options are now available to lower-income countries that would likely improve outcomes—irrespective of international rules—but they are, at best, imperfectly implemented. On the policy front, lower-income countries continue to sacrifice parts of their tax base through a combination of tax incentives and poor legislation. The challenges include poor management and monitoring of tax exemptions and incentives and the frequent absence of key antiavoidance provisions. On the administrative side, challenges include weak audit capacity (Pomeranz, Marshall, and Castellón 2014); poor access to and sharing of third-party data (Carrillo, Pomeranz, and Singhal 2017); inaccurate and bloated taxpayer registers (Mayega et al. 2019); suboptimal use of information technology (IT) facilities (Moore 2020); and an inability to track and audit VAT paper trails (Mascagni, Mukama, and Santoro 2019; Pomeranz 2015).

In seeking to build policy and administrative capacity, a critical but often overlooked challenge is staff recruitment and retention. In recent decades, countries have focused on modernizing their tax administrations and upskilling their workforce. A central goal of these reforms has been to improve salaries and working conditions in order to recruit and retain highly skilled technical staff. However, even with greater flexibility, recruitment and retention remain challenging in contexts where private sector firms can often offer salaries far higher than those available in the public sector. The result is often a limited supply of staff with the sophisticated audit skills required to confront larger corporate tax and legal departments (GIZ 2018).

Political Barriers

Underlying many of the challenges described so far are political barriers that slow or disrupt potential reform. These barriers are most obvious for tax incentives and exemptions, where discretion, opaqueness, and decentralized control make it easier to grant incentives that serve political rather than economic purposes (Li 2006; Moore, Prichard, and Fjeldstad 2018). Perverse tax treaties or a failure to abide by or ratify international rules also appear likely to reflect elites' engagement in (ineffective) tax competition. A lack of technical capacity and policies to guide treaty negotiations often creates ambiguity on matters such as who should be involved in the negotiations. This ambiguity, in turn, provides room for political and elite capture of the negotiation process and leads to the conclusion of treaties without adequate consideration of their technical implications (Hearson and Kangave 2016; Mutava 2019).

More broadly, weaknesses in tax enforcement are frequently rooted in the political influence exercised by large firms. A recent study describes how corporations influence the international tax regime by pressuring their home governments (Hearson 2018a). As for domestic taxation, a study from Bangladesh highlights the ways in which large corporate actors have traded financial contributions to political parties for relatively weak and predictable tax enforcement (Hassan and Prichard 2016). Work by Fairfield (2010) has also highlighted the broader ways in which corporate interests in Latin America have influenced political elites to limit taxation. Such political maneuvering can explain not only weak enforcement, or perverse tax incentives, but also more subtle weaknesses of reform such as inadequate or ineffective sharing of third-party data.

Taxing the extractives sector, and particularly mining, bears mention here. Mining taxation is an inherently difficult and politically fraught exercise given the ample opportunities for avoidance and evasion (Moore, Prichard, and Fjeldstad 2018). The available evidence for the mining sector suggests that the related revenue losses can be significant (Beer and Loeprick 2015; Lundstøl 2018)—see box 4.2.

BOX 4.2

Compliance Challenges in the Extractives Sector

Compliance challenges intersect most dramatically in the ineffective taxation of mining operations across much of the lower-income world. For lower-income countries, mining operations should be a major source of tax revenue—the primary social benefit expected from mining activities. In Botswana, for example, minerals contribute an estimated 40 percent of total government revenue (ANRC 2016). Yet in many countries, the tax revenue from mining operations has often been limited, although the data are also highly imperfect.

This shortfall reflects a variety of interconnected factors. Resource extraction firms have been particularly aggressive in exploiting international tax rules to reduce their tax liabilities, including through sector-specific strategies (Readhead 2016). They also have often been the beneficiaries of firm-specific resource extraction contracts that have offered significant tax incentives and holidays with limited transparency and seemingly driven by corruption and broader political interests (Lundstøl, Raballand, and Nyirongo 2015; Moore, Prichard, and Fjeldstad 2018; Prichard 2009; Prichard and Jibao 2010). In turn, the ability of firms to take advantage of international tax rules and otherwise avoid their tax obligations has been aided by the weak capacity of the agencies responsible for taxing resource extraction companies. These agencies frequently struggle to retain key staff and often experience political interference that disrupts reform (Lundstøl, Raballand, and Nyirongo 2015).

Tax Morale

Finally, to understand the challenge of compliance by larger corporate actors, it is equally necessary to consider the potential drivers of tax morale and quasi-voluntary tax compliance. Tax morale needs to be conceptualized quite differently for large firms than for individuals and smaller firms (Slemrod 2004). For larger firms, decisions about whether to be more voluntarily compliant are likely to be shaped by considerations less linked to tax morale and trust than to narrower corporate interests, especially when ownership and control are separated (Armstrong et al. 2015; Cai and Liu 2009; Chyz et al. 2013; DeBacker, Heim, and Tran 2015).

Limited research, however, does suggest that questions about fairness and equity are especially important for corporations (Alm and McClellan 2012; Hassan and Prichard 2016; Nur-tegin 2008; OECD 2019c). Will more voluntary compliance result in fairer treatment by tax authorities (for example, less harassment and lower compliance costs)? And are other firms in the same sector bearing roughly equivalent tax burdens? Somewhat fragmented evidence suggests that firms frequently fear that more cooperation will not protect them from harassment and may put them at a disadvantage relative to competitors, thereby spurring greater reliance on avoidance and evasion (Çule and Fulton 2009). Beyond these concerns, firms also are more likely to be compliant when they believe the government is funding services and activities that benefit them and when they have a voice in shaping those decisions (Prichard 2015). Labor-intensive firms, in particular, may have a vested interest in the state delivering on public services, as it lessens the need for firms to fill the gap.

Reform Progress—and Future Options

Strengthening the taxation of larger corporations likely requires a heavy emphasis on improving enforcement, along with specific facilitation and trust-building measures. Enforcement appears paramount given the likelihood that firms will focus on cost-benefit analysis in making tax compliance decisions. Their decisions are depersonalized and incentivized by shareholders, stock-based compensation, and financial markets, and thus are more likely to be driven by profit maximization.

Despite the primacy of enforcement, research also suggests the importance of combining investment in enforcement with parallel investments in facilitation and trust because very aggressive enforcement on its own may backfire by convincing firms to pursue tax minimization strategies more aggressively (Siglé et al. 2018). Consistent with this cooperative approach to compliance, over the last several decades large investments have been aimed at improving the business climate, including by reducing tax compliance costs. That said, evidence suggests that high costs of compliance are, in general, a more acute challenge for medium and small firms (Marcuss et al. 2013).

Enforcement

Strengthening enforcement entails both developing better enforcement tools and overcoming political and capacity-related barriers to applying those tools more effectively. International tax rules pose obvious challenges to effective enforcement and compliance, as do problematic tax treaties. Countries also face inescapable capacity challenges in trying to confront large firms staffed by teams of accountants and lawyers seeking to limit their firms' tax liabilities. Moreover, many countries continue to sacrifice parts of their tax base through tax exemptions. And yet where the political will to act can be mobilized, improved outcomes appear achievable in a variety of areas, even without any changes in the international environment. Of course, building political will may hinge, at least in part, on building greater trust among taxpayers. This feedback loop between trust and political will may not necessarily involve the corporate taxpayers directly involved, but it may build on a social contract with other taxpayers who might be perturbed by the low tax compliance or legal tax burdens of, in this case, larger companies.

Reform of International Rules and Representation

The OECD/G20 BEPS Action Plan has been an important step forward. It will improve the coherence of international tax rules and ensure a more transparent tax environment. The key to success will be implementation as well as ensuring that standards developed under the Action Plan and beyond fit the needs of all countries. To enable coordinated global implementation of the BEPS Action Plan and to ensure that interested countries and jurisdictions can participate on an equal footing in the development of standards on BEPS-related issues, OECD/G20 established the Inclusive Framework. The framework brings together 139 countries, and once excluded non-OECD and non-G20 countries (including lower-income countries) are now equal members of the decision-making processes (OECD 2013a, 2019a). As a result, new proposals are more likely to reflect the constraints and needs of lower-income countries. For example, OECD (2020b) simulations suggest that low-income countries stand to gain more than middle-income countries from recent proposals to address the tax challenges arising from the digitalization of the economy.

More can be done to address the needs and concerns of lower-income countries by ensuring the effective participation of all countries under the Inclusive Framework. Lower-income countries have become progressively more vocal about the challenges they face in implementing the existing rules. Initiatives such as the contributions of the Intergovernmental Group of Twenty-Four (G-24) to discussions on digitalization and of the African Tax Administration Forum's Cross Border Taxation Technical Committee show that lower-income countries are attempting to weigh in.[3]

Still, lower-income countries continue to struggle to achieve priority for their concerns, particularly at the technical level. In part this can be ascribed to, and is exacerbated by, some aspects of the decision-making processes, such as the pace and intensity of discussions, the culture of policy making, the costs of attending regular meetings in Paris, and the absence of routine and timely translation of documents and meetings. Meanwhile, negotiation of dynamics and outcomes is still being driven primarily by the interests of larger and wealthier countries to the relative exclusion of the concerns of lower-income countries. Expansion of initiatives aimed at deepening the knowledge of representatives from lower-income countries or at building the ecosystems of South-South collaboration could help to overcome these challenges (Christensen, Hearson, and Randriamanalina 2020).

Maximizing benefits for lower-income countries is likely to require further reform. Current rules are often still too complex to implement for administrations in low-capacity countries (Clavey et al. 2019; GIZ 2018; Picciotto 2018). To serve the interests of these countries, and arguably others as well, international tax reform is likely to need to prioritize both further simplification of international rules and investments in the capacity development of tax administrations in lower-income countries.

Building on an idea of the Tax Justice Network, an advocacy group, OECD and the United Nations Development Programme launched Tax Inspectors Without Borders (TIWB) in 2015 to strengthen the capacity of lower-income countries to effectively tax multinational enterprises. Via TIWB, expert tax auditors are embedded in lower-income country tax administrations to provide local officials with practical, hands-on help in dealing with tax audits and international tax issues. This capacity building complements efforts of other international and regional organizations, including World Bank technical assistance, and has resulted in significant extra revenue for lower-income countries (TIWB 2021).

Capacity-building efforts should be complemented with the simplification of international rules to make them easier to enforce and to provide more certainty. There have been some small but notable changes in this regard, drawing on the practices of lower-income countries. These include recognition in OECD's transfer pricing guidelines of a simplified approach to the treatment of commodities exports originating from Argentina and of the Chinese notion of location savings, which gives manufacturing countries a greater share of the tax base.[4] The United Nations, too, introduced a provision into its Model Double Taxation Convention allowing the imposition of withholding taxes on fees for technical services. Some other proposals push the boundaries of the existing paradigm (Durst 2016a; ICRICT 2018; IMF 2019; Picciotto 2016). Yet these reforms have been limited in scope and have focused primarily on larger middle-income countries (Hearson and Prichard 2018).

More ambitious has been a recent proposal by 130 countries to introduce a new international tax framework. The agreement builds on the OECD/G20 Inclusive Framework's work to address the tax challenges of a digitalized economy. The two-pillar package aims to ensure that large multinationals pay tax where they operate and earn profits, while adding much-needed certainty and stability to the international tax system. Pillar One would reallocate some taxing rights over multinationals to the markets where they have business activities, regardless of whether firms have a physical presence there. Pillar Two seeks to put a floor on competition over corporate income tax by introducing a global minimum corporate tax rate that countries can use to protect their tax base (OECD 2021).

The significance of this agreement is hard to overestimate. Yet the agreement also has limitations that may be particularly relevant for lower-income countries (Picciotto 2021). The proposal is restricted to the largest multinationals, which may be more important to larger countries and will likely be subject to carve-outs for specific industries. Lower-income countries have also raised concerns about the details of the design of both pillars, arguing that both remain biased toward increasing revenue for large economies and are administratively complex (ATAF 2021; G-24 2021). Moreover, a (small) number of key low-tax jurisdictions have yet to join the framework, raising additional challenges.

This progress is welcome, but the interests of lower-income countries still require greater priority and attention. Based on the World Bank's work in supporting tax policy and administration reforms in lower-income economies, a paper by Clavey et al. (2019) identifies five areas for further improvement to account for the specific (capacity) challenges faced by lower-income countries:

1. For proposals that require an allocation of a slice of all or part of an MNC's profit, a formulaic approach is desirable.

2. Work on the allocation of taxing rights should include the option to reallocate all nonroutine profit rather than only that part reflecting user value or marketing intangibles.

3. Approaches should consider both capital importing and exporting countries.

4. Detailed guidance is needed on the use of withholding tax and on the application of mandatory safe harbors.

5. Practical limitations to accessing relevant information for developing economies should be removed.

New Domestic Approaches to Taxing MNCs
Alongside efforts to further reform international rules to better suit the needs and realities of lower-income countries, such countries may rely on domestic policy options to reduce the scope for aggressive tax avoidance and evasion. These solutions are likely to share the characteristics of second-best policy options—that is, they sacrifice a measure of efficiency and equity in order to simplify administration and thus improve the quality of outcomes in practice in lower-capacity environments (Kleven, Khan, and Kaul 2016; Prichard and Moore 2018).

Withholding taxes. Although they likely distort production efficiency, withholding taxes have become increasingly popular, especially in lower-income countries, because they are relatively easy to implement and can raise significant revenue (Brockmeyer and Hernandez 2016). Usually, government institutions and large firms withhold a certain amount from their transactions with other parties. That revenue is then remitted to the tax administration and acts as a prepayment of taxes by those other parties.

Withholding taxes not only have potential for domestic transactions, but also can be effective tools for taxing outbound payments in cross-border transactions (Clavey et al. 2019; Durst 2016a). Although tax treaties often restrict their use, withholding taxes are back on the international agenda, especially in areas where they have not traditionally been applied such as to cross-border payments for technical services as proposed in the new UN model treaty provision (IMF 2019). Because of the risk of double taxation, especially when withholding taxes are placed outside tax treaties, alternatives such as diverted profit taxes have also been proposed (Clavey et al. 2019; Pemberton and Loeprick 2019).

Alternative minimum taxes. The governments of lower-income countries could rely more heavily on alternative minimum taxes (AMTs) to establish a floor for corporate tax payments. Thirty-six countries have provisions for an AMT in place, and although most are based on turnover, some implement an asset-based variant (Durst 2019).

The basic logic of a turnover-based AMT is that if the taxable profit declared by a firm falls below a predetermined threshold, then an AMT levied on total firm turnover is applied instead. The underlying concern is that firms may artificially reduce their taxable profit in two ways: by understating revenue or by inflating costs. Because an AMT focuses exclusively on turnover, it bypasses the need to verify the costs being claimed by the firms, thereby simplifying administration and reducing the scope for abuse.

But this approach comes at a cost. An AMT can be a rather blunt tool. It is more economically efficient to tax profits because an AMT risks imposing a significant tax on firms that are legitimately making little profit or incurring a loss, potentially disincentivizing investment. That said, the best study of AMTs in lower-income countries, focusing on Pakistan, concludes that the benefits of the AMT significantly outweigh the costs, at least in that case, thereby suggesting the value of further research (Best et al. 2015). According to the IMF (2019), minimum taxes, especially on inbound investments in lower-income countries, could be a powerful tool for addressing profit shifting and tax competition.

Mining sector tax reforms. In the mining sector, a range of policies have been proposed to help curb rampant abuses. Although the BEPS Action Plan has addressed some concerns, implementation often remains problematic because many tax administrations in lower-income countries lack the required technical expertise, sectoral knowledge, or proper risk assessment procedures (Readhead 2016). In response, toolkits have been developed to assist lower-income countries (Guj et al. 2017; Readhead 2017; UN 2017).

Transfer pricing risks remain, especially for minerals and specialized services in the mining sector (Durst 2016b; Readhead 2018). Nevertheless, some progress is being made on addressing the related information gaps (PCT 2017). Alternatives have also been proposed, such as a price-based royalty tax or index pricing, where values are based on publicly quoted prices (Clausing and Durst 2015; Readhead 2018). However, Readhead (2018) argues that for hard rock minerals, administrative pricing—where the government, not the taxpayer, sets the price—should be applied because it gives governments the presumptive advantage. Technical solutions aside, the combination of sector-specific risks and large rents creates distinct political economy challenges, making mining a hard-to-tax sector (Moore, Prichard, and Fjeldstad 2018; Readhead 2016).

Improved Data Quality and Deployment

The most widely cited path to improved compliance among corporate taxpayers lies in improving the collection and deployment of data to increase enforcement. One option is to focus on the collection, management, and sharing of data available within the tax administration or across government agencies (see more details in chapter 7). Many low-income countries have significant opportunities to improve the cross-checking of corporate income tax, VAT, and customs data to assess the credibility of tax returns (Mascagni, Mukama, and Santoro 2019). Another, often overlooked, option is better cross-referencing of information from other government activities, such as government contracts, to assess the completeness of tax reporting.

Greater reliance on both domestic and international third-party data, such as firms' transactions or banking information, is yet another option with significant potential. Although legal provisions enabling this access are improving, they are still often missing in the domestic legislation of certain countries, while other countries have yet to become signatories of information exchange treaties. New technologies are also expanding the possibilities to improve access to relevant data. For example, satellite imagery could be used to track changes in the physical footprints of firms, while changes in things such as taxi services and apartment rentals online can, in principle, provide tax authorities with detailed digitalized information about overall activities.

However, more third-party data are not a panacea. Although in Ecuador third-party information prompted businesses to declare more revenue, they simultaneously declared larger deductions (Carillo, Pomeranz, and Singhal 2017). Menkhoff and Miethe (2019) observe a similar dynamic: tax evaders adapt to both new and established information exchange treaties and find new ways to hide their income. Ultimately, information is needed from multiple sources, coupled with follow-up audit capacity and a capacity to pursue arrears where avoidance and evasion are detected (Menkhoff and Miethe 2019; Slemrod et al. 2017). Research on VAT enforcement suggests that tax administrations in lower-income countries often struggle to fully exploit data even though they are increasingly ubiquitous (Mascagni, Dom, and Santoro 2021).

Difficulty in taking full advantage of data also arises from political challenges within governments. Tax administrations may resist cooperating because of a desire to defend administrative fiefdoms or information monopolies, which can be a source of power and perks. Meanwhile, cross-government cooperation may lag as requests for sharing information move up and down hierarchical chains or because data formats and sources may not be readily compatible or available.

Investment in Administrative Capacity

Alongside specific policy and administrative strategies, building broad capacity and expertise within tax administrations is particularly important in strengthening the taxation of corporate actors. Properly taxing large corporate actors is inherently complex in legal and accountancy terms. Another acute challenge for tax authorities is retaining staff with the relevant skills (Moore 2014). Both challenges are amplified in international tax rules.

Effective enforcement thus requires both a sustained and a coordinated approach to building targeted capacity, as well as well-developed human resource strategies to support staff recruitment and retention. Meeting these needs has posed challenges for donors and governments alike in ensuring that capacity-building strategies are locally owned and driven, while moving beyond one-off training programs in favor of strategies for building broader and deeper capacity (Fjeldstad 2014; Fjeldstad and Heggstad 2012). It also means tax administrations must generate the right incentives for staff—for example, by increasing internal audit capacity (Schreiber 2018), improving performance incentives (Khan, Khwaja, and Olken 2016), or employing IT systems to introduce better data controls and assess staff performance (Moore 2020).

A Role for Social Sanctions and Recognition

The available research, although limited, suggests that social norms, rewards, and sanctions can strengthen compliance by large corporate taxpayers (Feld, Frey, and Torgler 2006). Compliance behavior among individual taxpayers may respond to social norms because of the importance of individual relationships or a desire to contribute to public welfare. By contrast, corporate responsiveness to social norms, rewards, and sanctions is likely to be rooted in a simpler logic: maintaining the corporation's reputation to maximize long-term profitability.

Where there are strong corporate norms of tax compliance, failure to pay taxes may undermine a firm's reputation in ways that affect its financial bottom line. For example, in Bangladesh the promise of exposing information about tax payments by all firms led to more tax compliance by previously non-compliant firms, specifically in areas in which some firms were already compliant (Chetty, Mobarak, and Singhal 2014). Meanwhile, Pakistan's government, instead of shaming firms, publicly recognized and rewarded the country's top 100 tax-paying firms. This approach significantly increased compliance, particularly among large incorporated firms, suggesting that they are best placed to monetize the goodwill generated by the program (Slemrod, Rehman, and Mazhar 2019).

The compliance effects of social sanctions are likely limited to firms with the greatest exposure to reputational damage (Austin and Wilson 2017). Nevertheless, by exploiting reputational concerns, public pressure can increase corporate tax compliance (Dyreng, Hoopes, and Wilde 2016). Whether firms become fully compliant because of these actions or merely ensure they pay enough taxes to avoid public scrutiny and critique—but no more than that—remains an open question.

Facilitation

Easing Tax Compliance

Over the last several decades, the issue of compliance costs has assumed more importance, buttressed by empirical evidence suggesting that greater compliance burdens negatively affect the business environment (Djankov et al. 2002; Marcuss et al. 2013; Slemrod and Yitzhaki 2002). In response, many countries have—often successfully—implemented measures to simplify their tax regimes to bring down compliance costs, frequently for large businesses. Central to this agenda has been seeking simplified tax design and improved tax administration. Tax systems had to become clearer, more transparent, more predictable, easier to administer, and less vulnerable to extortion and corruption. Tax administrations were reorganized and restructured to make processes more user-friendly. The idea that all taxpayers were potential evaders gradually gave way to the notion that taxpayers were customers (Fjeldstad and Moore 2008).

Similarly, international standards may reduce compliance burdens, especially for multinational enterprises. Harmonizing international tax rules and practices was one of the goals of the OECD/G20 BEPS process. By ensuring that predictable standards and procedures apply globally, compliance is simplified for corporations that operate across borders, even if international rules are still complex. Although a simple system would be best, a complex system that is the same everywhere is a good second-best.

Large Taxpayer Units

Many facilitation reforms began to focus on large corporate taxpayers by establishing large taxpayer units (LTUs). This approach was intended to improve the specialization of tax officials, while also facilitating compliance (Baer 2002). Because large corporate taxpayers are responsible for a disproportionally large share of total tax revenue (Slemrod and Velayudhan 2018), monitoring and improving the tax compliance of the largest taxpayers have often been the primary motivation for establishing LTUs. In line with the reorganization of many tax administrations from divisions dealing with tax types to those dealing with taxpayer segments, these units act as single windows for large corporate taxpayers. Typically, they are responsible for most tax administration functions, including taxpayer services, collection, enforcement of tax arrears, and audits (Baer 2002).

Despite the popularity of this reform, little evidence has emerged on its effectiveness, and its impact on revenue performance is not clear (Akhand 2015; Ebeke, Mansour, and Rota-Graziosi 2016). Anecdotal evidence suggests that greater specialization indeed strengthened risk management as well as taxpayer engagement. However, the available empirical evidence for lower-income countries suggests that at an aggregate level the revenue impact of LTUs has been insignificant (Ebeke, Mansour, and Rota-Graziosi 2016).

Meanwhile, taxpayers may respond strategically to size-dependent enforcement efforts, especially if they strengthen perceptions of increased or disproportionate monitoring. Evidence from Spain shows that firms tend to strategically bunch under the LTU threshold to avoid oversight (Almunia and Lopez-Rodriguez 2018). Research suggests that such bunching is not solely indicative of evasion efforts. Rather, it reflects real economic responses and therefore has real welfare implications. By affecting incentives for resource allocation, entry and exit, and investment in innovation, size-dependent enforcement (marginally) distorts the productivity of firms (Bachas, Jaef, and Jensen 2019).

On the other hand, given evidence that larger firms often benefit disproportionately from opportunities for avoidance and evasion, it may be that more intensive enforcement by LTUs merely levels the playing field. More evidence is needed to draw any strong conclusions. Nevertheless, at a minimum LTUs often appear to have acted as a pilot for other reforms.

Paying Taxes

Overall, the administrative burden associated with paying taxes seems to have lessened. Although it is hard to measure compliance costs precisely (Eichfelder and Hechtner 2018), the available evidence suggests that paying taxes has become increasingly less burdensome for businesses. Among the measures it tracks, the World Bank's Enterprise Survey assesses the extent to which firms identify tax administration as a constraint. Table 4.1 summarizes recent trends. Worldwide, with the exception of South Asia, it has become easier—as measured by the amount of time required—for a firm to fulfill its tax obligations. These results confirm that recent efforts aimed at facilitating tax compliance have had some success. Yet compliance costs remain an important factor in the business environment of large firms, with some studies suggesting they may affect investment decisions (Lawless 2013; World Bank 2018). However, compliance costs

TABLE 4.1 **Average Time Taken to Comply with Tax Laws, by Region, 2006–20**
Hours per year

Region	2006	2010	2015	2020
East Asia and Pacific	291	222	211	172
Europe and Central Asia	473	347	234	203
High-income: OECD	230	197	169	158
Latin America and the Caribbean	416	388	482	379
Middle East and North Africa	226	201	214	203
South Asia	268	248	303	295
Sub-Saharan Africa	332	304	307	283
Average	**324**	**280**	**281**	**245**

Source: World Bank, Doing Business (database), https://www.doingbusiness.org/en/data /exploretopics/paying-taxes.
Note: The Paying Taxes indicator measures the time it takes a firm to prepare, file, and pay three major types of taxes and contributions: corporate income tax, value added or sales tax, and labor taxes, including payroll taxes and social contributions. OECD = Organisation for Economic Co-operation and Development.

generally seem to be more binding for medium and small firms than for larger ones (Slemrod and Venkatesh 2002).

Trust

Fairness: Increasing Predictability and Certainty

The most essential component of strengthening trust among corporate taxpayers—and thus in fostering greater tax compliance and support for reform—is likely to lie in improving the predictability and certainty of tax enforcement. Uncertainty around enforcement can follow from discretionary applications of rules and procedures motivated by, for example, rent-seeking or political considerations. Moreover, time inconsistencies can prompt governments to promise low taxation in advance of a firm's investment decision, while afterward it has every incentive to increase taxation (see, for example, Fischer 1980). Most research, though not extensive, suggests that predictability is a critical concern of corporate taxpayers in lower-income countries—and, in some cases, perhaps more important than the overall payments required (Campos, Lien, and Pradhan 1999; Hassan and Prichard 2016; OECD/IMF 2017; World Bank 2018).

Tax uncertainty is likely to discourage investment and undermine quasi-voluntary tax compliance. From a firm's perspective, the importance of predictability is twofold: it allows them to plan for the future, and it provides assurance they will be treated like their competitors. Both aspects, in turn, are likely to encourage quasi-voluntary compliance. In the face of tax uncertainty, firms may think it better to rely on a lower tax declaration as a starting point for negotiation. However, a firm that knows taxes will be enforced in ways consistent with the law is more likely to declare honestly to avoid the costs, uncertainty, and potential informality of efforts to reduce tax burdens. Moreover, a firm that has confidence that its peers are paying broadly similar taxes will feel less pressure to engage in aggressive avoidance and evasion to remain competitive—or may even feel pressure to declare honestly for reputational reasons, as discussed earlier.

Building predictability and trust depends, in part, on the broad work of building reliable, rules-based tax administrations, which can also be supported by "rewarding" compliant taxpayers. Tax uncertainty can arise in various corners of the tax system: legislation may be unclear; administrative practices may be inconsistent; dispute resolution mechanisms may be slow; technological changes may complicate the applicability of existing rules; or taxpayers themselves may test the limits of the interpretation of tax provisions (OECD/IMF 2017). However, as spelled out in greater detail in the *OECD/IMF Report on Tax Certainty* (2017), there are alternatives for strengthening tax certainty such as by

- Developing principle-based tax laws

- Issuing timely rulings and technical interpretations

- Creating effective and timely dispute resolution mechanisms

- Investing in dispute prevention.

Cooperative Compliance

To improve predictability and certainty, several countries have introduced in recent years cooperative compliance programs. The notion of cooperative compliance goes back to a 2008 OECD report that defined it as "a relationship that favours collaboration over confrontation and is anchored more on mutual trust than on enforceable obligations" (OECD 2008, 39). Cooperative compliance programs usually require corporations to have an internal control framework in place to ensure they can comply with their tax obligations and can also detect uncertain tax positions and disclose these to the tax authority. In exchange, the tax authority ensures that tax matters are resolved quickly, quietly, fairly, and with finality (Goslinga, Siglé, and Veldhuizen 2019; van Dijk and Siglé 2015). This strategy can be summarized as "transparency in exchange for certainty" (OECD 2013b, 28).

No two cooperative compliance approaches are the same, but there are similarities across countries. In 2017, about 22 countries had a cooperative compliance program in place, while another 15, mostly higher-income, were either implementing or planning one. The nature of these arrangements varies and is often—though not always—formalized in specific regulations or a formal agreement (OECD 2019b). Most of these cooperative compliance programs entail commitments by the tax administration and taxpayer to share information on a real-time basis, as illustrated in figure 4.3.

Although the assumptions underlying the cooperative compliance framework seem supported by research (Kirchler, Kogler, and Muehlbacher 2014), the real-life effects of these programs are less clear owing to scant empirical research. Anecdotal evidence, mostly for high-income countries, suggests that the approach has led to less uncertainty in tax positions because tax issues are resolved before reporting and fewer issues are decided in court (Larsen and Oats 2019). Yet even in countries such as Sweden with a highly capable tax administration, success is not guaranteed, especially when businesses believe the initiative is skewed against them (Larsen 2019). Moreover, although these approaches may have been successful in establishing trust between the administration and

FIGURE 4.3 **Features of Cooperative Compliance Programs, 2017**

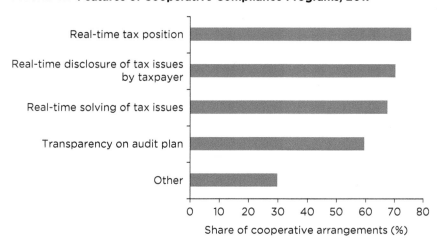

Source: International Monetary Fund, Revenue Administration Fiscal Information Tool (RA-FIT ISORA).

large businesses, they could lead to a diminution of trust from the broader public who does not enjoy such perks and may view the relationship as too "cozy" (Freedman 2018).

Little is known about the applicability and suitability of the framework for lower-income countries. Experiences so far seem to point to necessary preconditions for the successful implementation of cooperative compliance programs. Most important, both tax administrations and businesses must be able to gain from cooperation, such as cost savings or tax predictability. A report by OECD further identifies commercial awareness, impartiality, proportionality, openness, and responsiveness as crucial factors for the success of cooperative compliance programs (OECD 2013b). Also required are adequate accountability frameworks as well as skilled and specialized staff within tax administrations. This notion suggests that maturer administrations may benefit more from the implementation of cooperative compliance approaches, while less advanced administrations should prioritize strengthening basic functions and accountability frameworks.

Accountability: Expansion of Representation
Finally, several countries have made progress in recent years toward expanding forums for engagement between businesses and governments. These forums have in many countries served as spaces for discussing key tax questions and for building support for new taxation and expanded tax compliance. By doing so, they have offered businesses assurance that they have a space for engaging with government around their priorities.

Anecdotally, the existence of these forums appears to have fostered trust and engagement. However, because so little detailed research has been conducted (Moore 2014; Prichard 2015), much scope remains for learning more about how to foster corporate compliance and political support, including through targeted reciprocity and expanded representation.

Conclusion

Weak corporate tax compliance implies large revenue losses for governments, undermines tax morale among taxpayers in general, and can offer firms more able to avoid and evade taxes an unfair competitive advantage. Although global corporate tax revenue has risen in recent years because of rising corporate profits, collection as a share of GDP has been relatively stable, signaling declines in the taxation of corporations over time and the need for new approaches to reform.

Corporate taxation in low- and middle-income countries is undermined by international dynamics. In an era of capital and financial mobility, international tax competition has led to declining statutory corporate tax rates and generated continued pressure for often poorly designed and ineffective tax incentives and exemptions. Meanwhile, there is now extensive evidence of significant (albeit hard to measure) revenue losses due to international profit shifting by MNCs. These challenges have often been exacerbated by unbalanced tax treaties that reduce the taxing right of lower-income countries. The OECD/G20's BEPS process has generated substantial progress, but lower-income countries have had a limited say in the process, and most observers agree that reforms to date have failed to adequately prioritize and address their core concerns.

Yet despite international progress, many lower-income countries often still lack the capacity to adequately enforce international and domestic rules. Institutional weaknesses in national tax administrations, such as a lack of audit capacity, limited use of third-party data, and suboptimal use of IT continue to undermine effective administration. These weaknesses are often exacerbated by the difficulty of retaining staff with the sophisticated skills needed to audit large corporations given the frequently much higher salaries in the private sector.

Although recent debates have tended to focus on the technical challenges of taxing large corporate actors—many of them rooted in international tax rules—national political economy factors also pose a critical challenge to reform. Simply put, firms are able to exert significant political influence to limit taxation and enforcement. As with other tax types, the critical importance of politics tends to be revealed in the extent to which countries do not implement measures that are likely both effective and technically achievable. The persistence of poorly designed and poorly monitored tax incentives and exemptions is in many ways the largest and most striking challenge.

In recent decades, countries have pursued a wide range of reform directions, all of which appear individually useful but collectively not sufficient to counterbalance international challenges and domestic political barriers. For enforcement, governments have long emphasized trying to improve access to and use of third-party data, make new investments in audit capacity, pursue improved strategies to retain skilled staff, and strengthen IT systems. The last decade has also seen rapidly expanding international support for capacity building around international tax rules. Yet progress has been slow amid political and institutional obstacles. Countries have also increasingly emphasized efforts to facilitate compliance through institutional reform, efforts to simplify policy and administrative procedures, and a broader stress on customer service. These efforts appear to have enjoyed meaningful success, although the overall impact on compliance has not been widely studied.

Looking ahead, the central challenge for governments appears to be tackling international sources of tax avoidance and evasion, while addressing domestic political and institutional barriers to improved policy and administration.

At the international level, lower-income countries will continue to advocate through increasingly organized regional blocs for reforms that simplify international rules and allocate greater taxing rights to source countries. A range of options are available, including moving globally toward formulary apportionment; improving transparency and data sharing related to country-by-country reporting of corporate tax data; increasing reliance on withholding taxes or safe harbor rules; adopting a destination-based cash-flow tax; sharing residual profits; ascribing standardized profit margins to the operations of international firms; or using AMTs as a backstop on tax collection. In principle, some of these options could be adopted by individual countries or regional groupings, even in the absence of an international agreement, because many lower-income countries continue to debate whether the OECD-led reform process will meet their needs.

Any international reforms will need to be matched by domestic willingness to adopt and effectively implement new rules fairly and equitably. This willingness is, in part, a technical challenge, requiring investments in skilled staff, audit capacity, and better IT systems, among other things. Targeted research into the effectiveness of relatively new approaches to tax reform such as AMTs and cooperative compliance programs could be productive. On a more fundamental level, progress will require confronting corporate power by both mobilizing pro-tax coalitions and seeking to garner support from businesses themselves. Civil society organizations worldwide have been encouraging public pressure to improve corporate taxation by highlighting weak compliance and the social costs of lost revenue—often successfully (Dyreng, Hoopes, and Wilde 2016).

Firms that already bear significant tax burdens are natural allies of such efforts, and expanding effective, rules-based taxation to a critical mass of firms could tilt political dynamics further in that direction. Meanwhile, governments may be able to foster greater buy-in among firms through investments in trust-building. Two directions seem particularly promising: (1) taking steps to increase predictability through more transparent and consistent rules-based enforcement, adopting as much as possible principles of cooperative compliance; and (2) seeking to increase the collective dialogue with businesses to reduce the scope for bilateral rent-seeking, while increasing responsiveness to the concerns of businesses as a group. The question of how efforts to expand government engagement with corporate taxpayers affects trust and quasi-voluntary compliance, however, merits further research.

Notes

1. US Bureau of Economic Analysis, Gross National Product [GNP], retrieved from FRED, Federal Reserve Bank of St. Louis, https://fred.stlouisfed.org/series/GNP, November 4, 2020.

2. For further explanation and examples, see https://www.tax-platform.org/sites /pct/files/publications/PCT_Toolkit_The_Taxation_of_Offshore_Indirect _Transfers.pdf.

3. The Intergovernmental Group of Twenty-Four on International Monetary Affairs and Development was established in 1971 to help coordinate the positions of low- and middle-income countries on international monetary and development finance issues as well as to ensure that their interests are adequately represented in negotiations on international monetary matters.

4. *Location savings* refers to the cost savings stemming from differences in the cost of operations in high- and low-cost jurisdictions.

References

Abbas, S. M. A., and A. Klemm. 2013. "A Partial Race to the Bottom: Corporate Tax Developments in Emerging and Developing Economies." *International Tax and Public Finance* 20 (4): 596–617.

Akhand, Z. 2015. "How Compliant Are the Large Corporate Taxpayers? The Bangladesh Experience." *eJournal of Tax Research* 13 (2): 581–615.

Alm, J., and C. McClellan. 2012. "Tax Morale and Tax Compliance from the Firm's Perspective." *Kyklos* 65 (1): 1–17.

Almunia, M., and D. Lopez-Rodriguez. 2018. "Under the Radar: The Effects of Monitoring Firms on Tax Compliance." *American Economic Journal: Economic Policy* 10 (1): 1–38.

Andersen, M., B. Kett, and E. von Uexkull. 2018. "Corporate Tax Incentives and FDI in Developing Countries." In *Global Investment Competitiveness Report 2017/18*. Washington, DC: World Bank.

ANRC (African Natural Resources Center). 2016. "Botswana's Mineral Revenues, Expenditure and Savings Policy: A Case Study." ANRC, African Development Bank, Abidjan, Côte d'Ivoire.

Armstrong, C. S., J. L. Blouin, A. D. Jagolinzer, and D. F. Larcker. 2015. "Corporate Governance, Incentives, and Tax Avoidance." *Journal of Accounting and Economics* 60 (1): 1–17.

ATAF (African Tax Administration Forum). 2020. "Media Statement on the Outcomes of the Inclusive Framework Meeting 29 to 30 January 2020." Press release, ATAF, Pretoria, South Africa.

ATAF (African Tax Administration Forum). 2021. "ATAF Sends Revised Pillar One Proposals to the Inclusive Framework." Press release, ATAF, Pretoria, South Africa.

Austin, C. R., and R. J. Wilson. 2017. "An Examination of Reputational Costs and Tax Avoidance: Evidence from Firms with Valuable Consumer Brands." *Journal of the American Taxation Association* 39 (1): 67–93.

Bachas, P., R. N. Jaef, and A. Jensen. 2019. "Size-Dependent Tax Enforcement and Compliance: Global Evidence and Aggregate Implications." *Journal of Development Economics* 140: 203–22.

Baer, K. 2002. *Improving Large Taxpayers' Compliance: A Review of Country Experience*. Washington, DC: International Monetary Fund.

Beer, S., and J. Loeprick. 2015. "Profit Shifting: Drivers of Transfer (Mis)pricing and the Potential of Countermeasures." *International Tax and Public Finance* 22 (3): 426–51.

Beer, S., and J. Loeprick. 2018. "The Cost and Benefits of Tax Treaties with Investment Hubs: Findings from Sub-Saharan Africa." Working Paper No. 18/227, International Monetary Fund, Washington, DC.

Best, M., A. Brockmeyer, H. Jacobsen Kleven, J. Spinnewijn, and M. Waseem. 2015. "Production versus Revenue Efficiency with Limited Tax Capacity: Theory and Evidence from Pakistan." *Journal of Political Economy* 123 (6): 1311–55.

Brockmeyer, A., and M. Hernandez. 2016. "Taxation, Information, and Withholding: Evidence from Costa Rica." Policy Research Working Paper 7600, World Bank, Washington, DC.

Cai, H., and Q. Liu. 2009. "Competition and Corporate Tax Avoidance: Evidence from Chinese Industrial Firms." *Economic Journal* 119 (537): 764–95.

Campos, J. E., D. Lien, and S. Pradhan. 1999. "The Impact of Corruption on Investment: Predictability Matters." *World Development* 27 (6): 1059–67.

Carreras, M., P. Dachapalli, and G. Mascagni. 2017. "Effective Corporate Tax Burden and Firm Size in South Africa: A Firm-Level Analysis." Working Paper No. 2017/162, United Nations University World Institute for Development Economics Research (UNU-WIDER), Helsinki.

Carrillo, P., D. Pomeranz, and M. Singhal. 2017. "Dodging the Taxman: Firm Misreporting and Limits to Tax Enforcement." *American Economic Journal: Applied Economics* 9 (2): 144–64.

Chaurey, R. 2017. "Location-Based Tax Incentives: Evidence from India." *Journal of Public Economics* 156: 101–20.

Chetty, R., M. Mobarak, and M. Singhal. 2014. "Increasing Tax Compliance through Social Recognition." Policy Brief No. 31101, International Growth Centre, London.

Christensen, R. C., M. Hearson, and T. Randriamanalina. 2020. "At the Table, Off the Menu? Assessing the Participation of Lower-Income Countries in Global Tax Negotiations." Working Paper No. 115, International Centre for Tax and Development, Brighton, UK.

Chyz, J. A., W. S. C. Leung, O. Z. Li, and O. M. Rui. 2013. "Labor Unions and Tax Aggressiveness." *Journal of Financial Economics* 108 (3): 675–98.

Clausing, K. A., and M. C. Durst. 2015. "A Price-Based Royalty Tax?" Working Paper No. 41, International Centre for Tax and Development, Brighton, UK.

Clavey, C., J. L. Pemberton, J. Loeprick, and M. Verhoeven. 2019. "International Tax Reform, Digitalization, and Developing Economies." MTI Discussion Paper 16, World Bank, Washington, DC.

Cobham, A., and P. Janský. 2017. "Global Distribution of Revenue Loss from Tax Avoidance: Re-Estimation and Country Results." Working Paper No. 2017/55, United Nations University World Institute for Development Economics Research (UNU-WIDER), Helsinki.

Cooper, M., and Q. T. Nguyen. 2020. "Multinational Enterprises and Corporate Tax Planning: A Review of Literature and Suggestions for a Future Research Agenda." *International Business Review* 101692.

Crivelli, E., R. de Mooij, and M. Keen. 2016. "Base Erosion, Profit Shifting and Developing Countries." *FinanzArchiv: Public Finance Analysis* 72 (3): 268–301.

Çule, M., and M. Fulton. 2009. "Business Culture and Tax Evasion: Why Corruption and the Unofficial Economy Can Persist." *Journal of Economic Behavior and Organization* 72 (3): 811–22.

DeBacker, J., B. T. Heim, and A. Tran. 2015. "Importing Corruption Culture from Overseas: Evidence from Corporate Tax Evasion in the United States." *Journal of Financial Economics* 117 (1): 122–38.

Devereux, M. P., B. Lockwood, and M. Redoano. 2008. "Do Countries Compete over Corporate Tax Rates?" *Journal of Public Economics* 92 (5–6): 1210–35.

Djankov, S., R. La Porta, F. Lopez-de-Silanes, and A. Shleifer. 2002. "The Regulation of Entry." *Quarterly Journal of Economics* 117 (1): 1–37.

Dom, R., and N. McCulloch. 2019. "What Are 'Tax Expenditures' and How Big Are Energy-Related Tax Expenditures?" Policy Brief No. 18, International Centre for Tax and Development, Brighton, UK.

Durst, M. C. 2016a. "Beyond BEPS: A Tax Policy Agenda for Developing Countries." Working Paper No. 18, International Centre for Tax and Development, Brighton, UK.

Durst, M. C. 2016b. "Improving the Performance of Natural Resource Taxation in Developing Countries." Working Paper No. 60, International Centre for Tax and Development, Brighton, UK.

Durst, M. C. 2019. *Taxing Multinational Business in Lower-Income Countries: Economics, Politics and Social Responsibility.* Brighton, UK: International Centre for Tax and Development.

Dyreng, S. D., M. Hanlon, E. L. Mayhew, and J. R. Thornock. 2017. "Changes in Corporate Effective Tax Rates over the Past 25 Years." *Journal of Financial Economics* 124 (3): 441–63.

Dyreng, S. D., J. L. Hoopes, and J. H. Wilde. 2016. "Public Pressure and Corporate Tax Behavior." *Journal of Accounting Research* 54 (1): 147–86.

Ebeke, C., M. Mansour, and G. Rota-Graziosi. 2016. "The Power to Tax in Sub-Saharan Africa: LTUs, VATs, and SARAs." Working Paper No. 154, Foundation for Studies and Research on International Development (FERDI), Clermont-Ferrand, France.

Egger, P., W. Eggert, and H. Winner. 2010. "Saving Taxes through Foreign Plant Ownership." *Journal of International Economics* 81: 99–108.

Eichfelder, S., and F. Hechtner. 2018. "Tax Compliance Costs: Cost Burden and Cost Reliability." *Public Finance Review* 46 (5): 764–92.

Fairfield, T. 2010. "Business Power and Tax Reform: Taxing Income and Profits in Chile and Argentina." *Latin American Politics and Society* 52 (2): 37–71.

Feld, L., B. Frey, and B. Torgler. 2006. "Rewarding Honest Taxpayers." In *Managing and Maintaining Compliance*, edited by H. Elffers, P. Verboon, and W. Huisman, 45–61. The Hague: Boom Legal Publishers.

Fischer, S. 1980. "Dynamic Inconsistency, Cooperation and the Benevolent Dissembling Government." *Journal of Economic Dynamics and Control* 2: 93–107.

Fjeldstad, O-H. 2014. "Tax and Development: Donor Support to Strengthen Tax Systems in Developing Countries." *Public Administration and Development* 34 (3): 182–93.

Fjeldstad, O-H., and K. Heggstad. 2012. "Tax Administrations Working Together: Documentation of the Initial Phase of the Norwegian Tax Administration and the Revenue Authorities in Mozambique, Tanzania and Zambia." Report No. R 2012:3, Chr. Michelsen Institute, Bergen, Norway.

Fjeldstad, O.-H., and M. Moore. 2008. "Tax Reform and State-Building in a Globalised World." In *Taxation and State-Building in Developing Countries: Capacity and Consent*, edited by D. Bräutigam, O.-H. Fjeldstad, and M. Moore, 235–60. Cambridge, UK: Cambridge University Press.

Forstater, M. 2018. "Tax and Development: New Frontiers of Research and Action." Policy Paper No. 118, Centre for Global Development, Washington, DC.

Freedman, J. 2018. "Restoring Trust in the 'Fairness' of Corporate Taxation: Increased Transparency and the Need for Institutional Reform." In *Tax and Trust Institutions, Interactions and Instruments,* edited by S. Goslinga et al. The Hague: Eleven International Publishing.

G-24 (Intergovernmental Group of Twenty-Four). 2021. "Comments of the G-24 on the Pillar One and Pillar Two Proposals Being Discussed by OECD/G20 Inclusive Framework on BEPS." https://www.g24.org/wp-content/uploads/2021/06 /Comments-G-24-to-BEPS-IF-SG-May-2021_FINAL.pdf.

GIZ (German Agency for International Cooperation). 2018. "Implementing OECD/ G20 BEPS Package in Developing Countries: An Assessment of Priorities, Experiences, Challenges and Needs of Developing Countries." GIZ, Bonn.

Goslinga, S., M. Siglé, and R. Veldhuizen. 2019. "Cooperative Compliance, Tax Control Frameworks and Perceived Certainty about the Tax Position in Large Organisations." *Journal of Tax Administration* 5 (1).

Guj, P., S. Martin, B. Maybee, F. Cawood, B. Bocoum, N. Gosai, and S. Huibregtse. 2017. "Transfer Pricing in Mining with a Focus on Africa: A Reference Guide for Practitioners." Report No. 112346, World Bank, Washington, DC.

Hassan, M., and W. Prichard. 2016. "The Political Economy of Domestic Tax Reform in Bangladesh: Political Settlements, Informal Institutions and the Negotiation of Reform." *Journal of Development Studies* 52 (12): 1704–21.

Hearson, M. 2016. "Measuring Tax Treaty Negotiation Outcomes: The ActionAid Tax Treaties Dataset." Working Paper No. 47, International Centre for Tax and Development, Brighton, UK.

Hearson, M. 2018a. "Transnational Expertise and the Expansion of the International Tax Regime: Imposing 'Acceptable' Standards." *Review of International Political Economy* 25 (5): 647–71.

Hearson, M. 2018b. "When Do Developing Countries Negotiate Away Their Corporate Tax Base?" *Journal of International Development* 30 (2): 233–55.

Hearson, M., and J. Kangave. 2016. "A Review of Uganda's Tax Treaties and Recommendations for Action." Working Paper No. 50, International Centre for Tax and Development, Brighton, UK.

Hearson, M., and W. Prichard. 2018. "China's Challenge to International Tax Rules and the Implications for Global Economic Governance." *International Affairs* 94 (6): 1287–1307.

ICRICT (Independent Commission for the Reform of International Corporate Taxation). 2015. "Declaration." ICRICT, Oxford, UK.

ICRICT (Independent Commission for the Reform of International Corporate Taxation). 2018. "A Roadmap to Improve Rules for Taxing Multinationals: A Fairer Future for Global Taxation." ICRICT, Oxford, UK.

IMF (International Monetary Fund). 2002. "Improving Large Taxpayers' Compliance: A Review of Country Experience." Occasional paper, IMF, Washington, DC.

IMF (International Monetary Fund). 2014. "Spillovers in International Corporate Taxation." Policy paper, IMF, Washington, DC.

IMF (International Monetary Fund). 2019. "Corporate Taxation in the Global Economy." Policy Paper No. 19/007, IMF, Washington, DC.

IMF (International Monetary Fund). 2021. "Corporate Income Taxes: Why Reform Is Needed and How It Could Be Designed." IMF, Washington, DC.

IOTA (Intra-European Organization of Tax Administrations). 2008. "Definition of Large Taxpayer." IOTA Report for Tax Administrations, IOTA, Budapest.

James, S. 2014. "Tax and Non-Tax Incentives and Investments: Evidence and Policy Implications." World Bank, Washington, DC.

Kassim, L., and M. Mansour. 2018. "Tax Expenditures Reporting in Developing Countries: An Evaluation." *Revenue d'Économie de Développement* 26 (2): 113–67.

Keen, M., and K. Konrad. 2013. "The Theory of International Tax Competition and Coordination." *Handbook of Public Economics* 5: 257–328.

Keen, M., and M. Mansour. 2010. "Revenue Mobilisation in Sub-Saharan Africa: Challenges from Globalisation II—Corporate Taxation." *Development Policy Review* 28 (5): 573–96.

Khan, A., A. Khwaja, and B. Olken. 2016. "Tax Farming Redux: Experimental Evidence on Performance Pay for Tax Collectors." *Quarterly Journal of Economics* 131 (1): 219–71.

Kirchler, E., C. Kogler, and S. Muehlbacher. 2014. "Cooperative Tax Compliance: From Deterrence to Deference." *Current Directions in Psychological Science* 23 (2): 87–92.

Kleven, H. J., A. Khan, and U. Kaul. 2016. "Taxing to Develop: When 'Third Best' Is Best." Growth Brief Series 005, International Growth Centre, London.

Kronfol, H., and V. Steenbergen. 2020. "Evaluating the Costs and Benefits of Corporate Tax Incentives: Methodological Approaches and Policy Considerations." World Bank, Washington, DC.

Larsen, L. B. 2019. "What Tax Morale? A Moral Anthropological Stance on a Failed Cooperative Compliance Initiative." *Journal of Tax Administration* 5 (1): 26–40.

Larsen, L. B., and L. Oats. 2019. "Taxing Large Businesses: Cooperative Compliance in Action." *Intereconomics* 54 (3): 165–70.

Lawless, M. 2013. "Do Complicated Tax Systems Prevent Foreign Direct Investment?" *Economica* 80 (317): 1–22.

Li, Q. 2006. "Democracy, Autocracy, and Tax Incentives to Foreign Direct Investors: A Cross-National Analysis." *Journal of Politics* 68 (1): 62–74.

Lundstøl, O. 2018. "Revenue Sharing in Mining in Africa: Empirical Proxies and Determinants of Government Take." Working Paper No. 81, International Centre for Tax and Development, Brighton, UK.

Lundstøl, O., G. Raballand, and F. Nyirongo. 2015. "Low Government Revenue from the Mining Sector in Zambia and Tanzania: Fiscal Design, Technical Capacity or Political Will?" Working Paper No. 9, International Centre for Tax and Development, Brighton, UK.

Marcuss, R., G. Contos, J. Guyton, P. Langetieg, A. Lerman, S. Nelson, B. Schafer, and M. Vigil. 2013. "Income Taxes and Compliance Costs: How Are They Related?" *National Tax Journal* 66 (4): 833–54.

Markle, K. S., and D. Shackelford. 2009. "Do Multinationals or Domestic Firms Face Higher Effective Tax Rates?" Working Paper No. 15091, National Bureau of Economic Research, Cambridge, MA.

Mascagni, G., R. Dom, and F. Santoro. 2021. "VAT in Practice: Equity, Enforcement and Complexity." Working Paper No. 118, International Centre for Tax and Development, Brighton, UK.

Mascagni, G., and A. T. Mengistu. 2019. "Effective Tax Rates and Firm Size in Ethiopia." *Development Policy Review* 37 (S2): 248–73.

Mascagni, G., D. Mukama, and F. Santoro. 2019. "An Analysis of Discrepancies in Taxpayers' VAT Declarations in Rwanda." Working Paper No. 92, International Centre for Tax and Development, Brighton, UK.

Mayega, J., R. Ssuuna, M. Mubajje, M. I. Nalukwago, and L. Muwonge. 2019. "How Clean Is Our Taxpayer Register? Data Management in the Uganda Revenue Authority." African Tax Administration Paper No. 12, International Centre for Tax and Development, Brighton, UK.

McKinsey. 2015. "Playing to Win: The New Global Competition for Corporate Profits." McKinsey Global Institute Report, McKinsey and Company, London.

Menkhoff, L., and J. Miethe. 2019. "Tax Evasion in New Disguise? Examining Tax Havens' International Bank Deposits." *Journal of Public Economics* 176: 53–78.

Moore, M. 2014. "Revenue Reform and State Building in Anglophone Africa." *World Development* 60: 99–112.

Moore, M. 2020. "What Is Wrong with African Tax Administration?" Working Paper No. 111, International Centre for Tax and Development, Brighton, UK.

Moore, M., W. Prichard, and O-H. Fjeldstad. 2018. *Taxing Africa: Coercion, Reform and Development.* London: Zed Books.

Muller, A., and A. Kolk. 2015. "Responsible Tax as Corporate Social Responsibility: The Case of Multinational Enterprises and Effective Tax in India." *Business and Society* 54 (4): 435–63.

Mutava, C. 2019. "Review of Tax Treaty Practices and Policy Framework in Africa." Working Paper No. 102, International Centre for Tax and Development, Brighton, UK.

Nur-tegin, K. 2008. "Determinants of Business Tax Compliance." *B. E. Journal of Economic Analysis and Policy* 8 (1): 1–28.

OECD (Organisation for Economic Co-operation and Development). 2008. *Study into the Role of Tax Intermediaries.* Paris: OECD.

OECD (Organisation for Economic Co-operation and Development). 2013a. *Action Plan on Base Erosion and Profit Shifting.* Paris: OECD.

OECD (Organisation for Economic Co-operation and Development). 2013b. *Co-operative Compliance: A Framework—From Enhanced Relationship to Co-operative Compliance.* Paris: OECD.

OECD (Organisation for Economic Co-operation and Development). 2017. *Background Brief—Inclusive Framework on BEPS.* Paris: OECD.

OECD (Organisation for Economic Co-operation and Development). 2019a. "OECD/G20 Inclusive Framework on BEPS: Progress Report July 2018–May 2019." Third Annual Progress Report, OECD, Paris.

OECD (Organisation for Economic Co-operation and Development). 2019b. *Tax Administration 2019: Comparative Information on OECD and Other Advanced and Emerging Economies.* Paris: OECD Publishing.

OECD (Organisation for Economic Co-operation and Development). 2019c. "What Is Driving Tax Morale?" Public consultation document, OECD, Paris.

OECD (Organisation for Economic Co-operation and Development). 2020a. "Multilateral Convention to Implement Tax Treaty Related Measures to Prevent Base Erosion." Information brochure, OECD, Paris.

OECD (Organisation for Economic Co-operation and Development). 2020b. "Tax Challenges Arising from Digitalisation—Economic Impact Assessment." OECD, Paris.

OECD (Organisation for Economic Co-operation and Development). 2021. "130 Countries and Jurisdictions Join Bold New Framework for International Tax Reform." Press release, OECD, Paris.

OECD/G20 (Organisation for Economic Co-operation and Development/G20). 2014. *Two-Part Report to G20 Developing Working Group on the Impact of BEPS in Low Income Countries.* Paris: OECD.

OECD/IMF (Organisation for Economic Co-operation and Development/ International Monetary Fund). 2017. *OECD/IMF Report on Tax Certainty.* Paris: OECD.

Oppong, F., and S. James. 2016. "Tax Expenditure Estimates in Ghana." World Bank, Washington, DC.

PCT (Platform for Collaboration on Tax). 2015. "Options for Low Income Countries' Effective and Efficient Use of Tax Incentives for Investment." Report to the G-20 Development Working Group by the IMF (International Monetary Fund), OECD (Organisation for Economic Co-operation and Development), UN (United Nations), and World Bank, Washington, DC.

PCT (Platform for Collaboration on Tax). 2017. "A Toolkit for Addressing Difficulties in Accessing Comparables Data for Transfer Pricing Analyses Including a Supplementary Report on Addressing the Information Gaps on Prices of Minerals Sold in an Intermediate Form." International Monetary Fund, Organisation for Economic Co-operation and Development, United Nations, and World Bank Group, Washington, DC.

PCT (Platform for Collaboration on Tax). 2020. "The Taxation of Offshore Indirect Transfers—A Toolkit." International Monetary Fund, Organisation for Economic Co-operation and Development, United Nations, and World Bank Group, Washington, DC.

Pemberton, J., and J. Loeprick. 2019. "Low Tax Jurisdictions and Preferential Regimes: Policy Gaps in Developing Economies." Policy Research Working Paper 8778, World Bank, Washington, DC.

Piccioto, S. 2016. "Taxing Multinational Enterprises as Unitary Firms." Working Paper No. 53, International Centre for Tax and Development, Brighton, UK.

Picciotto, S. 2018. "Problems of Transfer Pricing and Possibilities for Simplification." Working Paper No. 86, International Centre for Tax and Development, Brighton, UK.

Picciotto, S. 2021. "Africa Follows Up the Biden Proposals for International Tax Reforms." ICTD blog, May 24, 2021, International Centre for Tax and Development, Brighton, UK. https://www.ictd.ac/blog/africa-biden-proposals -international-tax-reforms/.

Pomeranz, D. 2015. "No Taxation without Information: Deterrence and Self-Enforcement in the Value Added Tax." *American Economic Review* 105 (8): 2539–69.

Pomeranz, D., C. Marshall, and P. Castellón. 2014. "Randomized Tax Enforcement Messages: A Policy Tool for Improving Audit Strategies." *Tax Administration Review* 36: 1–21.

Prichard, W. 2009. "The Mining Boom in Sub-Saharan Africa: Continuity, Change and Policy Implications." In *A New Scramble for Africa? Imperialism, Investment and Development*, edited by Roger Southall and Henning Melber, 240–73. Durban, South Africa: Kwa-Zulu Natal Press.

Prichard, W. 2015. *Taxation, Responsiveness and Accountability in Sub-Saharan Africa: The Dynamics of Tax Bargaining.* Cambridge, UK: Cambridge University Press.

Prichard, W., and S. Jibao. 2010. "Building a Fair, Transparent and Inclusive Tax System in Sierra Leone." Sierra Leone Report, Tax Justice Network Country Report Series, Christian Aid Sierra Leone, Freetown.

Prichard, W., and M. Moore. 2018. "Tax Reform for Low Income Countries: Five Ideas for Simplifying Tax Systems to Fit Local Realities." Summary Brief No. 17, International Centre for Tax and Development, Brighton, UK.

Readhead, A. 2016. "Preventing Tax Base Erosion in Africa: A Regional Study of Transfer Pricing Challenges in the Mining Sector." Natural Resource Governance Institute, London.

Readhead, A. 2017. "Toolkit for Transfer Pricing Risk Assessment in the African Mining Industry." German Agency for International Cooperation, Bonn.

Readhead, A. 2018. "What Mining Can Learn from Oil: A Study of Special Transfer Pricing Practices in the Oil Sector, and Their Potential Application to Hard Rock Minerals." Policy Paper No. 128, Center for Global Development, Washington, DC.

Reynolds, H., and L. Wier. 2016. "Estimating Profit Shifting in South Africa Using Firm-Level Tax Returns." WIDER Working Paper 128/2016, United Nations University World Institute for Development Economics Research (UNU-WIDER), Helsinki.

Schreiber, L. 2018. "Broadening the Base: Improving Tax Administration in Indonesia, 2006–2016." Innovations for Successful Societies Case Study, Princeton University, Princeton, NJ.

Siglé, M., S. Goslinga, R. Speklé, L. van der Hel, and R. Veldhuizen. 2018. "Corporate Tax Compliance: Is a Change towards Trust-Based Tax Strategies Justified?" *Journal of International Accounting, Auditing and Taxation* 32: 3–16.

Slemrod, J. 2004. "The Economics of Corporate Tax Selfishness." Working Paper No. 10858, National Bureau of Economic Research, Cambridge, MA.

Slemrod, J., B. Collins, J. L. Hoopes, D. Reck, and M. Sebastiani. 2017. "Does Credit-Card Information Reporting Improve Small-Business Tax Compliance?" *Journal of Public Economics* 149: 1–19.

Slemrod, J., O. U. Rehman, and W. Mazhar. 2019. "Pecuniary and Non-Pecuniary Motivations for Tax Compliance: Evidence from Pakistan." Working Paper No. 25623, National Bureau of Economic Research, Cambridge, MA.

Slemrod, J., and T. Velayudhan. 2018. "Do Firms Remit at Least 85% of Tax Everywhere? New Evidence from India." *Journal of Tax Administration* 4 (1): 24–38.

Slemrod, J., and V. Venkatesh. 2002. "The Income Tax Compliance Cost of Large and Mid-Size Businesses." Ross School of Business Paper No. 914, University of Michigan, Ann Arbor.

Slemrod, J., and S. Yitzhaki. 2002. "Tax Avoidance, Evasion, and Administration." In *Handbook of Public Economics*, Vol. 3, 1423–70. Amsterdam: Elsevier.

TIWB (Tax Inspectors Without Borders). 2021. "Tax Inspectors Without Borders and Partners Pass USD 1 Billion Milestone in Additional Tax Revenues for Developing Countries." Press release, Organisation for Economic Co-operation and Development/United Nations Development Programme, Paris.

TJN-A (Tax Justice Network-Africa) and AAI (ActionAid International). 2012. "Tax Competition in East Africa: A Race to the Bottom?" Joint report, TJN-A, Nairobi; AAI, Johannesburg.

Tørsløv, T. R., L. S. Wier, and G. Zucman. 2018. "The Missing Profits of Nations."
Working Paper No. 24701, National Bureau of Economic Research,
Cambridge, MA.

Trigueros, M. P. 2014. "Tax Expenditures in Latin America: 2008–2012." Tax Studies
and Research Directorate Working Paper No. 2-2014, Inter-American Center of
Tax Administrations (CIAT), Panama City, Panama.

UN (United Nations). 2017. *United Nations Practical Manual on Transfer Pricing for
Developing Countries (2017)*. 2nd ed. New York: United Nations.

van Dijk, L. H., and M. Siglé. 2015. "Managing Compliance Risks of Large
Businesses: A Review of the Underlying Assumptions of Co-operative
Compliance Strategies." *eJournal of Tax Research* 13 (3): 760–83.

Villela, L., A. Lemgruber, and M. Jorratt. 2010. "Tax Expenditure Budgets: Concepts
and Challenges for Implementation." Working Paper Series 131, Inter-American
Development Bank, Washington, DC.

World Bank. 2018. *Global Investment Competitiveness Report 2017/2018: Foreign
Investor Perspectives and Policy Implications*. Washington, DC: World Bank.

CHAPTER 5

Taxing SMEs

Roel Dom and Wilson Prichard

The Tax Compliance Challenge

Tax reform initiatives have long sought to expand the taxation of micro, small, and medium enterprises (SMEs). Small firms constitute a large majority of firms in most low- and middle-income countries. They make up a large share of the gross domestic product (GDP) and generate at least as many jobs as large firms—in fact, often more. However, they are also frequently unregistered or noncompliant with tax laws (Ayyagari, Demirgüç-Kunt, and Maksimovic 2011; Benjamin and Mbaye 2012; Kumar 2017; Page and Söderbom 2015).

This chapter takes a closer look at the taxation of micro, small, and medium enterprises. Instead of focusing on a specific tax instrument, such as income tax, the chapter presents examples from different tax instruments to illustrate some of the barriers to taxing SMEs, as well as reforms proposed to address these challenges. Much like in chapter 4 for larger corporate taxpayers, no specific definition is offered for SMEs because they are highly diverse. They differ not only in terms of sectors and industries, but also in terms of their economic behavior, profitability, or growth potential (OECD 2015). Because this study draws on existing literature, it relies on the definitions there.

In low-income countries, the taxation of SMEs often overlaps with the goal of taxing the informal sector, as many or most SMEs in lower-income countries are to some degree informal. Although it is common for governments to call for expanded efforts to tax the *informal sector*, use of this term risks conflating a very diverse group of firms. At best this is unhelpful, and at worst it may be counterproductive if it leads to blanket approaches where more-targeted ones are needed. Therefore, it is important to understand the distinct varieties of informality instead of treating it like a uniform category.

In legal terms, some informal firms may operate in the shadow economy, implying that they intentionally hide their economic activity from all government authorities to escape not only taxation, but also the burdens imposed by, for example, health and safety standards (Medina and Schneider 2018). Other informal firms may have a more complex status that is formal from some perspectives but not others. For example, firms may have a business license but not necessarily be registered with the tax authority. For others, the opposite may be true, or they may be registered with subnational authorities but not national agencies. These different types of informality imply different challenges and opportunities. For those in the shadow economy, identification and registration may be the first step, while for firms that have business licenses the challenge lies in tax registration.

Alongside recognizing the diverse types of legal informality is the need to highlight the broader economic diversity of informal firms and tailor tax strategies accordingly. Some informal firms may be very large but operate in the shadows, whereas many informal firms are quite small. Likewise, some informal firms aspire to be long-lived and grow over time, while others are essentially subsistence-oriented. From the perspective of tax authorities, larger and more growth-oriented firms are the most important targets: they offer meaningful revenue potential; they may be unfairly benefitting relative to formal firms; and they may benefit from formalization. By contrast, focusing on micro, small, and subsistence firms may absorb scarce administrative resources and undermine the quality of taxpayer registers without significantly advancing revenue collection or other goals (Moore 2020).

Recognition of this diversity gives rise to two observations that permeate the rest of this chapter. First, although there are strong arguments for seeking to tax some parts of the informal sector more extensively, there are questions about the wisdom and benefits of making the taxation of all (informal) SMEs a major priority of reform efforts. Second, when tax reform is pursued, different groups of informal firms may warrant very different approaches to compliance. Thus any discussion of taxing SMEs should begin with an understanding of what reforms aim to achieve, which groups of firms should be targeted, and what kinds of strategies are most appropriate for those groups.

(Limited) Revenue Potential

Improving the taxation of (registered) SMEs and broadening the tax net by reducing the number of informal or unregistered SMEs could significantly increase government revenue. However, these benefits may be overstated because of high compliance and administration costs and limited revenue potential.

Taxing SMEs is notoriously difficult because they must first be brought into the formal part of the economy and then taxed. The shadow economy is often large in lower-income countries (Medina and Schneider 2018). But while the larger unregistered firms may offer significant revenue potential, the revenue potential from formalizing smaller firms will be limited because of their small size and small margins. Data from higher-income countries suggest that dedicated SME schemes on average account for only around 23 percent of total revenue (OECD 2019). Figures for lower-income countries are scarcer, but they suggest that around 90 percent of corporate tax revenue is collected from the largest 10 percent of firms (Mascagni and Mengistu 2019; URA 2020). In Rwanda, the bottom 50 percent of firms contributes less than 2 percent of total corporate income taxation (CIT) revenue, while the top 10 percent of firms is responsible for nearly 85 precent (Mascagni, Monkam, and Nell 2016)—see figure 5.1. This finding suggests that a drive to include smaller informal SMEs in the tax net is unlikely to result in substantial revenue gains. The largest revenue potential appears to lie with the largest informal SMEs.

Even when they are identified and registered, SMEs may be difficult to tax. They are frequently transient and hard to track, resulting in bloated and inaccurate taxpayer registers (Mayega et al. 2019). It can also be difficult to accurately estimate turnover and profit because of poor bookkeeping and a heavy reliance on cash transactions. In addition, research suggests that many such firms struggle to navigate the process for formalizing and paying taxes because of their limited knowledge and the complexity of formal systems (Joshi, Prichard, and Heady 2014). In view of these challenges, enforcement often relies heavily on face-to-face interactions between tax officials and taxpayers, resulting in high collection costs and extensive opportunities for informality and corruption (Fjeldstad and Heggstad 2011; Hassan and Prichard 2016).

FIGURE 5.1 Corporate Tax Contribution by Rwandan Firms, by Decile, 2012–14

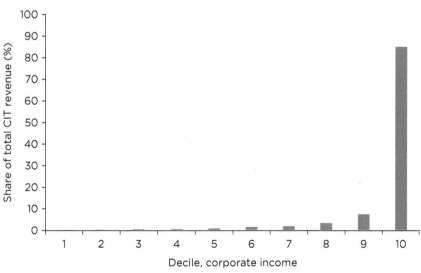

Source: Mascagni, Monkam, and Nell 2016.
Note: In addition to operating income, corporate income includes rental income, investment income, and nonoperating and extraordinary income. CIT = corporate income tax.

Meanwhile, the frequent claim that SMEs, and particularly unregistered ones, benefit unfairly from low tax burdens is open to question. Smaller firms, registered and unregistered, often bear significant burdens of small taxes and fees along with informal payments to state and nonstate actors (Paler et al. 2017). There is now evidence that, for example, small-market traders bear disproportionately high tax burdens relative to other firms (Akpan and Sempere 2019; Ligomeka 2019); effective tax rates are often substantial for small formal firms (Carreras, Dachapalli, and Mascagni 2017; Mascagni and Mengistu 2016); and formal and informal tax burdens are highest for informal firms (McCulloch, Schulze, and Voss 2010).

Benefits of Taxation and Formalization

Given the uncertain revenue benefits, the most persuasive alternative arguments for taxing SMEs tend to consider the possible ancillary benefits such as reducing unfair competition, promoting pro-poor economic growth, and improving governance (Joshi, Prichard, and Heady 2014).

One argument for improving taxation of SMEs is that it is important to ensuring equity and improving tax morale. The evidence suggests that the relationship between firm size and evasion is negative or U-shaped, implying that small firms are more likely to evade taxation (Abdixhiku et al. 2017; Cowell 2003; DeBacker, Heim, and Tran 2015; Hanlon, Mills, and Slemrod 2007; Slemrod 2004). This evasion may lead to unfair competition, which can undermine trust and negatively affect tax morale (Torgler and Schneider 2007). Yet although informality and low tax morale appear to be correlated, it remains unclear whether informality causes low tax morale: it may equally be that low tax morale (and poor government performance) encourages firms to remain unregistered (Williams and Horodnic 2017). Likewise, arguments that taxing SMEs can improve equity probably require greater nuance because, as previously noted, smaller firms may, in fact, bear more significant, though often fragmented and informal, burdens than is often assumed.

The formalization of SMEs could also support accelerated economic growth.[1] Formalization may reduce disincentives to growth and give small firms greater access to important resources such as legal protections, financing, and new business opportunities. Indeed, several studies in recent years have reported that formalization can have a positive impact on economic growth (Demenet, Razafindrakoto, and Roubaud 2016; Rand and Torm 2012; Ulyssea 2018), such as in Vietnam (box 5.1). Yet the most recent studies suggest that the potential benefits of formalization are likely limited to a subset of firms—often those somewhat larger and focused on growth rather than subsistence (Boly 2018; Ulyssea 2018). These studies find there are benefits to enabling and facilitating formalization, but they caution against aggressive enforcement, which may have negative impacts on many small firms.[2]

Formalizing and taxing SMEs may be a way to engage them with the state and to expand so-called tax bargaining, in which taxpayers negotiate demands for reciprocal service provision and greater accountability in exchange for tax payments (Prichard 2015). However, the empirical evidence on this score is mixed. The belief that taxing informal sector operators may spur popular engagement is intuitive: these taxes are highly visible, and informal sector associations are frequently relatively organized, making them well placed to engage

Benefits of Formalization: Evidence from Vietnam

Vietnam presents a unique opportunity to study informal businesses. Not only has it made formalization, and registration in particular, a government priority, but it also is one of the few countries to systematically and periodically survey both registered and nonregistered firms.

Studies have thus been able to assess the effects of formalization in Vietnam. Moreover, they all agree: firms gain from formalization. Rand and Torm (2012) find that registered firms have higher profits and investment than unregistered firms and use less casual labor, suggesting improvements in labor conditions. Demenet, Razafindrakoto, and Roubaud (2016) show that formalization causes significant increases in value added, while Boly (2018) confirms that these effects persist over time.

One prevailing view in the literature is that informal firms face barriers that prevent them from achieving their optimal size. If true, then formalization can spur productivity and economic growth by allowing firms to reach their most efficient size.

The evidence suggests that once they are released from informality, firms indeed grow quickly and considerably, which boosts productivity by allowing firms to take advantage of these new economies of scale. Formalization makes firms more competitive and makes it easier for them to access key services, such as electricity and internet service (Demenet, Razafindrakoto, and Roubaud 2016). In addition, registered firms advertise more, thereby increasing their customer base. Formalization also may make it easier for firms to voice their concerns and thus strengthen accountability because formal firms engage more with business associations (Boly 2018).

However, these effects appear to be true only for the largest informal firms. Demenet, Razafindrakoto, and Roubaud (2016) find that firms that formalize are already similar to the ones operating in the formal sector. They also show that the gains of formalization mostly benefit informal businesses that employ at least one person as opposed to the self-employed. This finding suggests that firms below a certain size may not benefit from legal existence. It may then be hard to persuade subsistence firms, in particular, to formalize because they may have no interest in doing so.

with government. Joshi and Ayee (2008) capture engagement between small businesses and government around the introduction of associational taxation. Prichard (2015) finds similar expanded engagement around small-business taxation in capital cities in Ethiopia, Ghana, and Kenya. And de Mel, McKenzie, and Woodruff (2013) find some expanded trust in the state among informal firms that formalized in Sri Lanka.

However, such positive outcomes may be the exception rather than the rule because small businesses—and especially the marginalized groups among them—can be highly vulnerable to government predation. Moreover, small-business associations are often poorly organized for engaging in effective advocacy with the state, and the expansion of taxation of these associations may sometimes reinforce hierarchical internal divisions (Meagher 2018). This finding prompts Meagher and Lindell (2013) to ask, "Does taxing informal traders strengthen public accountability, or just create new avenues of predation?" In practice, outcomes are likely to vary widely, dependent both on the character of the informal sector associations and on the details of reform efforts (Lindell 2010).

Barriers to Reform

Efforts to expand taxation of SMEs are likely to encounter both technical and political challenges. As a purely technical challenge, taxing SMEs, especially the smallest firms, often requires estimating the revenues (and potentially profits) of firms characterized by poor record keeping, cash transactions, and often a desire to avoid detection. It likewise requires managing large numbers of taxpayers as well as the tax collectors with whom they engage. These technical barriers to collection exist in parallel with significant political hurdles: weak revenue potential, potential resistance from large numbers of small firms, and resistance from tax officials threatened by a reduced scope for informality and uninterested in the laborious and unrewarding work of more effectively taxing small firms.

Technical Challenges

Obstacles to formalization. Convincing SMEs to register with the relevant authorities, in particular with the tax administration, is difficult when the benefits of formalization are not clear. For some firms, informality may be a choice (La Porta and Shleifer 2014; Williams and Gurtoo 2012). Despite the aggregate benefits of formalization, such as greater access to important resources and services, potentially larger profits and productivity, and a stronger voice through business associations, it may not be clear to individual firms that the benefits outweigh the costs—or the benefits of remaining unregistered. For example, evidence from India suggests that firms that start out unregistered have higher sales and employment growth than those registered from the outset (Williams and Kedir 2016).

Moreover, the costs linked to formalizing may be considerable. Firms need to go through the registration procedure; pay taxes; comply with labor, safety, and other legislation; and possibly require accountants. In a study of Brazilian firms, the cost of formalization was estimated to be around 15.6 percent of the baseline profits of the median firm (de Andrade, Bruhn, and McKenzie 2016). In many lower-income countries, formally registering a business still takes more than 20 days (World Bank 2019). It is therefore not surprising that it is mostly larger informal firms that formalize because they are likely to be more productive and therefore better placed to absorb these costs (McCulloch, Schulze, and Voss 2010).

High compliance costs. Once they are registered, complying with tax obligations requires firms to keep the necessary records, to complete and file the appropriate paperwork, and to pay the associated taxes. All of this consumes time and resources, representing a cost to the firm. Several factors can affect these compliance costs. Often it is the complexity of tax systems that drives up compliance costs. However, the number of taxes to be paid, the frequency of tax policy and administration changes, the clarity of laws and regulations, and the cost of hiring external or internal tax professionals—all have an impact on the financial burden that complying with tax obligations places on taxpayers.

The burden associated with paying taxes can itself be a deterrent to tax compliance, especially for SMEs. Compared with larger firms, SMEs often face higher tax compliance costs, in relative terms, due to their smaller size and the often significant fixed components of compliance costs (Faridy et al. 2014; Mascagni and Mengistu 2016; OECD 2015). In some cases, this burden can, in fact, be heavier than the tax payments themselves. A series of World Bank tax compliance cost surveys across developing and emerging markets documents the extremely regressive patterns of compliance costs among firms, with small businesses incurring costs up to 15 percent or more of turnover (Coolidge 2012). In Finland, these high compliance costs can force firms to remain small (Harju, Matikka, and Rauhanen 2019). To reduce the disproportionate burden on SMEs, governments worldwide have put in place provisions to reduce SME compliance costs.

Limited firm capacity. Compliance costs are closely intertwined with, and often exacerbated by, the (limited) administrative capacity of SMEs. Smaller firms typically struggle to keep good records and tend to rely heavily on cash transactions (World Bank 2016). An investigation of SMEs' accounting practices in Ghana's Kumasi Metropolitan Assembly revealed that most firms fail to maintain complete records because they do not see the need for them and also may not want to expose their financial position (Amaoka 2013). Low financial literacy among SMEs, especially among microenterprises, further compounds these issues (Fatoki 2014). The combination of a complex tax system and limited firm capacity may induce a certain level of confusion among taxpayers. This confusion often leads SMEs to adopt pragmatic strategies to cope with the tax system, not necessarily to evade taxes but rather to deal with a complex system and reduce compliance costs (Mascagni, Dom, and Santoro 2021; Mascagni et al. 2020).

Administrative difficulties and costs. Whatever the broad policy framework, taxing SMEs tends to present tax administrations with significant administrative and logistical challenges. These challenges are related to managing large numbers of small, sometimes mobile taxpayers. The frontline administrative task of identifying and ensuring compliance among large numbers of small firms can be particularly demanding—and poorly rewarded within administrative hierarchies. The administrative cost of taxing SMEs (that is, what it costs the administration to collect the taxes) is therefore likely to be high.

This administrative cost, much like the compliance cost, is endogenous; it depends on the design of the tax system. Moreover, it is compounded by the behavior of SMEs. Much like other taxpayers, SMEs have incentives to understate their taxable income and transactions, making monitoring and collection challenging and costly for the tax administrations. Meanwhile, the absence of reliable bookkeeping and the prevalence of cash transactions among SMEs can further complicate the tasks of the administration, as can the strategies adopted by SMEs to deal with the complexities of the system.

Combined with the low revenue potential of smaller SMEs in particular, high administrative costs leave tax administrations with only weak incentives to improve administrative efforts, to the extent that it may even be optimal not to pursue full enforcement (Keen and Slemrod 2017). However, little evidence is available on the importance of administrative costs and on the effectiveness of interventions to reduce them.

Opportunities for corruption and extraction. These administrative challenges are exacerbated by additional challenges from the often heavy reliance on face-to-face encounters between taxpayers and officials tasked with verifying revenue or other aspects of tax liabilities. These interactions create many opportunities for collusion or for corruption and extraction (Dube and Casale 2019), thereby diminishing trust (Cohen and Gershgoren 2016).

A handful of studies indicates that SMEs, including market traders, often pay significantly more to tax collectors than what reaches national budgets, and some are subject to significant harassment by tax officials. Meanwhile, technically informal firms may bear overall burdens of formal and informal payments on par with those of formal firms, pointing to pervasive informality in overall collection activities (Jibao and Prichard 2016; Jibao, Prichard, and van den Boogaard 2017; McCulloch, Schulze, and Voss 2010; Prichard and van den Boogaard 2017). A core challenge for governments thus lies in how to incentivize and effectively monitor frontline enforcement and collection of taxes on small firms where significant face-to-face interactions are involved.

Political Challenges

Resistance from politicians. Expanded taxation also faces a fundamental political challenge: SMEs may contribute relatively limited revenue, but they make up a large bloc of potential opposition voters and actors. Thus the political costs to government of expanded taxation of small firms may significantly outweigh the potential revenue benefits. Tendler (2002, 99) dubbed this the "devil's deal" between politicians and small informal taxpayers: "If you vote for me . . . I won't collect taxes from you; I won't make you comply with other tax, environmental, or labour regulations; and I will keep the police and inspectors from harassing you." In this account, not only are politicians unwilling to bear the political costs of expanding taxation; they may actually prefer continued informality to sustain the dependence of small firms on political leaders.

Resistance from SMEs. The political difficulty of taxing the SME sector reflects the extent to which sector associations are often well organized and can be organized politically. In Kenya, private bus services were shut down for several weeks in protest of the imposition of new taxes—although the government eventually prevailed thanks to sustained popular support (Prichard 2015). Similarly, in Bangladesh small businesses have long been recognized as a potentially powerful, disruptive political actor, which has helped to support a system of small-business taxation characterized by significant loopholes and subjectivity (Hassan and Prichard 2016).

Resistance from tax officials. A less widely cited political challenge lies within the tax administration itself, where tax officials may actively resist reform. Although research is limited, anecdotal evidence suggests that tax officials often view taxing small firms as unpleasant work lacking in prestige and opportunities for future advancement. At best, staff involved in this work are frequently undermotivated. As a result, the prospect of expanding these efforts—or transferring senior staff into strengthening SME taxation—poses significant internal challenges.

These challenges are likely to be all the more acute where reforms also remove opportunities for collusion and corruption, thereby possibly threatening the livelihood of frontline collectors. For example, shifting away from a system in which tax collectors directly assess small firms' tax liability to one in which firms can identify their presumptive tax category and pay by mobile phone may significantly threaten long-standing informal practices. Navigating these administrative politics is thus likely to be critical to successful reform.

Reform Progress—and Future Options

Strategies for taxing SMEs are likely to benefit from a realistic assessment of the potential costs and benefits and of the diverse potential objectives and impacts. Simply expanding enforcement may not be optimal; it risks generating only modest increases in revenue, at high cost, while imposing heavy formal and informal burdens on relatively low-income groups and expanding distrust between taxpayers and tax authorities. There may be greater potential in strategies that focus on higher-priority subsets of firms and that seek to combine strengthened enforcement with facilitation and trust-building to avoid undue burdens on low-income groups, encourage quasi-voluntary compliance, and seek to foster broader growth and governance gains. What follows considers options related to enforcement, facilitation, and trust, in turn, recognizing that any successful reform program will rely on elements of each.

Enforcement: Countering Avoidance and Evasion

As just described, there are limits to enforcement-led strategy approaches to improving compliance and tax collection among SMEs. These limits reflect the complexity of tracking and taxing large numbers of small firms, the correspondingly high costs of such enforcement, the political constraints on pursuing aggressive enforcement among large numbers of small firms, and the risk that expanded enforcement may fuel inequality. This does not, however, imply that improved enforcement is not a central concern. In the absence of a degree of credible enforcement, many firms will remain noncompliant, while there is also the risk that larger firms will seek to take advantage of special provisions designed for smaller firms.

Although there is no simple solution to managing the labor-intensive task of strengthening enforcement among smaller firms, recent research has pointed to the potential value of strategies that disaggregate between heterogeneous groups of SMEs, focus attention on higher-value firms, and seek to strengthen incentives among tax collectors.

Recognizing the Heterogeneous Nature of Informal Firms

References to taxing the informal sector can frequently obscure as much as they illuminate because the term *informal sector* masks enormous diversity among informal SMEs and thus distinct enforcement challenges. More-targeted approaches may allow for greater success.

A starting point for more effective revenue collection often lies in estimates of tax gaps—the difference between what should be collected and what is collected—as well as in understanding the broad characteristics of particular businesses. All of this may be more feasible at the sectoral level. Research has produced a variety of estimates of the size of the informal sector in low- and middle-income countries, but these estimates are so broad and incorporate so many disparate components that they have little value for concrete tax policy and administration (Schneider and Klinglmair 2004). By contrast, the estimation of sectoral tax gaps could help to target resources at not only the sectors most easily taxed but also those representing the greatest revenue-generating opportunity. Sectoral approaches have had comparative success in estimating revenue potential from market traders (Iversen et al. 2006; ODEP 2013) and private transport operators, while also being able to map both formal and informal payments to better understand actual tax burdens, dynamics, and concerns (Sánchez de la Sierra and Titeca 2016).

Targeting Higher-Value Firms
The overall revenue potential of SMEs is not only small, but also distributed unequally. Larger SMEs may have substantial tax liabilities, but there are risks of large revenue losses when larger firms pretend to be small to avoid taxes. A key challenge for tax authorities thus lies in identifying higher-value taxpayers within the SME sector on whom to focus resources. This process begins by taking a more disaggregated view of SMEs, as described earlier. A next step may be engaging in data analysis designed to flag larger and higher-risk SMEs for enforcement activities.

One example of this kind of approach is exploiting the now well-understood fact that taxpayers can situate themselves just below a threshold in a tax regime to minimize their tax liability—a phenomenon known as "bunching" (Almunia and Lopez-Rodriguez 2018; Kleven 2016; Saez 2010). In Pakistan, large numbers of taxpayers place themselves just below the thresholds in the country's income tax regime (Kleven and Waseem 2013). Similarly, in South Africa firms bunch just below the minimum threshold for VAT registration (Boonzaaier et al. 2016). In Pakistan, illicit evasion is estimated to account for most of the observed bunching in response to the cutoff between profit and turnover taxation (Best et al. 2015).

Bunching can be an indication that firms are illicitly evading taxation by underreporting their income. It can also be a sign that the tax system may be distorting real economic activity by encouraging firms to remain small (Harju, Matikka, and Rauhanen 2019; Velayudhan 2019). It is therefore critical to understand the source of the observed bunching: is it a real response, or is it evasion? In the case of a real response—economic distortions—the benefits of the simplified tax regime should be weighed against the loss in economic activity. In the case of evasion, audit capacity should be improved, particularly for firms around the cutoff, because bunching might result from income underreporting. When bunching below the threshold is observed, it can be used as a flag to trigger an audit.

Flagged declarations can then be cross-checked with other information available to the tax authority or followed up directly by tax authorities. For relatively larger firms, this may include relying on third-party data. However, this cross-checking must be comprehensive because evidence indicates that taxpayers will continue to evade through channels not covered by third-party information (Carrillo, Pomeranz, and Singhal 2017). Where third-party information is not easily available, it may be possible to identify risk using simple predictive algorithms to estimate turnover using available data within the tax administration (Arachi and Santoro 2007).

Strengthening Collection Incentives

Along with strategies for effective monitoring of firms, a key challenge for revenue agencies lies in motivating tax officials to collect revenue effectively. As noted earlier, determining the approximate revenue of informal firms and sectors is possible in principle through the painstaking work of identifying firms in the field and monitoring their activities. Digital innovations can help tax officials do this, while reducing opportunities for corruption (Okunogbe and Pouliquen 2018). However, the incentives for tax officers matter as well (Khan, Khwaja, and Olken 2019), especially because their work is labor-intensive but lacking in prestige and career advancement opportunities. Tax officials often seem undermotivated to perform effectively, particularly where opportunities for them to receive informal payments are constrained.

Several mechanisms may help, though few have been researched extensively. First, higher salaries or some form of reward payments matter for performance. Although it is important to carefully monitor all the incentives created by such payments and to pair them with effective monitoring, they can have positive effects (Khan, Khwaja, and Olken 2016). Similarly, evidence from the Kyrgyz Republic shows that linking tax inspectors' rewards to anonymous evaluations submitted by inspected firms can reduce corruption (Amodio, Choi, and Rahman 2018).

Second, a variety of methods can improve prestige and career trajectories for those involved in taxing SMEs. The creation of small taxpayer units with clear trajectories for advancement may help. Likewise, where simplification increases firms' voluntary compliance—for example, through simplified business registration or purchasing tax certificates at banks—the work of tax collectors could be shifted toward more "desirable" roles in monitoring and audit.

One indicator of the difficulty of motivating tax officials to tax SMEs is scattered evidence of a significant reliance on private revenue collectors to target the smallest firms. These private collectors have clear incentives to collect additional revenue because they can retain any surplus. And, indeed, limited evidence suggests that privatization does often improve revenue collection. However, this generally comes at excessively high cost: less protection for taxpayers, reduced long-term state capacity (and connections to the state), and potential corruption in the negotiation of revenue collection contracts (Fjeldstad, Katera, and Ngalewa 2009; Iversen et al. 2006). The challenge facing revenue agencies thus lies in finding ways to motivate revenue staff themselves instead of relying on outside contractors.

Facilitation: Encouraging Quasi-Voluntary Compliance

Given the limits of enforcement as a strategy for improving compliance and revenue mobilization among SMEs, governments are strongly motivated to invest in parallel in encouraging quasi-voluntary compliance. Reflecting that logic, there has been a significant focus, especially over the last two decades, on facilitating compliance among smaller firms through simplification and positive incentives for compliance.

Simplifying Formalization and Tax Compliance for Small Firms

The most straightforward but perhaps most valuable facilitation reforms are likely to be expanding efforts to simplify registration and tax compliance. These efforts have been at the core of reform movements in many countries, and there is meaningful—though fragmented and incomplete—evidence of the impact of such measures.

Simplified registration. Central to such efforts has been simplification of the process of business formalization by streamlining (tax) registration and reducing the numbers of permits and licenses required by small firms to start their operations. The creation of one-stop shops, for example, has been an integral part of many reforms aimed at reducing the number of steps necessary to start a business. One-stop shops are organizations that receive documents for business registration and carry out at least one other function related to business start-up, usually tax registration. New technologies, such as e-tax systems, have often been rolled out to support these reforms.

Despite differences across countries, progress has been compelling. Global measures of the ease of starting a business show a clear downward trend. In 2004, starting a business consumed an average of 53 hours, but only 19 hours in 2019 (World Bank 2019). Moreover, according to evidence from Kenya, simplification can result in significant formalization as well as improved conditions for small operators (Devas and Kelly 2001). Yet cross-country studies and meta-analysis indicate that success is not guaranteed. The ease of formalization alone is unlikely to spur firms to formalize if the benefits of doing so are small (Bruhn and McKenzie 2014; Floridi, Demena, and Wagner 2020).

Following formalization, efforts to simplify taxpayer registration have resulted in impressive expansions of taxpayer registries. However, the value of these registries depends on the quality of subsequent data management. Uganda's registration drive increased the number of taxpayers by 6,700 percent between 2010 and 2017. However, administration of this large assortment of new taxpayers remains difficult, resulting in a bloated and often inaccurate taxpayer register with many inactive taxpayers (Mayega et al. 2019). Similar problems have been observed elsewhere (Mascagni et al. 2020; Santoro and Mdluli 2019). Moreover, an obsession with registering informal firms may distract attention from the widespread failure to tax the wealthy (Moore 2020).

Therefore, if tax administrations are to take full advantage of the increased taxpayer registration, they must not lose sight of the more mundane but important task of following up, tracking those taxpayers over time, contacting them if they do not submit tax returns (or comply with alternative compliance regimes), and verifying the submitted tax declarations.

Simplified tax regimes. Alongside the facilitation of registration, governments have simplified tax systems to reduce compliance costs. These simplified regimes can take many forms, but they generally allow special treatment of small taxpayers that reduces both compliance and collection costs. Instead of levying a tax on the profit of small companies, some countries levy a tax on their turnover or gross income because it is easier to track than profits. Countries can also reduce administrative burdens by reducing the number of brackets, exemptions, or required documentation.

These changes are likely to reduce not only compliance costs but also incentives for informality, although their success in achieving the latter is less clear (Rocha, Ulyssea, and Rachter 2018). For example, although in Georgia such reforms led to a significant but one-off increase in the number of newly registered firms, the impact of the SIMPLES initiative in Brazil is less clear (Bruhn and Loeprick 2016; Fajnzylber, Maloney, and Montes-Rojas 2011; Piza 2018).[3]

Another commonly used tool to simplify tax regimes for SMEs is to relieve them from some of their tax duties by means of a threshold. For example, nearly all value added tax (VAT) regimes include a registration threshold below which registration for VAT is not compulsory, relieving SMEs from the need to file VAT returns and tax authorities from the need to cross-check all transactions (Ebrill et al. 2001). But it is important that the real value of thresholds be kept up to date if they are to retain their usefulness (Hirvonen, Mascagni, and Roelen 2018).

Presumptive taxation. Presumptive tax regimes are another example of simplified tax regimes for small firms that have been widely embraced and adopted. Presumptive taxes differ from standard taxes by using indirect approaches to estimating a firm's tax liability—that is, income is presumed rather than directly measured (Thuronyi 1996). Presumptive taxation reduces the compliance burdens on the firm and the administrative burdens on the tax administration, especially when accounts-based methods are unreliable. Moreover, the possibility of contesting the administration's presumption should encourage taxpayers to keep proper records (Thuronyi 1996).

Presumptive taxes can take many forms, but they typically calculate taxable income based on factors assumed to be associated with income generation such as sales, turnover, number of employees, size of firm, or assets of the taxpayer (Bird and Wallace 2005). In Ghana, a "tax stamp" regime requires small businesses below a certain threshold to pay a fixed rate (dependent on sector and size) quarterly in exchange for a stamp—a physical certificate of payment (Amponsah and Adu 2015). Ethiopia employs a revenue-based tax calibrated by sector and approximate firm size (Joshi, Prichard, and Heady 2014). These simplified taxes ease the burden of administration and bookkeeping—if well designed (box 5.2).

Paradoxically, the introduction of a presumptive tax regime can increase compliance costs if eligibility requirements become too complex (Memon 2013). Meanwhile, presumptive regimes can create other costs in terms of reduced equity and fairness; slow the progression of firms into the standard tax net; and leave significant discretion in the hands of tax collectors with risks of collusion

Challenges of Informal Sector Taxation: Evidence from the Presumptive Tax System in Zimbabwe

Recent research assessing Zimbabwe's efforts to tax the informal sector illustrates that presumptive tax systems need to be designed carefully and administered effectively if they are to improve compliance.

Zimbabwe operates a presumptive tax system consisting mostly of lump-sum taxes, or fixed fees, distinguished by sector. Although the country's informal sector is large, little revenue is collected from it. Dube and Casale (2019) identify low tax morale, caused by concerns about equity and fairness, as the major hurdle to improving the compliance of informal firms in Zimbabwe.

The Zimbabwean presumptive tax is characterized by both horizontal and vertical inequities. Horizontally, the effective tax rate for similarly placed firms is much higher under the presumptive regime than under the personal income tax regime—and in some cases higher than under the corporate income tax regime—because the fixed fee does not account for actual turnover or profitability. This also causes vertical inequalities because small firms end up paying proportionally more than larger ones.

Small and medium enterprises further complain about the selective application of tax rules, while many are not taxed at all. In part because of lack of resources, tax officers seem to target sectors that are highly visible, such as flea markets and hairdressers. However, in some instances the targeting appears to be politically motivated because businesses with connections to the incumbent party are apparently protected from taxation.

Design flaws in the presumptive tax system partly explain the equity outcomes. Fixed fees are largely based on guesswork by the Ministry of Finance about the profitability of different sectors in the informal economy. Research is important because sectors that have more credible estimates also have lower inequalities.

Yet politics also plays a role. Lack of cohesion between the finance ministry (which designs the regime) and the revenue authority (which administers it) hinders the effective use of evidence. There also seems to be little political appetite for reforming the system because the selective application of its rules provides opportunities for patronage.

and corruption (Dube and Casale 2019; Workneh, Baileyegn, and Stewart-Wilson 2019). Presumptive systems thus need to maximize simplicity for small firms, while also balancing the desire for simplicity against concerns about horizontal inequity.

National-subnational coordination. Effective simplification is likely to require cooperation between the national and subnational authorities in many countries. Despite enormous variation across countries, SMEs (particularly in more decentralized countries) generally pay taxes, levies, and fees as well as informal payments to both national and subnational authorities, leading many small firms to complain of double taxation.

A common model is that at the national level SMEs pay either the corporate income tax and VAT or a presumptive tax, while at the local level they are subject to business licenses or other fees (such as market taxes). Small businesses often lament the double taxation by multiple levels of government, along with the uncertainty and vulnerability that it can introduce. Research has also at times documented rivalry between levels of government in seeking to tax these groups (Prichard and van den Boogaard 2017).

At a minimum, greater coordination is sorely needed. More provocatively, some countries have explored fully decentralizing the taxation of smaller firms because the revenue raised from them is marginal for central governments and the collection costs are high, whereas for local authorities the same revenue may be relatively important and collected at lower cost (Joshi, Prichard, and Heady 2014). That said, based on the available evidence it is not clear that such decentralization would necessarily lower the tax burden for SMEs (Chen 2017; Lü and Landry 2014).

Positively Supporting Compliance by SMEs

Although simplification is a particularly attractive option for the smallest firms, for somewhat larger firms an argument could be made for specific strategies to support compliance with the standard tax regime. Small firms usually fall under presumptive regimes whose thresholds bar larger SMEs. Yet the general case for simplifying registration and compliance remains. For these firms, there may be options for simplifying registration and reporting requirements within the standard tax system.

One alternative is to implement concrete strategies to support SME compliance. In line with wider developments to make the collection process more user-friendly, as discussed elsewhere in this report, some countries have put in place not only offices for large taxpayers but also offices for small and medium taxpayers to address concerns specific to those segments. Although large taxpayers typically have dedicated caseworkers, taxpayer hotlines are emerging as the alternative for SMEs. In addition, tax authorities are increasingly and proactively reaching out to taxpayers. To deal with poor financial literacy among SMEs, especially among microbusinesses, taxpayer education campaigns are being launched with success, as Rwanda has demonstrated (Mascagni, Santoro, and Mukama 2019).

Some countries are going still further. In Georgia, dedicated tax outreach officials patrol the streets, not as enforcers but as facilitators to reduce the distance between the revenue authority and the taxpayer and to facilitate compliance (box 5.3). Meanwhile, Brazil has, with varying success, experimented with offering free accounting services to informal firms (de Andrade, Bruhn, and McKenzie 2016). Whereas programs that focus on enforcement assume that small firms are primarily interested in evading taxation, this kind of program assumes that a significant share of SMEs—including those with the greatest long-term tax potential—may be willing to join the tax net if it is simple and if presented with potentially broader accountancy benefits. This arrangement is a potential win-win for both governments and taxpayers.

The District Tax Officer in Georgia

The Georgia Revenue Service (GRS) operates a network of district tax officers whose primary responsibility is to facilitate tax compliance and reduce the distance between the GRS and the taxpayer—and small and medium enterprises, in particular.

Although the district tax officer is intended to facilitate compliance, taxpayers strongly perceive the position as an enforcement measure. Among surveyed firms, nearly 70 percent reported that they had been visited by a district tax officer in the last two years. When firms were asked what they believe the role of the district officer is, 60 percent said the officers are there to inspect them (figure B5.3.1). About 30 percent of firms believe district officers are there to help them.

FIGURE B5.3.1 **Perceived Role of the District Tax Officer in Georgia**

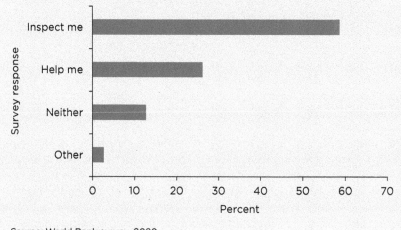

Source: World Bank survey, 2020.

Using Technology to Simplify Payments and Reduce Face-to-Face Interactions
Alongside the simplification of registration and tax systems for small businesses, there is significant interest in using technology to simplify payments and reduce the scope for corruption, thereby improving fairness. Because of the data-intensive nature of tax administration, digitalization holds many opportunities for the taxation of all taxpayer segments (Gupta et al. 2017; Moore 2020), but its use will likely be challenging for smaller SMEs (Efobi et al. 2019).

For filing, and especially for payments, there is a growing range of options for making payments directly to the tax agency instead of to tax officers, limiting opportunities for corruption (Okunogbe and Pouliquen 2018). Electronic filing and payment systems as well as tax management information systems are spreading rapidly (see chapter 7). Even where payments are based on in-person tax assessments, technology can be used both to calculate and display tax liabilities and to enable electronic payments to be directly registered in central databases. Efforts to join various scattered databases will increase the prevalence of prepopulated tax returns. Like e-filing, this development will further reduce compliance costs as well as opportunities for discretion.

However, limits persist to the use of digital solutions. Access to a computer, a stable supply of electricity, and an internet connection are not guaranteed, especially in low-income countries. In some countries, many SMEs still use manual accounts (Coolidge 2012). Meanwhile, comparative research from Nepal, South Africa, and Ukraine reveals that the learning curve for e-filing can be quite steep, particularly for small businesses, and that requirements to submit paperwork alongside e-filing can offset potential gains (Yilmaz and Coolidge 2013).

Trust: Strengthening the Social Contract

Trust-building is likely to be particularly important to taxation of SMEs in both seeking to change the political dynamics of reform and ensuring that such taxation generates broader social benefits. Ineffective taxation of SMEs appears, above all, to reflect limited political support and weak tax compliance. Efforts to build trust among taxpayers—including the kinds of facilitation reforms discussed so far— thus have substantial potential to both improve compliance and shift the political calculus of reform (Inasius 2018).

Providing Reciprocal Benefits

Many small businesses would willingly consider formalization and expanded tax compliance if they receive reciprocal benefits for doing so. According to experimental evidence from Brazil, many informal firms will not formalize even when compliance costs are lowered, suggesting that formality offers little private benefit to these firms (de Andrade, Bruhn, and McKenzie 2016). Therefore, improving the private benefits to formalization appears crucial.

Governments could expand the benefits of formalization in many ways. Benefits might include greater legal security; access to courts, credit, and training programs; and eligibility for government or private sector contracts. The value of such benefits is reflected in research showing the willingness of many firms to formalize if they received incentives to do so, as well as in the evidence of the improved growth of some firms after formalization (Boly 2018; Demenet, Razafindrakoto, and Roubaud 2016; Rand and Torm 2012). However, the extent to which firms benefit from formalization will vary across firms and be shaped by government efforts to make these benefits a reality.

Where governments proactively invest in providing these reciprocal benefits, the demand for formalization and tax compliance are likely to increase, particularly among somewhat larger SMEs. As important, a reform strategy premised on expanding trust and increasing the benefits of tax compliance is likely to draw into the tax net primarily those firms that stand to benefit most rather than expending resources on enforcement among small, subsistence-type firms—efforts that are not likely to raise much revenue and will impose new burdens on low-income groups.

Ensuring Equity

Efforts to ensure that tax regimes for SMEs (including various subnational taxes and user fees) are designed equitably are likely to be critical to building broad-based trust. Significant gains are possible by simplifying subnational regimes and coordinating them more effectively with central authorities, as described earlier. In many cases, there is also a worthy argument for examining market taxes and whether they impose an undue burden on the smallest businesses by virtue of their accessibility—as well as whether this burden, in turn, especially disadvantages female taxpayers. Meanwhile, measures to reduce complexity and face-to-face interactions between tax collectors and taxpayers can help to reduce informality, while also easing the disproportionate costs of compliance for smaller firms.

As discussed in box 5.2, another source of inequity is presumptive tax regimes that, being based on total firm turnover, impose heavier tax burdens on businesses with smaller profit margins (Getachew 2019). Furthermore, presumptive tax regimes that distinguish between firms of different sizes or in different sectors can be subject to significant instability when tax rules or rates are adjusted.[4] All of these effects can be exacerbated by pervasive informality in tax enforcement. The design of presumptive tax regimes requires a balancing act between the appeal of simplicity and the need for sufficient disaggregation to avoid major inequities. Where possible, SMEs should be given the choice to opt into the normal tax regime if they so desire.

Ensuring Fairness

Ensuring fairness is likely to be particularly important for SMEs, especially those in the informal sector that might be more vulnerable to abusive enforcement. Evidence suggests that informal firms perceive their tax burden as unfair, often because they feel the law is being applied selectively (Dube and Casale 2019; Getachew 2019).

Although recent reforms separating front-office functions (such as collection) from back-office functions (such as assessment) have reduced opportunities for extortion (Fjeldstad and Moore 2008), significant scope for arbitrariness remains. It is unlikely that this risk can be fully removed. Some aspects of assessments are intrinsically uncertain because at the margin tax officers have to make judgment calls, especially when rules and regulations are vague or do not cover all cases (Raaphorst 2017).

Such uncertainty only strengthens the case for an effective and accessible appeals system, which may or may not include the courts. Anecdotal evidence also suggests that SME taxpayers might prefer dispute resolution systems within revenue administrations to taking disputes to court. This is also likely to apply to larger corporate taxpayers. Although differential levels of trust in both institutions may play a role, lack of specialized knowledge within the judiciary has also been identified as a factor. Thus more research is needed.

Ensuring Accountability

Given the limited revenue potential from taxing SMEs, much of the recent interest in doing so stems from the potential to tax them as an entry point for popular public engagement and improved accountability. However, whether these efforts have resulted in an institutionalized voice for small taxpayers is uncertain. Evidence of this potential is mixed at best. Certainly, there are scattered examples of small- and medium-business associations responding to expanded taxation by engaging governments with demands for reciprocity (Joshi, Prichard, and

Heady 2014; Prichard 2015). However, in many other cases small-business associations appear either too weak to engage government meaningfully (Prichard and van den Boogaard 2017) or, worse, to have operated primarily for the benefit of their more powerful members—at least in the realm of taxation (Meagher 2018; Meagher and Lindell 2013).

For these and other reasons, it seems increasingly that reformers would be unwise to assume that expanded taxation of small firms would automatically result in accountability benefits from engagement. Instead, such benefits are likely to turn on explicit and complementary strategies to strengthen effective small-business associations and to create channels for their engagement with government. That said, little is known about how to best achieve these goals.

Associational taxation is a particularly interesting—but also fraught— example of governments working directly with small-business associations. Under systems of associational taxation, instead of taxing small firms directly, governments cooperate with small-business associations, which collect tax on behalf of governments. In principle, these arrangements can have significant benefits: tax collection costs are minimized; potential conflicts with tax collectors are largely eliminated; tax payments can be small and periodic for small taxpayers; a culture of tax compliance spreads slowly among small firms; small-business associations are institutionalized; and a clear channel is created for engagement between small-business associations and governments (Joshi and Ayee 2008).

However, the risks are equally significant because the benefits of these arrangements may be captured by association leaders at the expense of most of the small businesses. For example, association leaders may agree to expand taxation of their members to gain political influence—or patronage—from state elites for themselves, or they may re-create the role of state tax collectors by retaining a significant share of revenue for themselves. In these circumstances, the burden of taxation may expand more rapidly than would otherwise have been possible, but with few benefits and no expansion of popular engagement. Associational taxation thus remains a potentially interesting model, but one that must be approached with significant understanding of local power dynamics— and sufficient monitoring to ensure that revenue collected by the associations' leaders reach the state (Prichard 2009).

Conclusion

In many respects, the taxation of SMEs in low-income countries frequently reflects the worst of all worlds: it raises little revenue, appears to be relatively inequitable, is politically contentious, diverts scarce administrative resources to low-value activities and formalization, and when it does happen, carries few benefits for taxpayers. Because SMEs are often transient and cash-based in their operations with limited record keeping, it is a daunting task to maintain accurate taxpayer rolls and estimate taxable revenue. SMEs' limited financial and technical literacy also undermines tax compliance, leading to a reliance on face-to-face transactions with tax administrators that create opportunities for corruption and harassment of vulnerable firms. Meanwhile, efforts to expand taxation of SMEs must also confront political and institutional challenges. The sheer number of SME operators can create a fairly strong (and even well-organized) constituency in favor of the status quo. Tax officials may also lack incentives to devote more effort to the relatively cost-intensive and low-prestige task of increasing SME collections, especially if they prefer to maintain avenues for demanding informal payments. Meanwhile, general arguments in favor of taxing SMEs appear to be frequently overstated, which suggests a need to distinguish between types of SMEs and target reform efforts accordingly.

The larger informal SMEs are particularly likely to benefit from formalization, present more meaningful revenue potential, and, for the largest such firms, benefit unfairly relative to their competitors by avoiding taxation. For these firms, formalization may help long-term growth by opening the door to advantages such as legal protections, better access to utilities and financing, and opportunities for business networking and advertising. Governments also have stronger incentives to target larger SMEs because they are more likely to make longer-term contributions to tax revenue, and bringing them into the tax net may also increase equity. There seem to be good reasons for targeted government efforts to bring these larger firms into the tax net through a combination of targeted enforcement, easing the path to formalization, and efforts to expand and publicize the benefits of formalization.

By contrast, the case for aggressively targeting smaller firms appears far less compelling. These firms are less likely to benefit from formalization, and they are also more administratively difficult to tax, with greater risk of harassment by tax officials. Reform experience across countries suggests that the realistic revenue potential from taxing these firms is generally very limited. At the same time, many smaller SMEs (including those unregistered) paradoxically already face a relatively heavy fiscal burden of various taxes, fees, and demands for informal payments. In theory, expanding the tax net can benefit even these groups by increasing engagement between the government and these new constituencies, thereby strengthening accountability. Yet evidence is mixed on whether this happens in practice, or if it merely creates new channels for predation on vulnerable enterprises. For these firms, the best path for governments may be to rely less on the kinds of mass registration drives that have historically been common but often unproductive and more on encouraging quasi-voluntary compliance.

Emerging evidence points to an alternative approach to SME taxation that emphasizes encouraging quasi-voluntary compliance by promoting trust and building political support for taxation. Such strategies are likely to reflect four key elements. First, differentiation: target specific groups of relatively larger, growth-oriented firms for enforcement efforts instead of relying on blanket approaches that generate unproductive and bloated tax registers. Second, simplification: complex systems are costly to administer and costly to comply with, and they undermine trust. A wide variety of reform options are available, including eliminating unproductive subnational payments, taxes, and levies; reducing the number of brackets, exemptions, and paperwork required; introducing one-stop shops and electronic filing and payment systems; and expanding taxpayer education programs, hotlines, and technical support. Third, fairness: reduce opportunities for harassment of taxpayers and create appropriate incentives for tax collectors. Fourth, reciprocity: highlight and expand the benefits of formality by, for example, improving legal protections; expanding key services that benefit SMEs; and creating forums for direct engagement with government in ways likely to contribute to the progressive strengthening of the social contract.

Notes

1. Formalization includes but is not limited to registration for tax purposes. It refers to the broader process of obtaining all the necessary official licenses and complying with all relevant regulations when starting a business, which includes registering with the tax authority and paying the necessary taxes.
2. Fajnzylber, Maloney, and Montes-Rojas (2009) report benefits in either case, but most other recent studies suggest that aggressive efforts to bring firms into the tax net might yield some winners but also many firms that do not benefit or that suffer (Maloney 2004; Williams, Shahid, and Martínez 2016).
3. In 1996, Brazil introduced the Integrated System for Payment of Taxes and Contributions of Micro and Small Enterprises (SIMPLES) initiative—a business tax reduction and simplification scheme. Microenterprises (self-employed) and small firms in specified sectors could participate up to certain annual revenue limits. By combining six different federal taxes and social contributions into one single monthly-based rate, the reformed system considerably reduced the tax burden on these firms: instead of paying 5–11 percent of gross revenues on taxes, under SIMPLES microenterprises would pay 3–5 percent and small firms 5.4–8.6 percent (Piza 2018).
4. In 2005 in Ethiopia, there was a dramatic increase in rates amid such changes (Prichard 2015).

References

Abdixhiku, L., B. Krasiniqi, G. Pugh, and I. Hashi. 2017. "Firm-Level Determinants of Tax Evasion in Transition Economies." *Economic Systems* 41 (3): 354–66.

Akpan, I., and K. Sempere. 2019. "Hidden Inequalities: Tax Challenges of Market Women in Enugu and Kaduna States, Nigeria." Working paper, Research in Brief No. 97, International Centre for Tax and Development, Brighton, UK.

Almunia, M., and D. Lopez-Rodriguez. 2018. "Under the Radar: The Effects of Monitoring Firms on Tax Compliance." *American Economic Journal: Economic Policy* 10 (1): 1–38.

Amaoka, G. K. 2013. "Accounting Practices of SMEs: A Case Study of Kumasi Metropolis in Ghana." *International Journal of Business and Management* 8 (24): 73–83.

Amodio, F., J. Choi, and A. Rahman. 2018. "Bribes vs. Taxes: Market Structure and Incentives." Discussion Paper No. 11668, Institute of Labor Economics (IZA), Bonn.

Amponsah, S., and K. O. Adu. 2015. "Factors Influencing Tax Stamp Purchases in Ghana: A Case of Twifo-Atti Morkwa Sub-Tax District." *Journal of Accounting and Marketing* 5 (3): 1–7.

Arachi, G., and A. Santoro. 2007. "Tax Enforcement for SMEs: Lessons from the Italian Experience." *eJournal of Tax Research* 5 (2): 225–43.

Ayyagari, M., A. Demirgüç-Kunt, and V. Maksimovic. 2011. "Small vs. Young Firms across the World: Contribution to Employment, Job Creation, and Growth." Policy Research Working Paper 5631, World Bank, Washington, DC.

Benjamin, N., and A. A. Mbaye. 2012. *The Informal Sector in Francophone Africa: Firm Size, Productivity, and Institutions.* Washington, DC: World Bank.

Best, M., A. Brockmeyer, H. Jacobsen Kleven, J. Spinnewijn, and M. Waseem. 2015. "Production versus Revenue Efficiency with Limited Tax Capacity: Theory and Evidence from Pakistan." *Journal of Political Economy* 123 (6): 1311–55.

Bird, R. M., and S. Wallace. 2005. "Is It Really So Hard to Tax the Hard-to-Tax? The Context and Role of Presumptive Taxes." In *Taxing the Hard-to-Tax: Lessons from Theory and Practice,* edited by J. Alm, J. Martinez-Vazquez, and S. Wallace, 121–58. Bingley, UK: Emerald Group Publishing.

Boly, A. 2018. "On the Short- and Medium-Term Effects of Formalisation: Panel Evidence from Vietnam." *Journal of Development Studies* 54 (4): 641–56.

Boonzaaier, W., J. Harju, T. Matikka, and J. Pirttilä. 2016. "How Do Small Firms Respond to Tax Schedule Discontinuities? Evidence from South African Tax Registers." Working Paper No. 36, United Nations University World Institute for Development Economics Research (UNU-WIDER), Helsinki.

Bruhn, M., and J. Loeprick. 2016. "Small Business Tax Policy and Informality: Evidence from Georgia." *International Tax and Public Finance* 23 (5): 834–53.

Bruhn, M., and D. McKenzie. 2014. "Entry Regulation and the Formalization of Microenterprises in Developing Countries." *World Bank Research Observer* 29 (2): 186–201.

Carreras, M., P. Dachapalli, and G. Mascagni. 2017. "Effective Corporate Tax Burden and Firm Size in South Africa: A Firm-Level Analysis." Working Paper No. 2017/162, United Nations University World Institute for Development Economics Research (UNU-WIDER), Helsinki.

Carrillo, P., D. Pomeranz, and M. Singhal. 2017. "Dodging the Taxman: Firm Misreporting and Limits to Tax Enforcement." *American Economic Journal: Applied Economics* 9 (2): 144–64.

Chen, S. X. 2017. "The Effect of a Fiscal Squeeze on Tax Enforcement: Evidence from a Natural Experiment in China." *Journal of Public Economics* 147: 62–76.

Cohen, N., and S. Gershgoren. 2016. "The Incentives of Street-Level Bureaucrats and Inequality in Tax Assessments." *Administration and Society* 48 (3): 267–89.

Coolidge, J. 2012. "Findings of Tax Compliance Cost Surveys in Developing Countries." *eJournal of Tax Research* 10 (2): 250–87.

Cowell, F. A. 2003. "Sticks and Carrots." Research Paper No. DARP 68, Suntory and Toyota International Centres for Economics and Related Disciplines (STICERD), London School of Economics and Political Science.

de Andrade, G. H., M. Bruhn, and D. McKenzie. 2016. "A Helping Hand or the Long Arm of the Law? Experimental Evidence on What Governments Can Do to Formalize Firms." *World Bank Economic Review* 30 (1): 24–54.

DeBacker, J., B. T. Heim, and A. Tran. 2015. "Importing Corruption Culture from Overseas: Evidence from Corporate Tax Evasion in the United States." *Journal of Financial Economics* 117 (1): 122–38.

de Mel, S., D. McKenzie, and C. Woodruff. 2013. "The Demand for, and Consequences of, Formalization among Informal Firms in Sri Lanka." *American Economic Journal: Applied Economics* 5 (2): 122–50.

Demenet, A., M. Razafindrakoto, and F. Roubaud. 2016. "Do Informal Businesses Gain from Registration and How? Panel Data Evidence from Vietnam." *World Development* 84: 326–41.

Devas, N., and R. Kelly. 2001. "Regulations or Revenues? An Analysis of Local Business Licences, with a Case Study of the Single Business Permit Reform in Kenya." *Public Administration and Development* 21 (5): 381–91.

Dube, G., and D. Casale. 2019. "Informal Sector Taxes and Equity: Evidence from Presumptive Taxation in Zimbabwe." *Development Policy Review* 37 (1): 47–66.

Ebrill, L., M. Keen, J. P. Bodin, and V. Summers. 2001. *The Modern VAT*. Washington, DC: International Monetary Fund.

Efobi, U., I. Beecroft, T. Belmondo, and A. Katan. 2019. "Small Business Use of the Integrated Tax Administration System in Nigeria." African Tax Administration Paper No. 8, International Centre for Tax and Development, Brighton, UK.

Fajnzylber, P., W. F. Maloney, and G. V. Montes-Rojas. 2009. "Releasing Constraints to Growth or Pushing on a String? Policies and Performance of Mexican Micro-Firms." *Journal of Development Studies* 45 (7): 1027–47.

Fajnzylber, P., W. F. Maloney, and G. Montes-Rojas. 2011. "Does Formality Improve Micro-Firm Performance? Evidence from the Brazilian SIMPLES Program." *Journal of Development Economics* 94 (2): 262–76.

Faridy, N., R. Copp, B. Freudenberg, and T. Sarker. 2014. "Complexity, Compliance Costs and Non-Compliance with VAT by Small and Medium Enterprises (SMEs) in Bangladesh: Is There a Relationship?" *Australian Tax Forum* 29 (2): 281–328.

Fatoki, O. 2014. "The Financial Literacy of Micro Entrepreneurs in South Africa." *Journal of Social Sciences* 40 (2): 151–58.

Fjeldstad, O-H., and K. K. Heggstad. 2011. "The Tax Systems in Mozambique, Tanzania and Zambia: Capacity and Constraints." Report No. 2011:3, Chr. Michelsen Institute, Bergen, Norway.

Fjeldstad, O-H., L. Katera, and E. Ngalewa. 2009. "Outsourcing Revenue Collection to Private Agents: Experiences from Local Authorities in Tanzania." Special Paper No. 28, Research on Poverty Alleviation (REPOA), Dar es Salaam, Tanzania.

Fjeldstad, O-H., and M. Moore. 2008. "Tax Reform and State-Building in a Globalised World." In *Taxation and State-Building in Developing Countries: Capacity and Consent*, edited by D. Brautigam, O-H. Fjeldstad, and M. Moore, 235–60. Cambridge, UK: Cambridge University Press.

Floridi, A., B. A. Demena, and N. Wagner. 2020. "Shedding Light on the Shadows of Informality: A Meta-Analysis of Formalization Interventions Targeted at Informal Firms." *Labour Economics* 67: 101925.

Getachew, A. 2019. "Turnover-Based Presumptive Taxation and Taxpayers' Perceptions in Ethiopia." African Tax Administration Paper No. 7, International Centre for Tax and Development, Brighton, UK.

Gupta, S., M. Keen, A. Shah, and G. Verdier. 2017. *Digital Revolutions in Public Finance*. Washington, DC: International Monetary Fund.

Hanlon, M., L. Mills, and J. Slemrod. 2007. "An Empirical Examination of Corporate Tax Noncompliance." In *Taxing Corporate Income in the 21st Century*, edited by A. J. Auerbach, J. R. Hines, Jr., and J. Slemrod, 171–210. New York: Cambridge University Press.

Harju, J., T. Matikka, and R. Rauhanen. 2019. "Compliance Costs vs. Tax Incentives: Why Do Entrepreneurs Respond to Size-Based Regulations?" *Journal of Public Economics* 173: 139–64.

Hassan, M., and W. Prichard. 2016. "The Political Economy of Domestic Tax Reform in Bangladesh: Political Settlements, Informal Institutions and the Negotiation of Reform." *Journal of Development Studies* 52 (12): 1704–21.

Hirvonen, K., G. Mascagni, and K. Roelen. 2018. "Linking Taxation and Social Protection: Evidence on Redistribution and Poverty Reduction in Ethiopia." *International Social Security Review* 71 (1): 3–24.

Inasius, F. 2018. "Factors Influencing SME Tax Compliance: Evidence from Indonesia." *International Journal of Public Administration* 42 (5): 367–79.

Iversen, V., O-H. Fjeldstad, G. Bahiigwa, F. Ellis, and R. James. 2006. "Private Tax Collection—Remnant of the Past or a Way Forward? Evidence from Rural Uganda." *Public Administration and Development* 26 (4): 317–28.

Jibao, S., and W. Prichard. 2016. "Rebuilding Local Government Finances after Conflict: Lessons from a Reform Programme in Post-Conflict Sierra Leone." *Journal of Development Studies* 52 (12): 1759–75.

Jibao, S., W. Prichard, and V. van den Boogaard. 2017. "Informal Taxation in Post-Conflict Sierra Leone: Taxpayers' Experiences and Perceptions." Working Paper No. 66, International Centre for Tax and Development, Brighton, UK.

Joshi, A., and J. Ayee. 2008. "Associational Taxation: A Pathway into the Informal Sector?" In *Taxation and State-Building in Developing Countries: Capacity and Consent*, edited by D. Brautigam, O-H. Fjeldstad, and M. Moore, 183–211. Cambridge, UK: Cambridge University Press.

Joshi, A., W. Prichard, and C. Heady. 2014. "Taxing the Informal Economy: The Current State of Knowledge and Agendas for Future Research." *Journal of Development Studies* 50 (10): 1325–47.

Keen, M., and J. Slemrod. 2017. "Optimal Tax Administration." *Journal of Public Economics* 152: 133–42.

Khan, A., A. Khwaja, and B. Olken. 2016. "Tax Farming Redux: Experimental Evidence on Performance Pay for Tax Collectors." *Quarterly Journal of Economics* 131 (1): 219–71.

Khan, A. Q., A. I. Khwaja, and B. A. Olken. 2019. "Making Moves Matter: Experimental Evidence on Incentivizing Bureaucrats through Performance-Based Postings." *American Economic Review* 109 (1): 237–70.

Kleven, H. 2016. "Bunching." *Annual Review of Economics* 8: 435–64.

Kleven, H. J., and M. Waseem. 2013. "Using Notches to Uncover Optimization Frictions and Structural Elasticities: Theory and Evidence from Pakistan." *Quarterly Journal of Economics* 128 (2): 669–723.

Kumar, R. 2017. "Targeted SME Financing and Employment Effects: What Do We Know and What Can We Do Differently?" Jobs Working Paper No. 3, World Bank, Washington, DC.

La Porta, R., and A. Shleifer. 2014. "Informality and Development." *Journal of Economic Perspectives* 28 (3): 109–26.

Ligomeka, W. 2019. "Expensive to Be a Female Trader: The Reality of Taxation of Flea Market Traders in Zimbabwe." Working Paper No. 93, International Centre for Tax and Development, Brighton, UK.

Lindell, I. 2010. "Between Exit and Voice: Informality and the Spaces of Popular Agency Introduction." *African Studies Quarterly* 11 (2–3): 1–11.

Lü, X., and P. F. Landry. 2014. "Show Me the Money: Interjurisdiction Political Competition and Fiscal Extraction in China." *American Political Science Review* 108 (3): 706–22.

Maloney, W. F. 2004. "Informality Revisited." *World Development* 32 (7): 1159–78.

Mascagni, G., R. Dom, and F. Santoro. 2021. "VAT in Practice: Equity, Enforcement and Complexity." Working Paper No. 118, International Centre for Tax and Development, Brighton, UK.

Mascagni, G., and A. Mengistu. 2016. "The Corporate Tax Burden in Ethiopia: Evidence from Anonymised Tax Returns." Working Paper No. 48, International Centre for Tax and Development, Brighton, UK.

Mascagni, G., and A. Mengistu. 2019. "Effective Tax Rates and Firm Size in Ethiopia." *Development Policy Review* 37: O248–73.

Mascagni, G., N. Monkam, and C. Nell. 2016. "Unlocking the Potential of Administrative Data in Africa: Tax Compliance and Progressivity in Rwanda." Working Paper No. 56, International Centre for Tax and Development, Brighton, UK.

Mascagni, G., F. Santoro, and D. Mukama. 2019. "Teach to Comply? Evidence from a Taxpayer Education Programme in Rwanda." Working Paper No. 91, International Centre for Tax and Development, Brighton, UK.

Mascagni, G., F. Santoro, D. Mukama, and J. Karangwa. 2020. "Active Ghosts: Nil Filing in Rwanda." Working Paper No. 106, International Centre for Tax and Development, Brighton, UK.

Mayega, J., R. Ssuuna, M. Mubajje, M. I. Nalukwago, and L. Muwonge. 2019. "How Clean Is Our Taxpayer Register? Data Management in the Uganda Revenue Authority." African Tax Administration Paper No. 12, International Centre for Tax and Development, Brighton, UK.

McCulloch, N., G. G. Schulze, and J. Voss. 2010. "What Determines Firms' Decisions to Formalize? Evidence from Rural Indonesia." Discussion Paper No. 13, Department of International Economic Policy (IEP), University of Freiburg, Germany.

Meagher, K. 2018. "Taxing Times: Taxation, Divided Societies and the Informal Economy in Northern Nigeria." *Journal of Development Studies* 54 (1): 1–17.

Meagher, K., and I. Lindell. 2013. "ASR Forum: Engaging with African Informal Economies: Social Inclusion or Adverse Incorporation? Introduction." *African Studies Review* 56 (3): 57–76.

Medina, L., and F. Schneider. 2018. "Shadow Economies around the World: What Did We Learn over the Last 20 Years?" IMF Working Paper WP/18/17, International Monetary Fund, Washington, DC.

Memon, N. 2013. "Looking at Pakistani Presumptive Income Tax through Principles of a Good Tax?" *eJournal of Tax Research* 11 (1): 40–78.

Moore, M. 2020. "What Is Wrong with African Tax Administration?" Working Paper No. 111, International Centre for Tax and Development, Brighton, UK.

ODEP (Public Expenditure Observatory). 2013. "Rapport de l'enquête sur l'évaluation participative de la transparence dans la collecte et l'utilisation des taxes pour l'amélioration du marché central de Kinshasa" [Survey Report on the Participatory Assessment of Transparency in the Collection and Use of Taxes for the Improvement of the Central Market of Kinshasa]. Unreleased document, ODEP, Kinshasa, Democratic Republic of Congo.

OECD (Organisation for Economic Co-operation and Development). 2015. "Taxation of SMEs in OECD and G20 Countries." OECD Tax Policy Studies No. 23, OECD, Paris.

OECD (Organisation for Economic Co-operation and Development). 2019. *Tax Administration 2019: Comparative Information on OECD and Other Advanced and Emerging Economies.* Paris: OECD Publishing.

Okunogbe, O. M., and V. M. J. Pouliquen. 2018. "Technology, Taxation, and Corruption: Evidence from the Introduction of Electronic Tax Filing." Policy Research Working Paper 8452, World Bank, Washington, DC.

Page, J., and M. Söderbom. 2015. "Is Small Beautiful? Small Enterprise, Aid and Employment in Africa." *African Development Review* 27 (S1): 44–55.

Paler, L., W. Prichard, R. Sánchez de la Sierra, and C. Samii. 2017. "Survey on Total Tax Burden in the DRC, Final Report." Study for the Department for International Development (UK), Kinshasa, Democratic Republic of Congo.

Piza, C. 2018. "Out of the Shadows? Revisiting the Impact of the Brazilian SIMPLES Program on Firms' Formalization Rates." *Journal of Development Economics* 134: 125–32.

Prichard, W. 2009. "The Politics of Taxation and Implications for Accountability in Ghana 1981–2008." Working Paper No. 330, Institute of Development Studies, Brighton, UK.

Prichard, W. 2015. *Taxation, Responsiveness and Accountability in Sub-Saharan Africa: The Dynamics of Tax Bargaining.* Cambridge, UK: Cambridge University Press.

Prichard, W., and V. van den Boogaard. 2017. "Norms, Power, and the Socially Embedded Realities of Market Taxation in Northern Ghana." *African Studies Review* 60 (1): 171–94.

Raaphorst, N. 2017. "How to Prove, How to Interpret and What to Do? Uncertainty Experiences of Street-Level Tax Officials." *Public Management Review* 20 (4): 485–502.

Rand, J., and N. Torm. 2012. "The Benefits of Formalization: Evidence from Vietnamese Manufacturing SMEs." *World Development* 40 (5): 983–98.

Rocha, R., G. Ulyssea, and L. Rachter. 2018. "Do Lower Taxes Reduce Informality? Evidence from Brazil." *Journal of Development Economics* 134: 28–49.

Saez, E. 2010. "Do Taxpayers Bunch at Kink Points?" *American Economic Journal: Economic Policy* 2 (3): 180–212.

Sánchez de la Sierra, R., and K. Titeca. 2016. "The State as Organized Crime: Industrial Organization of the Traffic Police in the Democratic Republic of the Congo." Unpublished conference paper. https://editorialexpress.com/cgi-bin /conference/download.cgi?db_name=SAEe2016&paper_id=557.

Santoro, F., and W. Mdluli. 2019. "Nil-Filing in Eswatini: Should the Revenue Administration Be Concerned?" African Tax Administration Paper No. 6, International Centre for Tax and Development, Brighton, UK.

Schneider, F., and R. Klinglmair. 2004. "Shadow Economies around the World: What Do We Know?" Working Paper No. 1167, Center for Economic Studies and the ifo Institute (CESifo), Munich.

Slemrod, J. 2004. "The Economics of Corporate Tax Selfishness." Working Paper No. 10858, National Bureau of Economic Research, Cambridge, MA.

Tendler, J. 2002. "Small Firms, the Informal Sector, and the Devil's Deal." *IDS Bulletin* 33 (3).

Thuronyi, V. 1996. "Presumptive Taxation." In *Tax Law Design and Drafting*, edited by V. Thuronyi, 401–33. Washington, DC: International Monetary Fund.

Torgler, B., and F. Schneider. 2007. "Shadow Economy, Tax Morale, Governance and Institutional Quality: A Panel Analysis." Discussion Paper No. 2563, Institute of Labor Economics (IZA), Bonn.

Ulyssea, G. 2018. "Firms, Informality, and Development: Theory and Evidence from Brazil." *American Economic Review* 108 (8): 2015–47.

URA (Uganda Revenue Authority). 2020. *URA Annual Data Book FY2018/19*. URA, Kampala.

Velayudhan, T. 2019. "Misallocation or Misreporting? Evidence from a Value Added Tax Notch in India." Working paper, Department of Economics, Ohio State University, Columbus.

Williams, C. C., and A. Gurtoo. 2012. "Evaluating Competing Theories of Street Entrepreneurship: Some Lessons from a Study of Street Vendors in Bangalore, India." *International Entrepreneurship and Management Journal* 8 (4): 391–409.

Williams, C. C., and I. A. Horodnic. 2017. "Evaluating the Policy Approaches for Tackling Undeclared Work in the European Union." *Environment and Planning C: Politics and Space* 35 (5): 916–36.

Williams, C. C., and A. M. Kedir. 2016. "Business Registration and Firm Performance: Some Lessons from India." *Journal of Developmental Entrepreneurship* 21 (3): 1650016.

Williams, C. C., M. S. Shahid, and A. Martínez. 2016. "Determinants of the Level of Informality of Informal Micro-Enterprises: Some Evidence from the City of Lahore, Pakistan." *World Development* 84: 312–25.

Workneh, A. M., E. M. Baileyegn, and G. Stewart-Wilson. 2019. "Where the Gap Lay: Presumptive Income Tax Assessment for Small and Micro Enterprises in Addis Ababa City Administration." Working Paper No. 94, International Centre for Tax and Development, Brighton, UK.

World Bank. 2016. "Tax Compliance Cost Burden and Tax Perceptions Survey in Ethiopia." Working paper, World Bank, Washington, DC.

World Bank. 2019. *Doing Business 2019: Training for Reform*. Washington, DC: World Bank.

Yilmaz, F., and J. Coolidge. 2013. "Can E-filing Reduce Tax Compliance Costs in Developing Countries?" Policy Research Working Paper 6647, World Bank, Washington, DC.

CHAPTER 6

Taxing at the Local Level

Wilson Prichard and Roel Dom

The Tax Compliance Challenge

Recent decades have witnessed substantial decentralization across much of the developing world, but the strengthening of subnational revenue collection has lagged. Although governments have devolved expenditure decisions to lower levels, subnational revenue mobilization is often weak. Lower-level governments in high-income countries typically raise about 30 percent of total public revenue. Their counterparts in low-income countries raise less than 8 percent (Smoke 2019).

Decentralization is expected to improve the efficiency of government activities by moving the level of decision-making closer to those most affected by government action (Faguet 2014). Although there is no clear optimal model of tax assignment across levels of government, there is a strong case for a significant degree of tax autonomy at the subnational level. The basic argument is that subnational governments are more likely to allocate their spending effectively and efficiently if they are also responsible for their own revenue (Bird 2011; Sanogo 2019). Local revenue mobilization gives subnational governments the autonomy to respond to citizens' needs, while being a critical driver of engagement and ownership by taxpayers, thereby improving both accountability and responsiveness.

This chapter looks at local taxation, focusing, in particular, on efforts to strengthen property taxation and reform so-called nuisance taxes. But these are not the only sources of subnational revenue. Subnational governments can finance their expenditures from a range of revenue sources, which may include local taxes and fees, user fees for local services, financial transfers from the national government or revenue-sharing mechanisms, and nontax revenue such as revenue from commodity extraction. In several countries, subnational governments are also allowed to borrow. Three factors are therefore considered here. First, subnational revenue sources vary significantly across countries, driven by constitutional arrangements and political settlements and so warranting a closer look at a subset of issues of common concern. Second, although subnational governments can rely on a wide range of revenue-raising tools, property taxes are, or should be, the backbone of local revenue-raising almost everywhere. Third, although nuisance taxes are less critical to revenue-raising, there is growing evidence that they are very important to equity and broader trust in tax systems.

Low Revenue Mobilization

The most basic problem of subnational revenue-raising in low-income countries is the weakness of overall revenue-raising. As noted earlier, the average levels of subnational revenue collection lag far behind those of wealthier countries—a far larger gap than that for national revenue-raising. In many respects, even those average figures understate revenue challenges in many lower-income countries: total revenue collection even in midsize cities is often only a few dollars per capita, while in rural areas the amounts raised often barely cover the costs of collection. In both cases, the revenue is frequently inadequate to provide any meaningful services beyond paying some government salaries (van den Boogaard et al., forthcoming).

The weakness of subnational revenue-raising stems overwhelmingly from the weakness of the most important, and potentially most productive, subnational tax, the property tax. Although property taxes can encompass a variety of levies on the use, ownership, and transfer of property, most of this chapter focuses on the recurrent (annual) tax on immovable property (Norregaard 2013). Economists generally consider it to be the best local tax precisely because of the immovability of property. Thus the tax is, in principle, difficult to evade and does not distort economic decisions. Moreover, because it is a highly visible tax, it can be expected to promote taxpayer engagement and accountability (Slack and Bird 2015).

In Organisation for Economic Co-operation and Development (OECD) countries, property taxes almost universally are the backbone of local government finances, generally accounting for 1–2 percent of the gross domestic product (GDP) and in some cases significantly more. By contrast, admittedly imperfect data from lower-income countries suggest that property tax collection is often lower than 0.2 percent of GDP (see figure 6.1). Of all the major national and subnational taxes, property taxes are the most underperforming relative to higher-income countries. If property tax collection were to approach the levels seen in higher-income countries, it could transform local government finances in lower-income countries.

Differences in property tax collection reflect, in part, differences in income levels and demographics, but, most important, they reflect the limitations of policy and administration (Awasthi, Le, and You 2020; Sepulveda and

FIGURE 6.1 Subnational Tax Revenue as a Share of GDP, by Country Income Group, 2017

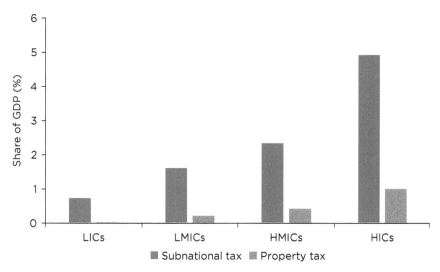

Source: Authors' calculations based on United Nations University World Institute for Development Economics Research (UNU-WIDER), Government Revenue Dataset of the International Centre for Tax and Development, https://www.wider.unu.edu/project/government-revenue-dataset.
Note: GDP = gross domestic product; HICs = high-income countries; HMICs = higher-middle-income countries; LICs = low-income countries; LMICs = lower-middle-income countries.

Martinez-Vazquez 2012). Available evidence suggests that limited collection is driven by weak collection among the most valuable properties owing to a combination of undervaluation of those properties, exemptions, and poor enforcement. A recent reform program in Freetown, Sierra Leone, sought to update the valuation of all properties using objective criteria. The result was that although the valuation of average properties remained effectively unchanged, tax liabilities on the lower-value properties decreased, whereas those on higher-value properties increased considerably (table 6.1). As a result, the updated valuation system increased the progressivity of the system (Prichard, Kamara, and Meriggi 2020).

TABLE 6.1 Change in Tax Liabilities in Freetown, Sierra Leone, by Property Value Quintile

Quintile	Existing system (US$)	New system (US$)	Average change (%)
1st	14.33	4.31	−70
2nd	15.85	9.48	−40
3rd	16.10	17.40	+8
4th	23.38	36.94	+58
5th	41.64	142.25	+242

Source: Prichard, Kamara, and Meriggi 2020.
Note: The table summarizes the impact of a new property valuation system in Freetown.

Inequity, Mistrust, and Disengagement

The weaknesses of subnational revenue systems go beyond weak revenue mobilization. Those systems also tend to be characterized by major inequities, substantial mistrust, and, as a result, disengagement by citizens.

Nuisance Taxes

Popular writing about subnational taxation in low- and middle-income countries often implies there is limited taxation at the local level and individual taxpayers pay few taxes (Fjeldstad, Chambas, and Brun 2014; Fjeldstad and Heggstad 2012). But this is not quite right. It is true that most subnational governments raise strikingly little revenue, as discussed previously, particularly because of the weakness of property taxes on the better-off. However, burdens on low-income groups are often substantial relative to their limited income because of the many small taxes, fees, and informal payments—nuisance taxes— they must pay (van den Boogaard 2020; van den Boogaard, Prichard, and Jibao 2019). The result is the worst of all possible worlds: subnational governments raise too little revenue to support effective decentralization, but low-income groups nonetheless bear significant formal and informal fiscal burdens.

A defining feature of nuisance taxes is that they raise little revenue and can result in inequitable tax burdens (Moore, Prichard, and Fjeldstad 2018). One study estimates that in North Kivu, Democratic Republic of Congo, 95 percent of the over 400 legal levies raise only negligible amounts of revenue if any (Paler et al. 2017). Moreover, they often affect the smallest taxpayers the most (Pimhidzai and Fox 2011). For example, *business licenses* are often applied at relatively flat rates to different types of businesses, effectively imposing much heavier burdens on smaller and lower-income firms (Fjeldstad and Heggstad 2012). *Market taxes* tend to fall disproportionally on smaller and more itinerant traders, who are often low-income women (Akpan and Sempere 2019; Ligomeka 2019; Prichard and van den Boogaard 2017; Sempere 2018; Siebert and Mbise 2018). *Poll taxes* are also highly regressive, which has led to their abolition in many but not all countries (Fjeldstad and Therkildsen 2008). And *user fees* usually impose a fixed burden irrespective of ability to pay.

The economic burden of nuisance taxes is often compounded by poor coordination between central and local authorities, as well as significant informal collection, which imposes multiple poorly coordinated demands for taxes and fees on businesses (Fjeldstad, Ali, and Katera 2019; Wanjiru et al. 2019).

Informal and Nonstate Taxation

Alongside formal revenue collection, recent research has also documented the prevalence of informal revenue generation at the subnational level, which may take the form of, among other things, informal user fees to access health care, education, or water and contributions to community development projects (van den Boogaard and Santoro, forthcoming). Some informal levies appear to be aimed at filling the gaps in the chronic underfunding of frontline activities by higher levels of government (De Herdt and Titeca 2016; van den Boogaard 2020; van den Boogaard and Santoro, forthcoming). This is most obviously true of informal fees for health, education, or water, but may also be reflected in informal levies to cover unpaid local salaries or to top up very low salaries. Critically, research suggests that these informal taxes are often even more regressive than formal taxes and fees, thus imposing a heavy burden on the lowest income groups (Olken and Singhal 2011; van den Boogaard, Prichard, and Jibao 2019).

Alongside informal payments to the state, research has also highlighted the role of informal payments to nonstate actors, such as customary authorities or rebel groups (Sánchez de la Sierra 2020; van den Boogaard and Santoro, forthcoming). Although these payments are not taxes in the legal sense, from the perspective of taxpayers they impose a similar burden. They should therefore feature in any discussion of the extent and nature of the burdens on citizens at the subnational level as well as of potential directions for reform.

Most critically, these fees further highlight the extent to which lower-income groups, in particular, may already face significant fiscal and quasi-fiscal burdens. They also signal the extent to which reform of subnational revenue systems should focus on improving revenue collection from the relatively wealthy (most notably through property taxation), while seeking to rationalize, and likely reduce, largely informal burdens on lower-income groups. That said, recent research also highlights the huge diversity of taxation by nonstate actors, which ranges from relatively popular and trusted strategies for funding public services (where the state is absent) to much more predatory forms of extraction (van den Boogaard, Prichard, and Jibao 2019).

Overall, the regressivity of small and informal payments means that while they are relatively modest for higher-income households, they impose a heavy burden on lower-income groups. In Sierra Leone, for example, lower-income households in smaller towns spend 10–15 percent of household income on smaller taxes, fees, and informal payments (van den Boogaard, Prichard, and Jibao 2019). Evidence from the Democratic Republic of Congo yields similar findings (Olsson, Baaz, and Martinsson 2020; Paler et al. 2017). Actual tax burdens on lower-income households and businesses are thus substantially higher than what is suggested by formal taxes alone or by the revenue that appears in government budgets.

This pattern of collection not only is disappointing in revenue and equity terms but also undermines the broader potential of decentralization to improve the government's responsiveness, accountability, and trustworthiness. At the core of arguments in favor of fiscal decentralization is the idea that it will bring political decision-making closer to citizens, make those decisions more responsive to local preferences, and encourage popular engagement in holding governments accountable (Prichard 2017). Yet this potential depends significantly on effective subnational taxation (Fjeldstad 2015). In the absence of subnational tax revenue, local governments are less able to respond to local preferences (Gervasoni 2010). And in the absence of taxation, taxpayers are less likely to engage politically and demand reciprocity and accountability from local governments (Prichard, Jibao, and Orgeira, forthcoming; Weigel 2020). The prevalence of inequitable and unfair forms of taxation is likely to further exacerbate these problems by undermining public trust in government.

Against this background, the broad contours of appropriate reform strategies look quite similar across many contexts: a dual-track strategy to both strengthen property taxation and curb nuisance taxes and the most problematic informal burdens. Critically, these two objectives are not only individually important but also closely intertwined and potentially reinforcing. Strengthening property taxation is likely critical to giving subnational governments the flexibility to curb nuisance taxes and informality. Meanwhile, curbing nuisance taxes and informality is likely important to generating the trust and political support needed to underpin a serious expansion of property taxation. So long as subnational tax systems remain characterized by significant unfairness and inequity, as well as limited reciprocity and accountability, building popular support for property tax reform is likely to be difficult.

Barriers to Reform

In many respects, the weakness of property taxation is surprising. Unlike income or sales, properties are both visible and immovable and thus seem to be an easy target for taxation. Yet in many countries (particularly lower-income ones), reforming property tax systems has proven to be exceptionally difficult (Norregaard 2013). To understand the barriers to reform, it is useful to consider issues within the various stages of the property taxation process—discovery, valuation, rate setting, billing, payment, and enforcement—as well as the political challenges and other cross-cutting issues (Fish 2018).

Discovery

Identification and registration of each property in a jurisdiction are a critical first step to effective property taxation. Yet it is not uncommon to observe coverage ratios (the number of registered properties divided by the total number of properties in a jurisdiction) of around 30 percent (Kelly 2000). In some countries, this ratio even falls below 10 percent. Such low rates reflect the fact that authorities often lack the capacity, or the will, to map all the properties within their jurisdictions and to keep such maps updated.

Properties can be mapped manually or by drawing on geographic information system (GIS), satellite, or drone imagery. This function is usually centralized within the national government as part of its broader responsibility for overseeing land use, land titling, and construction. As a result, the development of property registers is often subsumed within the broader and much more complex (as well as politically contentious) processes of titling and registering land. These processes have, in turn, frequently led to significant delays that have limited efforts to expand property tax rolls because the comparatively simple task of identifying all properties for tax purposes is slowed by challenges related to land titling; lack of coordination among players (such as the cadastral agency, the property registry, courts, tax authorities, geodetic institutes, and subnational authorities); and lack of central government resources for, or interest in, registering properties for taxation by subnational authorities (Martinez-Vazquez and Rider 2008).

The alternative is to make subnational governments responsible for the property tax register, thereby separating the process from land titling and reducing potential institutional hurdles. This change has been successful in a variety of jurisdictions (Jibao and Prichard 2016; Prichard, Kamara, and Meriggi 2020), but it faces challenges because local authorities often lack the capacity needed to maintain the registers. Accurate maps or qualified staff may not be available, or records are kept manually, making the change prone to error and manipulation.

Valuation

Once identified, the value of the properties must be established. Equitable, productive property taxation requires accurate valuation to ensure that more valuable properties are taxed more. However, determining the value of properties, or their (implied) rental value, is not straightforward: property prices and rental values are not always easily observed, and transactions may be infrequent, requiring efforts to estimate property values over time. This step has proven notoriously difficult in practice, even in high-income countries, owing to inaccurate valuations and the difficulty and cost of keeping valuation rolls up-to-date over time. Consequently, undervaluation can be dramatic, especially in lower-income countries. Valuation ratios (dividing the assessed value by the real market value) of 10–25 percent are not uncommon (Bahl 2009).

In addition, dominant models of property valuation in lower-income countries, usually inherited from the colonial period, frequently dictate that every property must be valued by a professional valuation officer (Moore, Prichard, and Fjeldstad 2018). Fulfilling this need is, however, enormously expensive, far beyond the resources of lower-income jurisdictions, and enormously slow because of the lack of professionally trained valuation officers (Kelly 2014). In Ghana, any subnational government wishing to update property valuations was required to contract the national valuation office, but many jurisdictions reported that they lacked the resources to do so or that too few valuation officers were available (Mohiuddin and Ohemeng, forthcoming). Such systems are also extremely vulnerable to collusion and corruption because expert valuations conducted in the absence of widely available market information leave much scope for subjectivity and negotiation.

Rate Setting

Once the tax base is determined, revenue collection and the distribution of the burden depend on the tax rates and exemptions adopted. Conventional policy advice is to broaden the tax base by limiting exemptions (which also increases equity and reduces administrative complexity), while setting rates according to revenue targets and taxpayers' ability to pay. In practice, however, tax systems across lower-income countries have been plagued by a proliferation of exemptions.

In Uganda, primary residences are exempt from property taxation (Kopanyi 2015). This policy is designed to protect property owners who may have valuable family homes but limited incomes. However, to protect a small subset of vulnerable taxpayers, it exempts a wide range of taxpayers who can and should pay, while also creating an enormous loophole through which owners of multiple properties can avoid tax liability by falsely claiming that properties are primary residences. Elsewhere, exemptions for government buildings or for charitable uses undermine revenue potential and increase administrative complexity (Franzsen and McCluskey 2017, 54–63).

Billing and Payment

Property taxation is relatively unique in that the assessment is generally conducted by the government, after which bills are sent to taxpayers. This seemingly straightforward task can, however, present additional challenges. In many cities in lower-income countries, street addressing and mapping are limited, which can complicate the task of identifying taxable properties and delivering tax bills. Similarly, in the absence of strong postal services, including methods for confirming such delivery, ensuring that tax bills are delivered can be difficult.

Thus most reform efforts now include plans to develop maps of relevant jurisdictions along with new systems of street addressing or property identification (Franzsen and Youngman 2009). These efforts are increasingly relying on satellite imagery or similar technology (Ali, Deininger, and Wild 2018; Richter and Georgiadou 2016). Technology can also be used to coordinate and confirm deliveries of tax bills (McCluskey et al. 2018). That said, mapping and addressing processes could remain a challenge in lower-capacity areas, as can organizing the complex logistics to ensure reliable delivery (Prichard and Fish 2017). One option is to attempt delivery everywhere—but also put the onus on taxpayers to seek their tax bill from government offices if it is not delivered for any reason.

The task of receiving payments also seems straightforward, but it can present problems, particularly in lower-income and lower-capacity environments (Nengeze 2018). Property tax systems have historically tended to rely on taxpayers making payments directly to tax collectors, either in the field or at government offices. These kinds of relationships are, however, ripe for corruption and collusion, which undermine trust (Fjeldstad 2003; Piracha and Moore 2016).

As a result, most reform programs are now attempting to set up payment via banks, with funds deposited directly in government accounts (Krolikowski 2014; Lall 2017). But here, too, capacity limitations within subnational governments can be a challenge. To facilitate compliance tracking and subsequent enforcement, payments must be credited against the accounts of individual taxpayers, but many subnational governments are limited in their capacity to match payments made at banks with individual taxpayer accounts. In some countries, taxpayers are expected to pay their tax at the bank and then bring their receipt to a government office for reconciliation. In others, governments have sought to establish direct links to the bank so payments are registered directly to taxpayer accounts. But doing that often means building new links between the bank's and the subnational government's information technology (IT) systems (Okunogbe and Pouliquen 2018). Some governments are also introducing mobile payments as a way to limit interaction between taxpayers and tax collectors, but here again it is important to get the technology right to ensure effective reconciliation of payments.

Enforcement

Finally, governments must be willing and able to take enforcement action against taxpayers who do not comply by the relevant deadline. In the absence of effective enforcement, taxpayers have few incentives to comply both because they face little penalty for noncompliance and because they have little confidence that other taxpayers are paying their fair share (Filippin, Fiorio, and Viviano 2013). Research from Sierra Leone found that compliance increased quite dramatically in city council areas where enforcement action was expanded (Jibao and Prichard 2016).

Although reliable and comparable data are not available, there is extensive anecdotal evidence of extremely large uncollected arrears across lower-income countries. Similarly, anecdotal evidence suggests that enforcement actions by government tend to be quite limited (Bodea and LeBas 2016). At times, lack of enforcement is indicative of a technical problem. As just noted, where governments cannot reliably link payments to individual taxpayer accounts, it is impossible to target enforcement action.

Political Challenges

Although property tax systems seem to be plagued by technical challenges, there is mounting evidence that many constraints are political (Grover et al. 2017; von Haldenwang 2017). This factor is most obvious in relation to poor enforcement and arrears collection—neither of which presents insurmountable technical challenges but both of which require confronting powerful interests.

Similarly, the absence of adequate valuation staff or sufficient IT capacity may reflect an unwillingness to recruit appropriately trained staff—or an unwillingness of central governments to allow subnational authorities to do so independently—rather than an inability to do so. Again anecdotally, many governments report significant numbers of unfilled government positions (Balogun 2019). In the same vein, continued reliance on "titling-led" approaches to reform or on extremely resource-intensive approaches to expert valuation of properties often indicates a political reluctance to challenge existing ways of working or to adopt reforms that would likely strengthen taxation (Chirambo and McCluskey 2019; Mohiuddin and Ohemeng, forthcoming).

The political barriers to improved property taxation appear to emerge from three sources: taxpayers, administrators, and elected officials.

Taxpayers. The first and most widely acknowledged political barrier is resistance from taxpayers themselves. In contrast to the taxes often withheld at the source or paid indirectly, the property tax is a visible tax. Its visibility makes it more salient to taxpayers and thus more difficult for politicians to reform (Slack and Bird 2014). Moreover, robust collection of property taxes depends on taxation of the most valuable properties, which are often owned by elites who successfully, actively and passively, resisted increased taxation of their properties (Fjeldstad 2005; Goodfellow 2017). Meanwhile, the close link with local service provision has made it difficult to build popular support for reform wherever the quality of those services is poor, reflecting a lack of trust in governments. Consequently, governments often shy away from effective but politically costly property tax reforms (von Haldenwang 2017).

Administrators. Revenue administrations are the second major source of resistance to improved property taxation because they may benefit from opportunities for collusion and corruption within unreformed systems. Research has begun to document the importance of bureaucratic politics, the scope of informality, and the agency of collectors (Cirolia and Mizes 2019). One case study illustrates how in Pakistan the relationships among field staff, taxpayers, departmental superiors, and politicians shape incentives for reform (Piracha and Moore 2016). There, a dysfunctional property tax system generates a continual stream of modest rents for many of the actors involved, who, in turn, resist any effort to undermine their activities. Field staff collude with taxpayers and both monopolize and manipulate the information they report to their superiors. Senior staff, in turn, often have few incentives to engage in longer-term structural reform because they are frequently rotated among jurisdictions to keep them disempowered and dependent on their political masters. Across jurisdictions, this kind of pattern is repeated, with some administrators resisting reform that threatens rent-seeking activities.

Elected officials. Finally, and closely related, is the resistance or passivity of elected officials. Case studies from emerging economies in Europe and Central Asia demonstrate that property tax reforms often lack a political champion (Grover et al. 2017). This lack of support has three possible sources. First, central governments may express public support for decentralization but in practice seek to limit the fiscal autonomy of local governments. Alternatively, municipal governments may hinder national efforts to revise property tax systems if change implies a loss of power or revenue, as in Slovenia (Žibrik 2016). Second, because of their salience, property taxes are more likely than other taxes to generate political costs and may therefore be more difficult for politicians to support (Cabral and Hoxby 2012). For example, von Haldenwang (2017) documents how Indonesian local governments shied away from using the property tax because of the high political cost. Third, rents from more informal modes of property tax administration—much as in other areas of tax administration—may flow not only to senior administrators but to political officials as well (Hassan and Prichard 2016).

Quasi-Voluntary Compliance

Against this background of both technical and political challenges, it is not surprising that quasi-voluntary compliance among taxpayers remains limited in many places. More broadly, the relative absence of fairness, equity, reciprocity, and accountability appears to further undermine compliance (Fjeldstad 2016).

Part of the foundation for quasi-voluntary compliance is credible, fair enforcement. Few taxpayers will voluntarily comply if they do not believe their neighbors are also paying their fair share (Alm, Bloomquist, and McKee 2016). When undervaluation of properties is coupled with poor enforcement, most owners of high-value properties appear to pay only a fraction of what they should, further undermining public confidence in the fairness and equity of the system (Zebong, Fish, and Prichard 2017). In terms of reciprocity and accountability, case studies consistently report that taxpayers have little confidence that property tax revenues will translate into concrete benefits, despite the obvious potential for drawing such links more clearly (Prichard 2017).

Nuisance Taxes

Strengthening property taxation presents a particular set of technical and political challenges, whereas the parallel challenge facing subnational revenue-raising is the continued prominence of nuisance taxes.

The persistence of these nuisance taxes, despite their unpopularity, appears to reflect a combination of bureaucratic inertia and broader rent-seeking. Once a particular revenue instrument has been created, the public officials tasked with its collection will have incentives to resist abolishment. In the simplest cases, public officials may be defending their small fiefdoms and opportunities to engage in informality. The preservation of such opportunities may be more deeply entrenched where resources flow upward within the public sector—or where central governments wish to expand public sector employment as part of a broader logic of patronage politics but lack the ability to pay adequate salaries. The latter is widely understood to help explain the enormous prevalence of nuisance taxes in the Democratic Republic of Congo, where former president Mobutu famously encouraged state officials to self-finance their salaries and operating costs through informal and predatory taxation (Weijs, Hilhorst, and Ferf 2012).

Reform Progress—and Future Options

Despite the challenges of strengthening subnational revenue-raising and the limited revenue potential relative to national tax sources, there remain compelling reasons to reform subnational revenue collection.

Property taxes, more than perhaps any other tax type, could lead to virtuous cycles of improved compliance and service delivery (Prichard 2017). Whereas for national taxes the connections between additional revenue collection and improved service delivery are often distant and vague, these connections are much more immediate and visible at the subnational level. Meanwhile, although other subnational taxes, fees, and levies tend to be relatively small in absolute terms, they may have significant welfare and livelihood implications for lower-income people (van den Boogaard, Prichard, and Jibao 2019).

The sections that follow describe strategies for achieving the most critical priorities for subnational reform: strengthening property taxes and improving the equity and fairness of other aspects of local revenue-raising.

Enforcement
Strengthening Collection of Property Tax Liabilities
The most basic priority for any property tax reform is likely to be strengthening enforcement of existing property tax liabilities. Moreover, complementary investments in strengthening property identification or valuation will not translate into increased revenue unless they are paired with the technical and political capacity to pursue enforcement of unpaid taxes. It is thus sensible for reformers to first ask whether there is the capacity and political will to strengthen enforcement before undertaking costlier, more extensive reform initiatives.

That said, efforts to strengthen enforcement will often best be paired with other kinds of reforms to ensure fairness and therefore avoid further undermining public trust. An aggressive push to strengthen enforcement when many properties are not captured within property tax rolls, or when many higher-value properties are severely undervalued, could further expand inequities and frustrations. Similarly, an aggressive push to expand enforcement without adopting mechanisms to reduce face-to-face payments or allow for appeals against unfair treatment could lead to increased extraction, albeit distributed inequitably and with significant collection not reaching government budgets.

Moving Away from Title-Led Taxation
A critical question and challenge revolve around whether formal land titling must precede the expansion of property taxation. Historically, many reform projects have adopted a titling-led approach to reform in which public authorities first seek to formally register the ownership of properties and land before subjecting them to property taxation (Deininger 2003). Conceptually, this

approach makes sense: property taxes are almost universally levied on property owners. Practically, however, it has often posed an enormous constraint on property taxation because of both capacity constraints and the pervasiveness of land title disputes in many low-income countries (Boone 2014; Earle 2014; Goodfellow and Owen 2018). Land titling processes can often take years and become politically fraught, creating delays that, in turn, have limited efforts to expand property tax rolls.

Reflecting the challenges of implementing titling-led approaches to building property tax registers, some countries, including Brazil and Colombia, have moved to tax properties even if formal titling is incomplete (Norregaard 2013; Smolka and De Cesare 2006). Conceptually, this approach rests on the idea that one can tax a visible, immovable property without necessarily knowing the identity of the legal owner or having a perfect cadastral survey of the land.

Practically, this approach is straightforward. Freetown, Sierra Leone, initiated its property tax reform (box 6.1) by mapping all properties in the city using satellite imagery (Prichard, Kamara, and Meriggi 2020). When it came time to distribute the tax bills, they were simply addressed to "The Owner" along with the legal instruction that tax liability did not depend on being able to name the owner. Where contact information was available for an owner, that information was also included on tax bills. Owners were also invited to contact the authorities to add their information to the government database; otherwise, the information would be recorded about those making payments. Unlike other taxes, if the owner does not pay and if the owner is not known to the tax authorities, enforcement action can still target the property itself. Instead of struggling to formally register properties as a prerequisite to raising property taxes, such an approach moves ahead in issuing property tax notices and uses the existence of those tax demands as a means of identifying owners.

Implementing Simpler, More Equitable Valuation
In attempting to keep valuation rolls up-to-date and ensure progressivity and equity, countries have explored alternative approaches to valuing properties. Most countries follow some form of market-based valuation, based on either sales or rental values (Martinez-Vazquez and Rider 2008). These market values have traditionally been established either through access to concrete sales and rental data or, where such data are not available, by relying on expert opinion. The latter approach is most common in lower-income jurisdictions, where sales and rental values are often nonexistent, unavailable, or unreliable, but it is enormously costly, capacity-intensive, and prone to subjectivity, collusion, and corruption (Franzsen and McCluskey 2017).

Several alternative strategies seek to lower the cost, complexity, and subjectivity of maintaining valuation rolls:

- *Computer-assisted mass appraisal* approaches develop models that automate the translation of available property characteristics (including historical sales and rental values, where available) into estimated market values. However, a lack of data about properties or about market transactions (including underdeclaration of prices) can make it administratively complex and costly to implement (McCluskey and Adair 1997; McCluskey and Franzsen 2005).

- *Self-assessment* approaches ask taxpayers to declare the value of their property, but they depend on the ability of governments to assess the quality of that information, which is often limited. One frequent result is undervaluation of high-value properties, which tends to make systems regressive (Bird 2015).

BOX 6.1

Points-Based Property Valuation in Freetown, Sierra Leone

In 2019, Sierra Leone's capital, Freetown, implemented a points-based system to simplify and improve the valuation of properties. Before this reform, Freetown, like many other cities across the developing world, used a valuation system from its colonial days. But that manual system, based on floor area, had become obsolete.

The new points-based system relies on a hybrid methodology that uses both surface area and easily observable characteristics to arrive at an estimated market value. It can be thought of as a simplified form of computer-assisted mass appraisal (CAMA). Properties are assigned a standard number of points based on the surface area of the building (measured with satellite imagery), and additional points are awarded for positive features or deducted for negative features, such as location, quality of materials, and access to services. Accurate valuation data for a sample of properties are then used to calibrate the values implied by the scores.

The appeal of the points-based methodology is that it combines the relative simplicity of implementation with significant accuracy and progressivity as well as a high level of transparency to both curb the potential for revenue leakages and encourage voluntary compliance by taxpayers.

Although an evaluation of the new system is still under way, the project doubled the number of properties in the tax register. Moreover, it increased the overall size of the tax base fivefold by expanding coverage and taxing higher-value properties that had long gone undertaxed. The tax payable on the top 20 percent of properties more than tripled, while the burden on the bottom 20 percent was more than halved.

The project has been a technical success, but it also highlights the political challenges and dynamics of reform. Shortly after distribution of the new property tax bills began in 2020, central government authorities intervened and demanded a pause to the reform, while senior staff of the city council began a series of strikes and work disruptions. Formally, they argued the reform had failed to follow the appropriate processes. Informally, most observers believe that the central government's opposition to reform reflected its efforts to curb the fiscal autonomy of the opposition-led city council, and that staff resistance was driven by concerns that a more transparent, objective system would reduce opportunities to engage in informality.

Resistance from the central government eventually forced a six-month pause in the reform program, during which new national guidelines were negotiated. Here the value of a simple, transparent system was put on display: supporters of the Freetown reform were able to make a compelling case, both publicly and in formal government meetings, in favor of the reform. Gradually resistance to reform declined, and it was successfully relaunched in February 2021.

- *Area-based systems* tax parcels at a specific rate per area unit. These systems are far more administrable, but they tend to be highly inequitable because they do not account for differences in the quality of properties (Carolini, Gelaye, and Khan 2020). Although some adjustment is typically made for the quality or location of the property, it is often inadequate in the complex urban environments of lower-income countries. It is not unusual, for example, to encounter large but relatively low-value property compounds within large urban areas (Connolly and Bell 2009; Norregaard 2013).

There is growing interest in models that seek to strike a balance between simplicity and equity. Points-based approaches, for example, use enumeration teams equipped with data collection applications to record the easily observable external characteristics of every property in a given jurisdiction (Grieco et al. 2019). Simple models, which can easily be communicated to and checked by taxpayers, can then be developed to translate those property characteristics into estimated values that broadly mimic market values (Fish 2018; Franzsen and McCluskey 2017). This approach has been most successfully implemented in Sierra Leone (box 6.1), where it has resulted in dramatic increases in both revenue collection and progressivity (Prichard, Kamara, and Meriggi 2020).

Yet simplicity needs to avoid incentives for evasion and related losses. There are plenty of examples in which properties are modified based on the characteristics that affect taxation (Oates and Schwab 2015). By deploying a wide enough range of property features, points-based systems can minimize these incentives so that no single and easily modified feature has a major impact on valuation.

Ultimately, how jurisdictions address the trade-off between accuracy and simplicity will depend on local capacity and political constraints (figure 6.2). Although a market-based valuation may be highly accurate, the data requirements are enormous while transparency can be low. Area-based methods, at the other end of the spectrum, may be simple and transparent but lack accuracy

FIGURE 6.2 **Property Valuation Systems**

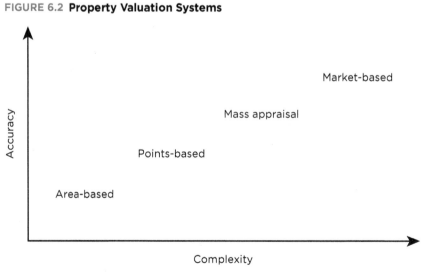

Source: World Bank study team.

and equity. These findings suggest that where registration levels are high, transactions are properly recorded, and technical capacity is good, a market-based valuation or mass appraisal may be possible. Elsewhere, area-based methods or points-based systems may be more appropriate and more readily accepted because of their relative transparency (Collier et al. 2018).

Developing Locally Appropriate Approaches to IT
Virtually all plans to reform property tax systems in lower-income countries now include a push toward automation of administrative systems. This push reflects the obvious advantages of automation for managing large volumes of data; the growing use of satellite imagery and GIS to identify and measure properties; the potential for automation to increase transparency and trust in tax systems; and the growing use of IT systems to translate information about property characteristics into estimated property values using standardized formulas and models (Ali, Deininger, and Wild 2018; Prichard, Kamara, and Meriggi 2020; Richter and Georgiadou 2016).

However, new technologies will not on their own always suffice to ensure better outcomes. Reformers need to assess where new IT systems are likely to be an appropriate target for reform (see box 6.2). In many countries, the property tax administration could be immediately improved even without new IT tools—most obviously where there are large uncollected arrears, property tax registers are incomplete, or broad, poorly enforced exemptions are undercutting the

---

BOX 6.2
Reforming Cadastral Mapping in Kaduna, Nigeria

A pilot assessment of Kaduna's property tax reform under the World Bank's Innovations in Tax Compliance program shifted the direction of reform. Kaduna State, Nigeria, recently abolished its Land Ministry and replaced it with the Kaduna Geographic Information Service (KADGIS). The creation of KADGIS facilitated transformative investments in new information technology systems aimed at modernizing cadaster management and automating the billing system for the ground rent levy. The new systems resulted in an impressive digitalization of the administration.

To ensure that these capabilities were put to good use, the World Bank, at the request of the Kaduna state government, assessed the reform progress. The assessment found that core administrative processes needed to be strengthened in parallel to the ongoing technology reforms to ensure that the benefits of the latter would materialize. The assessment reprioritized the direction of short-term reform toward

- Investing in robust frontline administrative systems
- Improving facilitation by lowering information-related transaction costs
- Strengthening trust, specifically through investments in fairness.

The assessment revealed that new technologies will not on their own always ensure improved outcomes. To sustainably improve tax compliance, they need to be part of a holistic reform.

tax base. It is only where governments have shown a willingness to confront the political barriers to reform—both among taxpayers and within their own administrations—that automation is likely to contribute to significant improvements in outcomes (McCluskey et al. 2018).

When IT systems are reformed, new technologies must be appropriate to the jurisdiction. Particularly where subnational governments administer property tax systems, IT capacity is often quite limited, as are financial resources (McCluskey et al. 2018). An IT system that is practical and administrable for a national revenue agency may be both too complicated and too expensive for subnational governments. And what works for larger cities is unlikely to be the right answer for smaller cities and towns with more limited capacity and resources.

Thus IT systems should be relatively simple, inexpensive, and tailored to the needs of subnational governments. In practice, these requirements call for balancing the benefits and costs of off-the-shelf solutions, often from wealthier countries (which offer reliability, stability, and often shorter rollout times), with more tailored, locally developed solutions (which may be more adaptable and less costly)—see Prichard (2014).

Asymmetric Approaches

Where local authorities differ widely in capacity, asymmetric approaches to the administration of a property tax system could be considered. Larger cities are likely to possess more resources and administrative capacity than smaller jurisdictions, and some may also enjoy more independence in setting policy and deciding on administrative variables for revenue and expenditure management. In such settings, the creation of a national—or perhaps regional—"back office" could be considered to support smaller jurisdictions in the administration of their property taxes. These back-office functions could include valuation and the administration of the fiscal cadaster. Some examples of this approach can be found in the provinces of British Columbia and Ontario in Canada and in Colombia, the Philippines, and Spain. In the Philippines, designated cities administer the property tax, but the province handles administration for local governments that are not cities (Awasthi and Nagarajan 2020).

Facilitation

In facilitating tax compliance, one of the most important places to begin at the subnational level is by allowing payments through banks or mobile money accounts and simplifying the administrative processes associated with making those payments. Such a shift would not have to be limited to property tax payments. They could be applied equally to the payment of business licenses, market fees, or any other fees collected by local authorities (Krolikowski 2014).

The motivations for such a shift are straightforward. First, it seeks to remove opportunities for harassment, extraction, or corruption by government officials. Second, it increases simplicity by making it possible for taxpayers to make payments when they want and at a variety of locations, thereby eliminating the need to travel to sometimes distant government offices. Mobile payments are even better than bank payments because they allow taxpayers to make payments without traveling to a payment point.

The key challenge for subnational governments in setting up such systems often lies not in setting up the payment system itself but in ensuring that such systems are secure and in establishing systems for recording and reconciling those payments to taxpayer accounts. In many localities, payments can be made at banks or through mobile platforms, but taxpayers are then required to travel to government offices to have those payments recorded against their accounts and to receive receipts. More ambitious reform efforts are seeking to establish direct links from banks and mobile money providers to a government's IT systems, so that payments are linked to a unique taxpayer identification (ID) or tax bill ID. This link, in turn, allows payments to be recorded directly in taxpayer accounts without requiring taxpayers to travel to government offices and can allow receipts to be generated directly by banks by mobile phone or email (Jankeeparsad, Jankeeparsad, and Nienaber 2016; Maphumula and Njenga 2019).

Trust

Expansion of property taxation, especially where explicitly targeting more valuable properties, should unambiguously benefit the vast majority of citizens. Intuitively, such reforms should be popular with the public, but largely anecdotal evidence suggests this is often not the case, thereby undermining the broad-based support needed to overcome entrenched resistance to reform by wealthy taxpayers, some administrators and politicians, and higher levels of government (Jibao and Prichard 2016). Addressing the lack of trust stemming from perceptions around fairness, equity, reciprocity, and accountability appears critical to building political support for more effective subnational taxation.

Linking Revenue to Services

A critical part of building trust is an ability to demonstrate, concretely and visibly, that expanded tax revenue is resulting in services and broader benefits for taxpayers (Ali, Fjeldstad and Sjursen 2014; Fjeldstad 2004). This outcome is, in principle, straightforward at the subnational level, where there are many opportunities for using local revenue to support highly visible local services such as road repairs, bus services, improved markets, and expanded and improved sanitation services (Bird 2010).

Available research suggests that when governments can demonstrate those connections, it is possible to build meaningful popular support for more effective taxation and compliance (Prichard et al., forthcoming; Sanogo 2019). For example, Korsun and Meagher (2004) found that market traders in Guinea were more willing to pay taxes if they saw at least part of those revenues reinvested in improving market facilities. Recent experimental evidence from Haiti confirms the same dynamic for property taxation. In collaboration with a local mayor's office, Krause (2020) cross-randomized property tax collection and the provision of a public good (municipal garbage removal). The results are clear: providing the public good increased tax compliance by 27 percent. By contrast, where quality local services are lacking it may be hard to build political support for property tax reform, causing politicians to shy away from trying (von Haldenwang 2017).

Consistent with this logic, in some countries local politicians have successfully allowed improved revenue collection to play a central role in their political platforms by demonstrating broader benefits to the community. For example, successful property tax reform in Bo City, compared with other councils in Sierra Leone, followed significant public education programs and new forums for engagement between taxpayers and the city council (Jibao and Prichard 2015).

Improving Meaningful Transparency

Alongside better efforts to link revenue to better service delivery, governments may benefit from broader investments in enhancing transparency to reinforce popular trust.

Transparency in expenditures. Research suggests that it is not enough to simply give the public access to budget information, which can be extremely difficult for most taxpayers to access and understand. More important are efforts to present revenue and spending information that is widely accessible and easily understandable (Krause 2020). Better still may be forums that facilitate interaction between taxpayers and government to increase public understanding of revenue-raising and public expenditures (Prichard et al., forthcoming).

Most ambitious is the introduction of participatory budgeting processes by which taxpayers can have a direct say in how new revenue is being spent. Although it is hard to establish a causal link between participation and tax compliance, experiences from Latin American cities suggest links between participatory budgeting, less tax delinquency, and higher revenue from property taxation (Biderman and da Silva 2007; Cabannes 2004). A World Bank paper describes how Brazilian municipalities that voluntarily adopt participatory institutions collect significantly higher levels of taxes, especially property taxes, than similar municipalities without these institutions (Touchton, Wampler, and Peixoto 2019). Support for the notion that participation may lead to greater compliance also comes indirectly from recent evidence showing that when taxpayers pay more taxes, they become more engaged in making demands on government for reciprocity (see box 6.3).

Transparency in tax collection. There are also opportunities to improve transparency in revenue collection to build taxpayer trust in the fairness and equity of revenue-raising. Although research on this aspect is limited, anecdotal evidence from the field suggests that taxpayers generally have little confidence that property taxes are assessed consistently and fairly. This is in many ways not surprising because of the subjectivity and opacity of many existing systems.

Simplified systems of assessment that use satellite images to map and identify properties, as well as consistent criteria to assess property value, can help to build trust that everyone is paying their fair share (Ali, Deininger, and Wild 2018; Prichard, Kamara, and Meriggi 2020). Along these lines, one strategy is to make property valuation lists publicly available for scrutiny.

Similarly, limited survey data suggest that taxpayers have little confidence that enforcement will be applied to those who do not meet their tax obligations, particularly when those taxpayers are politically well connected. Highly visible and consistently applied enforcement targeting higher-profile taxpayers—and not just those from the political opposition—can build public confidence (Hasegawa et al. 2013; Jibao and Prichard 2016; Slemrod, Rehman, and Mazhar 2019).

Transparency through recourse. Transparency can also be pursued by introducing appeals processes that offer taxpayers recourse if they feel their tax burden is unreasonable, as well as access to information about how tax assessments are carried out. For property taxes, this would mean allowing taxpayers to request information from the government about the basis for their assessment and to request changes to the assessment if the explanation does not match the

The Participation Dividend of Taxation in the Democratic Republic of Congo

Theories of state-building and taxation argue that a link exists between accountability and taxation—a narrative to which policy makers and donors often appeal when supporting tax reforms. Yet causal evidence for this relationship has long been elusive. A recently published article on property taxation in the Democratic Republic of Congo (DRC) provides such evidence.

Weigel (2020) explores the participation dividend of tax collection in Kananga, the capital city of Kasaï-Central Province in the DRC. In 2016, the provincial government launched its first citywide citizen tax campaign to raise property tax revenue. Citizens were asked to register for property taxation and subsequently to pay the tax. To facilitate evaluation, the government randomized the rollout of the campaign across the city's neighborhoods. Because the rollout was random, the only difference between neighborhoods was whether they were affected by the campaign. Therefore, any differences in measured outcomes could be attributed to the tax campaign.

To test the hypothesis that taxation prompts citizens to become more vocal in making demands on the government, the study examines participation in town hall meetings and anonymous evaluations of the provincial government, which were submitted in drop boxes.

The results are astonishing. By both measures, the tax campaign increased participation. Residents of treated neighborhoods were about 5 percentage points more likely to attend a town hall meeting or to submit an evaluation—a 31 percent increase relative to the control group. The campaign also raised property tax compliance by more than 11 percentage points, from 0.1 percent in control to 11.6 percent in treatment. These findings are consistent with the existence of a virtuous circle between taxation, accountability, trust, and quasi-voluntary compliance.

characteristics of the property. Such a process allows taxpayers not only to challenge their own property assessment but also to access information about the broader functioning of the system.

The same principles could be applied to business licenses or other subnational levies, where the ability to lodge appeals—and to receive transparent, detailed information about the basis for assessment—can address taxpayer concerns that the system is fundamentally inequitable or arbitrary.

Abolishing Nuisance Taxes

Although the greatest revenue potential for subnational governments lies in strengthening property taxes, reforming other aspects of the revenue system can be important as well for building popular trust. This is most obviously true of nuisance taxes, which can appear arbitrary and are often subject to significant informality and negotiation with tax collectors.

These characteristics, in turn, lend themselves to a simple solution: eliminate the wide range of levies and fees that fit the nuisance tax description while focusing attention on larger revenue sources. As noted earlier, in North Kivu in the Democratic Republic of Congo the government could have eliminated 95 percent of all provincial taxes and levies while having only a negligible impact on total revenue collection (Paler et al. 2017).

Efforts to abolish nuisance taxes will, however, likely confront significant political barriers because such taxes usually reflect a combination of (1) inadequate subnational financing of key governance functions and public services and (2) a lack of effective mechanisms for limiting extraction by state officials.

The biggest challenge lies in inadequate governance mechanisms for monitoring and limiting rent extraction. Although revenue from nuisance taxes may be small compared with the overall budget, it can be very material for those who levy the taxes. China's experience with outlawing such practices suggests that efforts are likely to fail if the incentive structure of public servants is not changed (Ang 2020). These challenges point to the importance of ensuring adequate transfers from the central government and simplifying local systems to reduce both incentives and opportunities for informal extraction.

Developing Hybrid Forms of Service Delivery

Many governments considering directions for subnational revenue reform face the complex question of how to respond to informal revenue-raising by nonstate actors. A growing body of evidence indicates that such informal revenue collection, either in cash or in kind, is relatively widespread in many lower-income contexts and that such payments are often more extensive than formal tax payments, particularly for lower-income groups (van den Boogaard, Prichard, and Jibao 2019).

But how should governments respond? On the one hand, there is an incentive to seek to formalize revenue collection and limit informal collection. On the other hand, some forms of informal revenue generation by nonstate actors are widely accepted and supported by citizens and play an important role in local service delivery (van den Boogaard and Santoro, forthcoming). A handful of surveys suggest that informal payments to nonstate actors are often more trusted than payments to the state (van den Boogaard, Prichard, and Jibao 2019).

In broad terms, governments might be best served by seeking to curb the more extractive forms of informal collection and implicitly or explicitly supporting "hybrid" forms of service delivery where appropriate (MacLean 2017; MacLean and Brass 2015; Stel, de Boer, and Hilhorst 2012; Trefon 2009). At times, informal revenue-raising by nonstate actors appears to be relatively extractive and regressive; there is less broad public benefit and little oversight of funds (Meagher 2012, 2016). In these cases, the rightful role of the state is in curbing such informality. But elsewhere, informal revenue generation by nonstate actors may help to fill gaps in service delivery and enjoy significant public legitimacy (van den Boogaard and Santoro, forthcoming). Thus governments might tacitly accept or even endorse those community projects or seek to play a regulatory role that brings additional accountability to the use of these funds. Recent research suggests that this can sometimes be a more efficient way of supporting local service delivery while fostering broader public support for the state (van den Boogaard 2020).

Conclusion

Two challenges underlie weak local revenue systems in many low- and middle-income countries, and they may undermine the broader potential benefits of decentralization. The first is the weakness of property taxes, which should be the foundation of local revenue mobilization but are, in practice, vastly under-collected and often highly inequitable, resulting in the wealthy often paying very little tax. The second is the heavy reliance instead on a regressive, cumbersome, and economically distorting mix of nuisance taxes, user and license fees, and demands for informal payments or contributions to community projects. These payments impose substantial burdens on lower-income groups and undermine broader public trust because of the often widespread corruption and extraction.

The overall message from this chapter is therefore not surprising: local tax reforms are urgently needed to strengthen property taxes while curbing nuisance taxes and more informal forms of extraction. As with other tax types, strengthening property taxes is, in part, a technical challenge. Improved property mapping and registration are needed to identify all those who should be taxed. Valuation and rate setting are complicated by difficulties in assessing property values in an illiquid and nontransparent market. Billing and receipt of payment are logistically challenging and vulnerable to abuse. And the introduction of new IT systems often poses significant challenges, particularly in lower-capacity environments. In turn, there is growing evidence that approaches guided by best practices drawn from wealthier contexts have been relatively ineffective. Although they are successful in some cases, approaches that have relied on quite sophisticated technology, an emphasis on land titling as a precursor to property taxation, and an emphasis on complex models of valuation have tended to disappoint (Deininger 2003; Grieco et al. 2019; McCluskey et al. 2018).

More promising are the technical strategies emerging from recent research; they are better suited to the challenges of lower-income contexts. Property identification for tax purposes may be simplified by disconnecting it from longer-term land titling exercises. Valuation can be simplified by adopting methods such as points-based valuation that emphasize the need to combine equity, administrability, and transparency for taxpayers. IT systems can be simplified to their core functionality, while reform programs may also benefit from focusing first on more basic problems before initiating technology-driven reforms. The right solution will vary across localities. For example, large cities may adopt more complex systems and methods than smaller jurisdictions, and some localities might support hybrid forms of service delivery in which some services are provided by nonstate actors.

In view of advances in research and practice on the technical aspects of reform, the most important challenges of subnational revenue reform thus appear to be political rather than technical. In many cases, property tax collection could be improved immediately simply by making more concerted efforts to collect arrears, enforce taxation of high-income households, or review and update property rolls and property valuation, starting with high-income areas. Further research on the effect that taxpayer perceptions of fairness in the administration of property taxes have on compliance and ways to level the playing field—perhaps via increased transparency—would also be useful.

Reducing the burdens on the poorest and curbing extractive behavior by state officials could technically be easily achieved by eliminating many nuisance taxes and simplifying the rules and processes for other taxes. Facilitation-oriented reforms, such as shifting payments to banks or mobile money, require slightly more technical capacity, but they are nonetheless achievable almost everywhere and could significantly increase trust and reduce abuses. Yet these reforms are frequently not undertaken, or they face sharp resistance from public officials.

Because of the primacy of the political economy context in shaping reform outcomes, one critical question for reformers is how to identify genuine political support for reform. As with other areas of tax reform, the best indicator of such political commitment is likely to lie in the willingness of officials to take politically challenging but technically feasible reform steps early in the process. None of the steps just mentioned requires large new investments. Instead, they rely on a willingness to confront strong vested interests among taxpayers who see little benefit in compliance, public administrators who prefer to maintain rent-seeking opportunities, or public officials at higher levels of government who do not wish to pay what they perceive to be a big political price for strengthening taxation.

Reform strategies should also seek to proactively construct and sustain political support for reform—and in so doing also strengthen the local social contract. Central to such efforts is likely to be building trust by emphasizing equity and fairness, strengthening visible links between revenue collection and service delivery, and expanding accountability. Strengthening fairness and equity—and doing so transparently, including through measures such as public valuation lists—could be useful not only for building support among the broad base of taxpayers, but also for responding systematically to political resistance. Introducing appeals procedures for taxpayers and publicizing enforcement efforts against high-profile taxpayers could also boost tax morale. Most ambitious—and the subject of multiple ongoing studies—are commitments to allocating a share of property tax revenue via participatory budgeting processes or other forms of engagement with taxpayers. These kinds of measures can be strategies for building political support, thereby fostering a virtuous circle of increased collection and improved outcomes for taxpayers.

References

Akpan, I., and K. Sempere. 2019. "Hidden Inequalities: Tax Challenges of Market Women in Enugu and Kaduna States, Nigeria." Working paper, Research in Brief No. 97, International Centre for Tax and Development, Brighton, UK.

Ali, D. A., K. W. Deininger, and M. Wild. 2018. "Using Satellite Imagery to Revolutionize Creation of Tax Maps and Local Revenue Collection." Policy Research Working Paper 8437, World Bank, Washington, DC.

Ali, M., O-H. Fjeldstad, and I. H. Sjursen. 2014. "To Pay or Not to Pay? Citizens' Attitudes toward Taxation in Kenya, Tanzania, Uganda, and South Africa." *World Development* 64: 828–42.

Alm, J., K. M. Bloomquist, and M. McKee. 2016. "When You Know Your Neighbour Pays Taxes: Information, Peer Effects and Tax Compliance." *Fiscal Studies* 38 (4): 587–613.

Ang, Y. Y. 2020. *China's Gilded Age: The Paradox of Economic Boom and Vast Corruption.* Cambridge, UK: Cambridge University Press.

Awasthi, R., T. M. Le, and C. You. 2020. "Determinants of Property Tax Revenue: Lessons from Empirical Analysis." Policy Research Working Paper 9399, World Bank, Washington, DC.

Awasthi, R., and M. Nagarajan. 2020. "Property Taxation in India: Issues Impacting Revenue Performance and Suggestions for Reform." Governance Global Practice Discussion Paper, World Bank, Washington, DC.

Bahl, R. 2009. "Property Tax Reform in Developing and Transition Countries." Paper for Fiscal Reform and Economic Governance project, United States Agency for International Development (USAID), Washington, DC.

Balogun, T. F. 2019. "An Assessment of Property Tax Administration in Edo State, Nigeria." *Indonesian Journal of Geography* 51 (1): 69–77.

Biderman, C., and G. P. da Silva. 2007. "Estimating the Impact of Participatory Budget on Observed Outcomes." In *Proceedings of the 35th Brazilian Economics Meeting*, 70. Recife: Brazilian Association of Graduate Programs in Economics (ANPEC).

Bird, R. 2010. "Subnational Taxation in Developing Countries: A Review of the Literature." Policy Research Working Paper 5450, World Bank, Washington, DC.

Bird, R. 2011. "Subnational Taxation in Developing Countries: A Review of the Literature." *Journal of International Commerce, Economics and Policy* 2 (1): 139–61.

Bird, R. 2015. "How to Reform the Property Tax: Lessons from around the World." Institute on Municipal Finance and Governance Papers on Municipal Finance and Governance No. 21, University of Toronto.

Bodea, C., and A. LeBas. 2016. "The Origins of Voluntary Compliance: Attitudes toward Taxation in Urban Nigeria." *British Journal of Political Science* 46 (1): 215–38.

Boone, C. 2014. *Property and Political Order in Africa: Land Rights and the Structure of Politics*. New York: Cambridge University Press.

Cabannes, Y. 2004. "Participatory Budgeting: A Significant Contribution to Participatory Democracy." *Environment and Urbanization* 16 (1): 27–46.

Cabral, M., and C. Hoxby. 2012. "The Hated Property Tax: Salience, Tax Rates, and Tax Revolts." Working Paper No. 18514, National Bureau of Economic Research, Cambridge, MA.

Carolini, G. Y., F. Gelaye, and K. Khan. 2020. "Modelling Improvements to Property Tax Collection: The Case of Addis Ababa." Working Paper No. 103, International Centre for Tax and Development, Brighton, UK.

Chirambo, A., and R. McCluskey. 2019. "Property Tax Reform Increases Municipal Revenue in Mzuzu, Malawi." Blog post, March 1, 2019, International Centre for Tax and Development, Brighton, UK. https://www.ictd.ac/blog/property-tax -reform-increases-municipal-revenue-in-mzuzu-malawi/.

Cirolia, L. R., and J. C. Mizes. 2019. "Property Tax in African Secondary Cities: Insights from the Cases of Kisumu (Kenya) and M'Bour (Senegal)." Working Paper No. 90, International Centre for Tax and Development, Brighton, UK.

Collier, P., E. Glaeser, A. Venables, P. Manwaring, and M. Blake. 2018. "Land and Property Taxes for Municipal Finance—Version 2." IGC Cities that Work Policy Paper, International Growth Centre, London.

Connolly, K., and M. E. Bell. 2009. "Area-Based Property Tax Systems: Current Practice and Equity Concerns." Working paper, Lincoln Institute of Land Policy, Cambridge, MA.

De Herdt, T., and K. Titeca. 2016. "Governance with Empty Pockets: The Education Sector in the Democratic Republic of Congo." *Development and Change* 47 (3): 472–94.

Deininger, K. 2003. *Land Policies for Growth and Poverty Reduction*. Policy Research Report. Washington, DC: World Bank and Oxford University Press.

Earle, L. 2014. "Stepping Out of the Twilight? Assessing the Governance Implications of Land Titling and Regularization Programmes." *International Journal of Urban and Regional Research* 38 (2): 628–45.

Faguet, J. P. 2014. "Decentralization and Governance." *World Development* 53: 2–13.

Filippin, A., C. V. Fiorio, and E. Viviano. 2013. "The Effect of Tax Enforcement on Tax Morale." *European Journal of Political Economy* 32: 320–31.

Fish, P. 2018. "Practical Guidance Note: Training Manual for Implementing Property Tax Reform with a Points-Based Valuation." African Tax Administration Paper No. 2, International Centre for Tax and Development, Brighton, UK.

Fjeldstad, O-H. 2003. "Fighting Fiscal Corruption: Lessons from the Tanzania Revenue Authority." *Public Administration and Development* 23 (2): 165–75.

Fjeldstad, O-H. 2004. "What's Trust Got to Do with It? Non-Payment of Service Charges in Local Authorities in South Africa." *Journal of Modern African Studies* 539–62.

Fjeldstad, O-H. 2005. "Corruption in Tax Administration: Lessons from Institutional Reforms in Uganda." Working Paper No. 2005: 10, Chr. Michelsen Institute, Bergen, Norway.

Fjeldstad, O-H. 2015. "When the Terrain Does Not Fit the Map: Local Government Taxation in Africa." In *Perspectives on Politics, Production and Public Administration in Africa: Essays in Honour of Ole Therkildsen*, edited by Anne Mette Kjær, Lars Engberg Pederson, and Lars Buur, 147–58. Copenhagen: Danish Institute for International Studies.

Fjeldstad, O-H. 2016. "What Have We Learned about Tax Compliance in Africa?" Summary Brief No. 5, International Centre for Tax and Development, Brighton, UK.

Fjeldstad, O-H., M. Ali, and L. Katera. 2019. "Policy Implementation under Stress: Central-Local Government Relations in Property Tax Administration in Tanzania." *Journal of Financial Management of Property Construction* 24 (2): 129–47.

Fjeldstad, O-H., G. Chambas, and J-F. Brun. 2014. "Local Government Taxation in Sub-Saharan Africa: A Review and an Agenda for Research." Working Paper No. 2014: 2, Chr. Michelsen Institute, Bergen, Norway.

Fjeldstad, O-H., and K. Heggstad. 2012. "Local Government Revenue Mobilisation in Anglophone Africa." Working Paper No. 7, International Centre for Tax and Development, Brighton, UK.

Fjeldstad, O-H., and O. Therkildsen. 2008. "Mass Taxation and State-Society Relations in East Africa." In *Taxation and State-Building in Developing Countries: Capacity and Consent*, edited by D. Brautigam, O-H. Fjeldstad, and M. Moore, 114–34. Cambridge, UK: Cambridge University Press.

Franzsen, R., and W. McCluskey, eds. 2017. *Property Tax in Africa: Status, Challenges, and Prospects*. Cambridge, MA: Lincoln Institute for Land Policy.

Franzsen, R. C. D., and J. M. Youngman. 2009. "Mapping Property Taxes in Africa." *Land Lines* (July): 8–13, Lincoln Institute of Land Policy, Cambridge, MA.

Gervasoni, C. 2010. "A Rentier Theory of Subnational Regimes: Fiscal Federalism, Democracy, and Authoritarianism in the Argentine Provinces." *World Politics* 62 (2): 302–40.

Goodfellow, T. 2017. "Taxing Property in a Neo-Developmental State: The Politics of Urban Land Value Capture in Rwanda and Ethiopia." *African Affairs* 116 (465): 549–72.

Goodfellow, T., and O. Owen. 2018. "Taxation, Property Rights, and the Social Contract in Lagos." Working Paper No. 73, International Centre for Tax and Development, Brighton, UK.

Grieco, K., A. B. Kamara, N. F. Meriggi, J. Michel, W. Prichard, and G. Stewart-Wilson. 2019. "Simplifying Property Tax Administration in Africa: Piloting a Points-Based Valuation in Freetown, Sierra Leone." Summary Brief No. 19, International Centre for Tax and Development, Brighton, UK.

Grover, R., M-P. Törhönen, P. Munro-Faure, and A. Anand. 2017. "Achieving Successful Implementation of Value-Based Property Tax Reforms in Emerging European Economies." *Journal of European Real Estate Research* 10 (1): 91–106.

Hasegawa, M., J. Hoopes, R. Ishida, and J. Slemrod. 2013. "The Effect of Public Disclosure on Reported Taxable Income: Evidence from Individuals and Corporations in Japan." *National Tax Journal* 66 (3): 571–608.

Hassan, M., and W. Prichard. 2016. "The Political Economy of Domestic Tax Reform in Bangladesh: Political Settlements, Informal Institutions and the Negotiation of Reform." *Journal of Development Studies* 52 (12): 1704–21.

Jankeeparsad, R. W., T. R. Jankeeparsad, and G. Nienaber. 2016. "Acceptance of the Electronic Method of Filing Tax Returns by South African Taxpayers: An Exploratory Study." *Journal of Economic and Financial Sciences* 9 (1): 120–36.

Jibao, S., and W. Prichard. 2015. "The Political Economy of Property Tax in Africa: Explaining Reform Outcomes in Sierra Leone." *African Affairs* 114 (456): 404–31.

Jibao, S., and W. Prichard. 2016. "Rebuilding Local Government Finances after Conflict: Lessons from a Reform Programme in Post-Conflict Sierra Leone." *Journal of Development Studies* 52 (12): 1759–75.

Kelly, R. 2000. "Designing a Property Tax Reform Strategy for Sub-Saharan Africa: An Analytical Framework Applied to Kenya." *Public Budgeting and Finance* 20 (4): 36–51.

Kelly, R. 2014. "Implementing Sustainable Property Tax Reform in Developing Countries." In *Taxation and Development: The Weakest Link? Essays in Honor of Roy Bahl*, edited by Jorge Martinez-Vazquez and Richard M. Bird, 326–63. Cheltenham, UK: Edward Elgar Publishing.

Kopanyi, M. 2015. "Local Revenue Reform of Kampala Capital City Authority." Working paper, International Growth Centre, London School of Economics.

Korsun, G., and P. Meagher. 2004. "Failure by Design? Fiscal Decentralization in West Africa." In *Devolution and Development: Governance Prospects in Decentralizing States*, edited by Mwangi S. Kimenyi and Patrick Meagher, 137–96. Aldershot, UK: Ashgate Publishing.

Krause, B. 2020. "Balancing Purse and Peace: Tax Collection, Public Goods and Protests." Unpublished paper, University of California, Berkeley.

Krolikowski, A. 2014. "Can Mobile-Enabled Payment Methods Reduce Petty Corruption in Urban Water Provision?" *Water Alternatives* 7 (1): 235–55.

Lall, A. 2017. "The Federal Reserve and Faster Payments: 'Umbrella' or 'Rails'?" *Journal of Payments and Strategy and Systems* 11 (2): 134–44.

Ligomeka, W. 2019. "Expensive to Be a Female Trader: The Reality of Taxation of Flea Market Traders in Zimbabwe." Working Paper No. 93, International Centre for Tax and Development, Brighton, UK.

MacLean, L. 2017. "Neoliberal Democratisation, Colonial Legacies and the Rise of the Non-State Provision of Social Welfare in West Africa." *Review of African Political Economy* 44 (153): 358–80.

MacLean, L., and J. Brass. 2015. "Foreign Aid, NGOs and the Private Sector: New Forms of Hybridity in Renewable Energy Provision in Kenya and Uganda." *Africa Today* 62 (1): 57–82.

Maphumula, F., and K. Njenga. 2019. "Innovation in Tax Administration: Digitizing Tax Payments, Trust, and Information Security Risk." Study presented at 2019 Open Innovations Conference, Institute of Electrical and Electronics Engineers (IEEE), October 2–4, Cape Town, South Africa.

Martinez-Vazquez, J., and M. Rider. 2008. "The Assignment of the Property Tax: Should Developing Countries Follow the Conventional Wisdom?" International Studies Program Working Paper No. 08-21, Andrew Young School of Policy Studies, Georgia State University, Atlanta.

McCluskey, W., and A. S. Adair, eds. 1997. *Computer Assisted Mass Appraisal: An International Review*. Oxon, UK, and New York: Ashgate Publishing.

McCluskey, W., and R. Franzsen. 2005. "An Evaluation of the Property Tax in Tanzania: An Untapped Fiscal Resource or Administrative Headache?" *Property Management* 23 (1): 43–69.

McCluskey, W., R. Franzsen, M. Kabinga, and C. Kasese. 2018. "The Role of Information Communication Technology to Enhance Property Tax Revenue in Africa: A Tale of Four Cities in Three Countries." Working Paper No. 88, International Centre for Tax and Development, Brighton, UK.

Meagher, K. 2012. "The Strength of Weak States? Non-State Security Forces and Hybrid Governance in Africa." *Development and Change* 43 (5): 1073–1101.

Meagher, K. 2016. "Taxing Times: Taxation, Divided Societies and the Informal Economy in Northern Nigeria." *Journal of Development Studies* 54 (1): 1–17.

Mohiuddin, F., and F. L. K. Ohemeng. Forthcoming. "The Enigma of Central and Local Governments Relationship and the Impact on Property Tax Administration in Ghana." Research project, International Centre for Tax and Development, Brighton, UK.

Moore, M., W. Prichard, and O-H. Fjeldstad. 2018. *Taxing Africa: Coercion, Reform and Development*. London: Zed Books.

Nengeze, M. 2018. "How Local Authorities Can Exploit the Potential for Effective Property Taxes: A Case Study of Harare." African Tax Administration Paper No. 4, International Centre for Tax and Development, Brighton, UK.

Norregaard, M. J. 2013. "Taxing Immovable Property: Revenue Potential and Implementation Challenges." Working Paper No. 13-129, International Monetary Fund, Washington, DC.

Oates, W. E., and R. M. Schwab. 2015. "The Window Tax: A Case Study in Excess Burden." *Journal of Economic Perspectives* 29 (1): 163–80.

Okunogbe, O. M., and V. M. J. Pouliquen. 2018. "Technology, Taxation, and Corruption: Evidence from the Introduction of Electronic Tax Filing." Policy Research Working Paper 8452, World Bank, Washington, DC.

Olken, B., and M. Singhal. 2011. "Informal Taxation." *American Economic Journal: Applied Economics* 3 (4): 1–28.

Olsson, O., M. E. Baaz, and P. Martinsson. 2020. "Fiscal Capacity in 'Post'-Conflict States: Evidence from Trade on Congo River." *Journal of Development Economics* 146: 102506.

Paler, L., W. Prichard, R. Sanchez de la Sierra, and C. Samii. 2017. "Survey on Total Tax Burden in the DRC, Final Report." Study for the Department for International Development (UK), Kinshasa.

Pimhidzai, O., and L. Fox. 2011. "Taking from the Poor or Local Economic Development: The Dilemma of Taxation of Small Informal Enterprises in Uganda." Paper prepared for Africa Regional Project on Improving the Productivity and Reducing Risk of Household Enterprises, World Bank, Washington, DC.

Piracha, M., and M. Moore. 2016. "Revenue-Maximising or Revenue-Sacrificing Government? Property Tax in Pakistan." *Journal of Development Studies* 52 (12): 1776–90.

Prichard, W. 2014. "Using Local IT Solutions to Improve Local Government Tax Reform." Policy Briefing No. 58, Institute of Development Studies, Brighton, UK.

Prichard, W. 2017. "Linking Property Tax Revenue and Public Services." Summary Brief No. 13, International Centre for Tax and Development, Brighton, UK.

Prichard, W., R. Beach, F. Mohiuddin, and V. van den Boogaard. Forthcoming. "The Micro-Links between Taxation and Accountability Initiatives." Working paper, International Centre for Tax and Development, Brighton, UK.

Prichard, W., and P. Fish. 2017. "Strengthening IT Systems for Property Tax Reform." Summary Brief No. 11, International Centre for Tax and Development, Brighton, UK.

Prichard, W., S. Jibao, and N. Orgeira. Forthcoming. "Sub-National Tax Reform and Tax Bargaining: A Quasi-Randomized Evaluation from Sierra Leone." Working paper, International Centre for Tax and Development, Brighton, UK.

Prichard, W., A. B. Kamara, and N. Meriggi. 2020. "Freetown Just Implemented a New Property Tax System That Could Quintuple Revenue." Blog post, May 22, 2020, International Centre for Tax and Development, Brighton, UK. https://www.ictd.ac/blog/freetown-new-property-tax-system-quintuple-revenue/.

Prichard, W., and V. van den Boogaard. 2017. "Norms, Power, and the Socially Embedded Realities of Market Taxation in Northern Ghana." *African Studies Review* 60 (1): 171–94.

Richter, C., and Y. Georgiadou. 2016. "Practices of Legibility Making in Indian Cities: Property Mapping through Geographic Information Systems and Slum Listing in Government Schemes." *Information Technology for Development* 22 (1): 75–93.

Sánchez de la Sierra, R. 2020. "On the Origins of the State: Stationary Bandits and Taxation in Eastern Congo." *Journal of Political Economy* 128 (1): 32–74.

Sanogo, T. 2019. "Does Fiscal Decentralization Enhance Citizens' Access to Public Services and Reduce Poverty? Evidence from Côte d'Ivoire Municipalities in a Conflict Setting." *World Development* 113: 204–21.

Sempere, K. 2018. "Tax Unrest among Market Traders: The Local Side of ActionAid's International Tax Justice Campaign in Nigeria." Working Paper No. 80, International Centre for Tax and Development, Brighton, UK.

Sepulveda, C., and J. Martinez-Vazquez. 2012. "Explaining Property Tax Collections in Developing Countries: The Case of Latin America." In *Decentralization and Reform in Latin America*. Cheltenham, UK: Edward Elgar Publishing.

Siebert, M., and A. Mbise. 2018. "Toilets Not Taxes: Gender Inequity in Dar es Salaam's City Markets." Working Paper No. 89, International Centre for Tax and Development, Brighton, UK.

Slack, E., and R. M. Bird. 2014. "The Political Economy of Property Tax Reform." OECD Working Papers on Fiscal Federalism No. 18, Organisation for Economic Co-operation and Development, Paris.

Slack, E., and R. Bird. 2015. "How to Reform the Property Tax: Lessons from around the World." IMFG Papers on Municipal Finance and Governance No. 21, University of Toronto.

Slemrod, J., O. U. Rehman, and W. Mazhar. 2019. "Pecuniary and Non-Pecuniary Motivations for Tax Compliance: Evidence from Pakistan." Working Paper No. 25623, National Bureau of Economic Research, Cambridge, MA.

Smoke, P. 2019. "Improving Subnational Government Development Finance in Emerging and Developing Economies: Toward a Strategic Approach." Working Paper No. 921, Asian Development Bank Institute, Tokyo.

Smolka, M. O., and C. De Cesare. 2006. "Property Taxation and Informality: Challenges for Latin America." *Land Lines* 18 (3): 14–19, Lincoln Institute of Land Policy, Cambridge, MA.

Stel, N., D. de Boer, and D. Hilhorst. 2012. "Policy Brief. Multi-Stakeholder Service Provision and State Legitimacy in Situations of Conflict and Fragility: Experiences from Burundi, DR Congo, Nepal and the Palestinian Territories." Monograph, Peace, Security and Development Network, Utrecht, Netherlands.

Touchton, M. R., B. Wampler, and T. C. Peixoto. 2019. "Of Governance and Revenue: Participatory Institutions and Tax Compliance in Brazil." Policy Research Working Paper 8797, World Bank, Washington, DC.

Trefon, T. 2009. "Public Service Provision in a Failed State: Looking beyond Predation in the Democratic Republic of Congo." *Review of African Political Economy* 36 (119): 9–21.

van den Boogaard, V. 2020. "Informal Revenue Generation and the State: Evidence from Sierra Leone." PhD diss., University of Toronto.

van den Boogaard, V., W. Prichard, R. Beach, and F. Mohiuddin. Forthcoming. "Enabling Tax Bargaining: Supporting More Meaningful Tax Transparency and Taxpayer Engagement in Ghana and Sierra Leone." *Development Policy Review*.

van den Boogaard, V., W. Prichard, and S. Jibao. 2019. "Informal Taxation in Sierra Leone: Magnitudes, Perceptions and Implications." *African Affairs* 118 (471): 259–84.

van den Boogaard, V., and F. Santoro. Forthcoming. "Hybrid Tax Collection and Public Goods Provision in Somalia: Building the State through Informal Revenue Generation." Working paper, International Centre for Tax and Development, Brighton, UK.

von Haldenwang, C. 2017. "The Political Cost of Local Revenue Mobilization: Decentralization of the Property Tax in Indonesia." *Public Finance and Management* 17 (2): 124–51.

Wanjiru, R., A. Wanyagathi Maina, E. Onsomu, and G. Stewart-Wilson. 2019. "Local Government Property Tax Administration and Collaboration with Central Government: Case Studies of Kiambu, Laikipia and Machakos Counties, Kenya." Working Paper No. 95, International Centre for Tax and Development, Brighton, UK.

Weigel, J. L. 2020. "The Participation Dividend of Taxation: How Citizens in Congo Engage More with the State When It Tries to Tax Them." *Quarterly Journal of Economics* 135 (4): 1849–1903.

Weijs, B., D. J. Hilhorst, and A. Ferf. 2012 "Livelihoods, Basic Services and Social Protection in Democratic Republic of the Congo." Secure Livelihoods Research Consortium; Overseas Development Institute, London.

Zebong, N., P. Fish, and W. Prichard. 2017. "Valuation for Property Tax Purposes." Summary Brief No. 10, International Centre for Tax and Development, Brighton, UK.

Žibrik, N. 2016. "The Process of Introducing a Modern Real Property Tax in Slovenia." *Land Tenure Journal* 15 (2): 83–99.

CHAPTER 7

The Tax and Technology Challenge

Moyo Arewa and Stephen Davenport

The Tax and Technology Challenge

Tax administration is inherently data-intensive, and digitalization has enormous potential to enhance various administrative functions, including the collection, sharing, and use of tax information. Investments in information technology (IT) are thus a central component of many tax reform efforts, and so technology is a central theme of this report. This chapter explores the promise and limitations of digital technologies in greater detail and how revenue authorities use these technologies to address critical gaps in enforcement, facilitation, and trust.

Tax administration tends to be laborious for both taxpayers and tax officials. It often involves face-to-face interactions, the use of manual systems for administration, inadequate human and technical resources, rigid bureaucracy, and insufficient access to or use of data for enforcement and tax compliance purposes. These factors ultimately result in high enforcement and tax compliance costs and therefore relatively high levels of tax noncompliance, fraud, evasion, and avoidance (Okunogbe and Pouliquen 2018).

Digital technologies can, in theory, alleviate many of these challenges. For that reason, countries have invested heavily in technological systems and platforms, including taxpayer portals, automation, integrated databases, e-filing/returns systems, and e-payment platforms (Awasthi et al. 2019; Bird and Zolt 2008; Gupta et al. 2017; Moore 2020; Okunogbe and Pouliquen 2018).

However, these investments do not always deliver, and the potential of digitalization has not always been fully realized. In general, many government-led digital technology and IT projects underperform, suffering from scope creep, benefits shortfalls, cost overruns, or schedule delays. These projects are often abandoned entirely or provide limited benefits because they are misaligned with local contexts and capabilities (Mayega et al. 2019; World Bank 2016). Part of the problem has been implementation. Growing evidence points to the underutilization of existing IT systems and frequent challenges in delivering new systems, reflecting broader bureaucratic, political, social, legislative, and capacity constraints. It is also a question of scope. Most digitalization efforts have focused on improving enforcement and compliance, but less is known about the power of digital technologies to strengthen trust between governments and taxpayers—and thus to reshape the often-challenging politics of reform.

Many countries still struggle to improve their revenue performance or to make their tax systems more efficient and equitable. The shortcomings in digitalization efforts reflect three dynamics:

1. There are inherent difficulties in designing useful technology systems in low-capacity contexts.

2. In retrospect, major IT projects have often proven to be overly ambitious in view of both technical and political constraints.

3. There has been a tendency to expect technology to solve the various challenges facing tax administrations—but with no emphasis on understanding the current processes and the forces inhibiting the effective adoption of technology. As a result, the introduction of new technologies has often been insufficient on its own to overcome the underlying barriers to establishing more effective tax administration (World Bank 2016).

Despite the challenges of digitalization, it is practically impossible to run an effective and modern tax administration without relying on digital technologies and IT systems (Junquera-Varela et al. 2017). Moreover, the economies of many low- and middle-income countries are rapidly becoming more digitally connected, spurred by the ubiquity of mobile technologies, the advent of new citizen-facing digital platforms, increased internet penetration, and broad improvements in IT infrastructure and digital literacy (IMF 2020).[1]

Yet many countries remain in the nascent stages of their digital transformation, which can take several years, if not decades, as it has in many wealthy countries (Awasthi et al. 2019, 67). This lag has vital implications for efforts to digitalize tax administration functions.

In line with previous chapters, this chapter explores a wide range of barriers to successful IT projects and discusses the current landscape of reform efforts, emphasizing the importance of tailoring IT projects to local contexts and capabilities while responding to binding constraints. The chapter does not exhaustively cover the wider government technology ecosystem, nor does it delve deeply into the legal, regulatory, or legislative interdependencies often critical to technology investments. Instead, its focus is specifically on the direct political and administrative dynamics underpinning revenue authorities' investments in digital technologies and IT.

Innovations in Tax Compliance

Barriers to Reform

IT projects are challenging by nature, even in the best circumstances. Regardless of their scale, they tend to confront a range of technical, administrative, political, and economic barriers, although the height of these barriers depends on country-specific realities. Some of the challenges include the broader enabling environment and the need to integrate IT systems into the broader institutional framework, but they also reflect factors related to political economy or capacity that fall outside revenue authorities' remit. Other barriers reflect bureaucratic dysfunction, misaligned incentives, or other weaknesses within the tax administration itself. Technology investments are more likely to succeed if managers and champions of the project understand precisely which factors are most likely to impede progress in their unique context and plan accordingly.

This section, which is by no means exhaustive, examines some of the common challenges that revenue authorities face when implementing digital technology and IT projects. Although the barriers discussed in this section may appear numerous or too high to climb, they are often not unique to revenue authorities in low- and middle-income countries. Governments everywhere struggle to get technology right, and tax administration—including the technology ecosystem supporting it—is especially complex. There is no one-size-fits-all approach to making IT investments succeed, even despite the proliferation of internationally validated IT solutions. A key lesson here is that technology is not a panacea. Rather, it should be accompanied by broader organizational improvements, human capacity development, and business process reengineering to be successful.

Gaps in Technology Infrastructure

IT projects are constrained by the level of sophistication of the underlying countrywide technological infrastructure. Infrastructure limitations could include an unstable electricity supply, inadequate access to computers and other consumer technology, limited availability of data centers, or low mobile and internet connectivity.

Although many low- and middle-income countries are rapidly closing the digital gap and becoming more digitally connected (see figure 7.1), the depth of this connection is still relatively shallow (Gnangnon and Brun 2018; IMF 2020).[2] Moreover, low- and middle-income countries are especially at a disadvantage because of the rapidly evolving advancement of mobile and internet (including cloud) technologies, which are intensifying the adverse effects of weak or outdated infrastructure (World Bank 2021b).

The general improvements in IT and data infrastructure, internet use and quality, and other technology infrastructure are notable but ultimately not enough to create an enabling environment for large-scale, whole-of-government digital transformation projects (IMF 2020). The proliferation of mobile technology does, however, present many novel opportunities for tax administrations, notably by creating new platforms for taxpayers to settle tax liabilities and access taxpayer services. Although several low- and middle-income countries have embraced this avenue for electronic payments and taxpayer engagement, efforts may be constrained by poor-quality mobile connection and, perhaps more

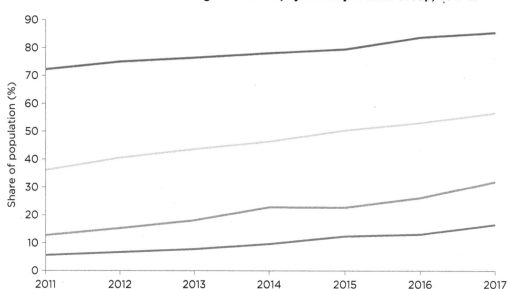

Source: International Telecommunication Union (ITU), World Telecommunication/ICT Indicators Database, https://www.itu.int/en/ITU-D/Statistics/Pages/publications/wtid.aspx (updated July 2021).
Note: Internet use includes use of computers, mobile phones, digital TV, and game machines. HICs = high-income countries; LICs = low-income countries; LMICs = lower-middle-income countries; UMICs = upper-middle-income countries.

important, lack of integration between traditional and mobile payment systems (Awasthi et al. 2019).

The infrastructure gap also extends to cybersecurity and data protection. Many low- and middle-income countries have untenably insecure cyberdefense capabilities. As cyber threats become even more sophisticated and internationalized, revenue authorities, which control and process volumes of sensitive personal and financial data, are especially at risk—even more so without robust investments in systemwide cybersecurity and cyber risk mitigation frameworks and systems (Adelmann et al. 2020).

Digital Literacy and the Human Capacity Gap

Low digital literacy further dampens the positive effects of adopting digital technologies and IT. From the perspective of taxpayers, it limits their ability or desire to use the digital taxpayer platforms and services in which many revenue authorities have invested. Individuals in low- and middle-income countries, where digital literacy and internet penetration levels are lowest, overwhelmingly report not knowing what the internet is or how to use it (Bhuasiri et al. 2016; Okunogbe and Pouliquen 2018; World Bank 2016; Yilmaz and Coolidge 2013). The few who do have internet access do not consume much data, with monthly per capita data consumption sitting at just 0.2 gigabytes (World Bank 2021b).

The digital literacy gap is also a question of affordability. In many low- and middle-income countries, the cost of a smartphone can be up to 80 percent of the monthly income of the poorest, with high taxes and duties making these products even more out of reach (GSMA 2019).

From a tax administration's perspective, the human capacity gap hinders tax officials' ability to make productive use of the various internal technology and data analytics tools now available to revenue authorities, even in low-capacity contexts. Moreover, tax administrations struggle to manage new data systems and use the resulting data to improve core administrative functions, including audit management, revenue forecasting, business intelligence, and fraud detection (Awasthi et al. 2019; Mascagni, Monkam, and Nell 2016).

Tax administrations also struggle to recruit, train, and retain appropriately skilled staff, including the programmers and developers, business and data analysts, statisticians, user researchers, systems integrators, and product and project managers needed to sustain IT projects. This struggle stems, in part, from the frequent immobilization of administrations by inflexible job classifications and salaries (making them uncompetitive in the market for talent), a lack of sustainable employee training programs, and poorly suited civil service frameworks (Awasthi et al. 2019).

Taken together, limited technology infrastructure, low levels of digital literacy, and the human capacity gap suggest that some countries may not be ready to adopt many advanced technological solutions for tax administration. This unreadiness also underscores the need to tailor digital technology and IT projects to local contexts and capabilities lest they maintain or exacerbate existing inequities and tax enforcement and compliance challenges (Awasthi et al. 2019; World Bank 2016).

Political and Administrative Constraints

On the political and institutional fronts, key decision-makers often face perverse incentives when it comes to implementing IT projects and new technologies. Senior bureaucrats, wealthy taxpayers, and politicians—that is, those on whom reform efforts depend to be successful—often face greater incentives to maintain collusive opportunities through rent-seeking networks than to invest smartly in technologies that may improve transparency and accountability (AlphaBeta and BMGF 2018; Bird and Zolt 2008; CIAT 2020; Prichard and Fish 2017). Unlike their counterparts in the private sector, they do not need to respond to market competition and, in some cases, are patronage-based rather than performance-oriented (World Bank 2016, 177).

In some contexts, reform projects are curtailed even before they begin. In other settings, they are disrupted either tacitly or explicitly, ensuring that the final products fail to deliver entirely or fail to provide critical components. The efficiency gains from technology adoption may also threaten existing departmental mandates and budgets within government or the revenue authority (World Bank 2016, 179). Moreover, the high cost and long duration of many technology projects are misaligned with the typical political or election cycles that underpin government decision-making. This combination of political and administrative disincentives can blunt the impact of IT projects unless there is strong, sustained political leadership moving the machinery of government and the tax administration at all levels (see box 7.1).

Weak institutional and administrative structures also effectively entrench inefficiencies and rigidities, while precluding coordination within revenue authorities and with other relevant agencies (Heeks 2003; Kangave et al. 2016, 25). Several reports have emerged of departments competing for both budgetary and

IT-Supported Property Tax Reform in Freetown, Sierra Leone

Many low- and middle-income countries operate ineffective property tax systems, which often fall under the authority of subnational and local governments. These systems, especially in Sub-Saharan Africa, are frequently vestiges of the colonial era, heavily manual, and based on antiquated property valuation methods. One African city has taken bold steps to remedy this situation (also see box 6.1 in chapter 6). In Freetown, Sierra Leone, the International Centre for Tax and Development (ICTD) and the International Growth Centre (IGC) have embarked on an ambitious property tax reform in collaboration with the Freetown City Council (FCC).

Backed by the city's reformist mayor, Yvonne Aki-Sawyerr, the reform began in 2019 with a pilot project to implement the points-based valuation method described in box 6.1. This method departs from both market-based and surface area–based approaches to property valuation. The market-based method can be subjective, especially where data on property market values are not readily available. The surface area–based method, though transparent, does not always pay enough attention to qualitative property features, including location and the quality of structures. The points-based system is a simplified (and more progressive) hybrid of the two methods and reflects both surface area and observable characteristics of properties to estimate market value—and, subsequently, to determine the appropriate mill rate.

Central to these reform efforts is a new information technology (IT) system to facilitate the administration of property taxes, including data collection, valuation, billing, payments, appeals, and enforcement. Reformers have also used technology in simple yet effective ways to build trust and improve the taxpayer experience. These efforts include automating and providing more pertinent information to taxpayers about their tax bills and liabilities, initiating electronic communications with taxpayers, and allowing mobile payments to reduce face-to-face interaction with officials. It also includes digital town halls to improve two-way communication between taxpayers and officials and facilitate participatory budgeting.

Freetown's reform experiences emphasize both the importance of political will and the benefits of situating tax reform efforts—and the IT investments that often underpin them—within the local context, informed by local expertise. The mayor's political courage, coupled with sustained engagement of FCC staff and local vendors, might have prevented reform efforts from faltering in the face of significant administrative and political constraints. Instead, after a successful pilot period, the project is now expanding to the broader population and is expected to generate a five-fold increase in revenue for the city of Freetown.

Source: Prichard, Kamara, and Meriggi (2020).

informational resources in counterproductive ways, resulting in a silo mentality and insufficient horizontal collaboration (Kangave et al. 2016, 25; World Bank 2016, 179). Tax administration and associated IT projects almost always require collaboration and information sharing between various internal and external stakeholders, often within the context of misaligned priorities, information asymmetries, and competing or overlapping mandates (Prichard and Fish 2017, 3). Improving and automating internal and external data sharing is often incredibly challenging because individual units or officials guard access to information. After all, information can be a source of power, an enabler of collusion or corruption, or a mechanism for protecting well-connected taxpayers from tax enforcement (Kangave et al. 2016, 25; Ligomeka 2019, 5).

Lack of IT System Integration
A related but distinct barrier is the lack of integration between IT systems both within revenue authorities and governmentwide. Revenue authorities may operate several IT systems, often with departments or units owning components of a bigger system or running their own departmental IT systems (Ligomeka 2019; Moore 2020). This fact alone does not necessarily impede technology investments. Some countries that benefit from a highly sophisticated digital tax infrastructure also operate multiple systems (Awasthi et al. 2019). They may have one payment system for processing value added tax (VAT) payments and returns; a taxpayer portal to handle registration and collections; another system to manage third-party information internally; and perhaps one overarching integrated tax administration portal and data warehouse that allows staff to access, query, and use data from all the component systems.

The profusion of systems reflects a few realities. The first is that tax administrations have multiple mandates and may require different IT solutions, depending on the type of tax being collected or the nature of the taxpayers themselves. It also reflects the trial-and-error nature of technology investments generally and the need for government agencies, including revenue administrations, to adopt flexible institutional and procurement approaches that respond to changing technologies and dynamics on the ground.

However, the problem in many low- and middle-income countries is that these systems are often incompatible and do not speak to each other, either because of technical barriers—including inconsistent data parameters, low system integration capacity, or little to no scope for application programming interfaces (APIs)—or because of a lack of basic horizontal cooperation. This lack of integration reduces the usefulness of existing IT systems and increases the complexity (and cost) of future technology investments. To improve the chances of overcoming the lack of integration, technology investments should be preceded by assessments of business processes, with a view toward consensus building, bridging departmental silos, and understanding the technical and nontechnical drivers of weak system integration.

"Tech Solutionism" and the Allure of Big IT Projects
Donors and governments alike often prioritize investments in big, costly, and sometimes overly ambitious IT projects that may not reflect on-the-ground system requirements and user needs. Many donors are occasionally more

concerned about the disbursement of funds than the impact and outcome of the technical assistance projects they fund. Likewise, senior politicians and governments may find it beneficial to prioritize grand, citizen-facing digital technologies (such as taxpayer portals and registries) that capture international attention, while investing less in essential back-end reforms that could improve accounting, data sharing, and data management.

Moreover, tax administrations in low- and middle-income countries often have added incentives to invest in technological solutions that improve their scoring on international indexes—for example, the Tax Administration Diagnostic Assessment Tool (TADAT)—even if these solutions may be cost-ineffective or otherwise inappropriate to case-specific user needs and system requirements (AlphaBeta and BMGF 2018; Moore 2020).

Decision-makers may also be moved by "tech solutionism," whereby various technological tools are presented as the solution to administrative and revenue shortcomings that may or may not be technology-related. These decisions are often driven more by the need to demonstrate the usefulness of technology than by assessments of which interventions would be appropriate for or feasible within the local context (Morozov 2013; World Bank 2016, 133). The success of investments in technology by revenue authorities—especially in low-capacity contexts where there may be less fiscal room to experiment with untested technologies—will depend on decision-makers adhering to a careful, continual assessment of their tax administration's technical and administrative requirements or risk committing resources to big IT solutions that are unsustainable or entirely ill-suited to their needs.

Procurement Issues

The success of technology investments depends heavily on how the technology is procured, but many administrations do not get procurement right. Government IT projects often suffer from inflexible and linear procurement and development procedures that are incompatible with local capacity. Decision-makers also face several procurement options, each with benefits and drawbacks. Given the importance of procurement arrangements to IT projects' outcomes, this section considers some of these alternatives and how making the wrong procurement decision can limit the impact of technology investments.

International versus Local Vendors

When procuring IT systems, revenue authorities must often decide whether to employ international vendors—which is typical for large donor-funded projects—or local vendors. International vendors often provide technically sound software solutions. However, these solutions tend to be expensive and sometimes poorly suited to local contexts and needs because of their complexity, high cost, and the broader challenges of ensuring sustained, long-term support. They often require revenue authorities to remain dependent on vendors that may be inaccessible or otherwise unable to provide the type of hands-on IT development and change management support critical to success.

Although working with international vendors tends to come with specific challenges, there are some notable exceptions. Over the past three decades, several countries have successfully introduced the Automated System for Customs

Data (ASYCUDA) for customs management and the Debt Management and Financial Analysis System (DMFAS) for debt management. These noncommercial systems developed internationally by the United Nations Conference on Trade and Development (UNCTAD) have become global standards. In the Philippines, a World Bank–supported computerization project in the 1990s included development of the second-generation ASYCUDA++, and several African countries now rely on this system—or the third-generation ASYCUDA World—for customs management (Engelschalk 2000). Some equally unique international commercial software solutions include Sogema Technologies' SIGTAS system for integrated tax and income tax management. This system has been deployed in dozens of countries in Sub-Saharan Africa and Latin America and the Caribbean.

Despite the appeal of some internationally developed systems, at times local private sector vendors may be better placed to meet the context-specific IT needs and requirements of revenue administrations. Such vendors tend to cost less, are more flexible and less "tied in," and because of their proximity to end users, they can better scope the scale of the technological gap and engage with governments to ensure that the solutions can be sustained (Engelschalk 2000). However, their solutions may be less cutting-edge, and they may otherwise lack the capacity to provide enterprisewide solutions for tax administration.

The choice between international and local vendors is necessarily dependent on revenue authorities' resource constraints and realities. International vendors are not inherently efficient, just as local vendors are not always convenient. Where administrations are especially constrained by weak in-country capacity, it may be prudent to contract international vendors with a proven track record across various contexts. Likewise, where administrations benefit from a somewhat established IT sector, it may be just as prudent, and possibly much cheaper, to contract local vendors and software firms to provide technology solutions.

The choice of option does not have to be binary. In Nigeria, SIGTAS provides the core integrated tax administration system used by the Federal Inland Revenue Service (FIRS) and several state revenue agencies, but a local software firm, SystemSpecs, provides the most prevalent electronic payments system (Remita) for business-to-government (B2G) and person-to-government (P2G) payments.[3]

Commercial Off-the-Shelf versus Custom-Built Solutions

Whether to build solutions in-house (custom-built) or opt for commercial off-the-shelf (COTS) solutions depends heavily on the technological maturity and capability of the revenue authority. COTS solutions often face significant implementation challenges in low- and middle-income countries with weak foundational technological infrastructure. These countries' processes and capacities do not always adequately accommodate existing commercial solutions. COTS systems tend to require significant customization and reengineering of existing business processes, which can be cost-prohibitive in low-capacity environments. Governments also encounter financial, political, and technical difficulties when integrating a COTS solution into existing systems and may be unable to mount the sustained effort required to implement a solution over several years or possibly decades (OECD 2019, 5).

Despite the drawbacks of COTS solutions, they are the most prevalent mode of procurement among revenue authorities in low- and middle-income countries (figure 7.2). Although these solutions are more costly initially, the costs often level out sooner than those for custom-built solutions, which may become more expensive as maintenance and system requirements balloon. COTS solutions are also more up-to-date with industry standards and best practices. They are rigorously tested and have shorter implementation cycles, and they tend to be fully integrated enterprise solutions capable of streamlining both back-end and front-end functions. Nevertheless, many low- and middle-income countries often do not reap these benefits either because of their inchoate institutional and technological contexts or because of the high costs of customization.

By contrast, custom-built solutions can offer revenue authorities greater control and flexibility at lower initial costs while ensuring that solutions are locally relevant. However, they require sizable internal expertise that may not be available or easily retained in many tax administrations. They also often do not yet conform with best practices, take much longer than COTS solutions to reach full development, and suffer system maintenance challenges of their own.

Ultimately, no one approach is inherently perfect, and tax administrations often make these decisions based on unique budgetary, political, and circumstantial factors rather than just on specific technical merits. Many IT projects necessarily arise from a hybrid of various procurement options. For example, administrations may choose an international vendor or COTS system, which provides a sophisticated technical backbone, but also increases investment in either (1) developing local ownership and capacity to support the system or (2) procuring versions of the system that can be simplified to reflect local realities and constraints. Decision-makers should assess their own tax administration's

FIGURE 7.2 **Adoption of Tax Management Information Systems in Low- and Lower-Middle-Income Countries, by Type, 2017**

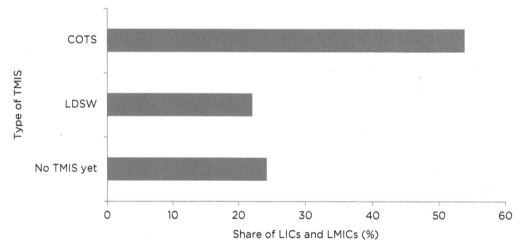

Source: World Bank Public Financial Management Systems and eServices Global Dataset, https://datacatalog .worldbank.org/dataset/public-financial-management-systems-and-eservices-global-dataset (last updated 2017). *Note:* COTS = commercial off-the-shelf; LDSW = locally developed software; LICs = low-income countries; LMICs = lower-middle-income countries; TMIS = tax management information system.

capabilities and user needs, as well as the total cost of ownership of the alternative chosen, before committing significant resources to technology investments.[4]

Open-Source versus Closed-Source Software

Tax administrations must also decide between procuring and developing open-source or proprietary closed-source software products. Again, there is no one correct approach. Tax administrations and their IT vendors tend to follow the traditional closed-source software development model, which often requires rigorous coordination and sometimes lacks transparency about the source code and how the system is built. Although closed-source software may be more costly, rigid, and opaque, it also may be better standardized and more reliable and secure. Tax administrations may find closed-source software solutions more practical if their unique circumstances call for more standard, rigorously tested, and established systems.

By contrast, open-source software (OSS) solutions may be practical for tax administrations whose local contexts and system requirements demand more cost-effective, flexible, and innovative solutions. OSS is developed and tested openly, with transparent access to the source code, thereby improving oversight and accountability about how the system is built (Joia and Vinhais 2017; Paulson, Succi, and Eberlein 2004). It often requires no license fee, and its quality can be evaluated and reviewed by a community of programmers—a fact that may encourage innovation and reduce the costs of development for tax administrations.

Limits of Rigid and Linear Procurement Processes

IT development and procurement are also limited by rigid and heavily bureaucratic procurement processes that prevent revenue authorities from engaging with vendors flexibly and iteratively. Traditionally, vendors—whether local or international—are selected based on requests for proposals (RFPs) with detailed specifications and milestones that do not always reflect user needs or IT requirements and can be difficult to alter even when new information or requirements surface (Bhatnagar 2009; Dunleavy and Carrera 2013; Fountain 2001; World Bank 2016). This linear "waterfall" style of development is a common and reflexive practice in government, owing mainly to the need for accountability and control during the procurement process.

However, given the complexity of tax information systems and the need to secure buy-in from local staff, this style of development process often creates systems that are not well aligned with users' needs and over which users feel little ownership. In fact, this approach runs counter to the nimbler, more "agile" procurement and development procedures using RFPs that are not too prescriptive in the early stages. This alternative approach reflects a rigorous, adaptive, and continual requirements-gathering process; a clear-eyed assessment of existing capabilities and needs; and a well-defined, long-term digital strategy that accounts for potential economic, political, and technological limitations.

Rigid procurement processes can also be counterproductive for ensuring accountability and closing channels for corruption. The opaqueness of inflexible IT procurement processes often plays into a status quo that incentivizes corruption and entrenches weak accountability. This dynamic remains the same even when procurement and contract management systems have been automated or otherwise digitalized, suggesting that potential efficiency gains from e-procurement systems will be elusive without concomitant reforms of the processes that underpin the system (Kochanova, Hasnain, and Larson 2016).

Weak Project Management

IT projects are time-consuming and complex, even under ideal circumstances. Influenced by the intense revenue pressures facing tax authorities, many reform programs underestimate the complexity of IT projects and fail to adequately plan for project management, change management, development and testing, staff training, and taxpayer sensitization (Prichard and Fish 2017). The length and complexity of IT projects (some taking up to 15 years) create various project risks, including scope creep, cost overruns, and schedule delays (Awasthi et al. 2019).

These risks were evident in a World Bank–supported tax computerization project in Thailand. The 1992 project set out to overhaul Thailand's tax IT system, but it suffered from lack of strategic planning, fuzzy objectives, poor project preparation and planning, insufficient and overprescribed technical specifications, and inadequate procurement and project management (Barbone et al. 1999). Without the proper project and change management protocols in place—including adaptive, scrum-style development and sequencing; education; marketing; engagement; and training—the inherent complexities of IT projects are bound to multiply.

Reform Progress—and Future Options

Despite the enormous potential of technology to transform tax administration, investments in IT have often yielded disappointing results, in part because of some of the barriers mentioned. Findings on the performance of IT systems in low- and middle-income countries are sparse not only because of the inadequate evaluation of such systems but also because of the difficulty in measuring and demonstrating impact. This section reviews the available evidence on the various IT investments that revenue authorities in low- and middle-income countries can make or have made to improve tax enforcement capacity, facilitate compliance, and build trust.

Enforcement: IT for Audits, Data Sharing, and Access to Electronic Transaction Data

Revenue authorities have long targeted their reform efforts at enforcement and have developed increasingly sophisticated tools to deter tax noncompliance. This focus on enforcement extends to IT projects aimed at monitoring taxpayers and accessing the information—including third-party—needed to collect taxes and detect and punish malfeasance.

In many countries, the emphasis on enforcement necessarily considers wrongdoing not only by taxpayers but also by tax officials (for example, through internal audits) for whom opportunities and incentives to engage in bribery and corruption are rife. As a result, IT projects meant to bolster enforcement capacity often involve two types of investments. The first seeks to improve automated data-sharing protocols, facilitate accessing third-party information, boost audit and risk management capacity, and improve debt collection methods for various types of taxes. The second seeks to enhance the transparency and auditability of internal processes to incentivize good administrative performance and reduce the scope for collusion and corruption.

Building Audit Capacity

Revenue authorities have employed various IT tools to improve their capacity to assess the veracity of taxpayers' self-declared returns. These efforts sometimes include setting up risk-based audit protocols and improving automation to flag inconsistencies in taxpayers' declarations. Specifically, to better identify non-compliant taxpayers and the riskiest returns, a sophisticated risk-based audit procedure uses risk-scoring algorithms to create reference points with which to quantify and compute risk for every taxpayer (Junquera-Varela et al. 2017). These algorithms can be fed with information on taxpayers' characteristics, including age, profession, marital status, assets, and liabilities.

In Malaysia, as part of its Self-Assessment System (SAS), the tax authority replaced its manual audit screening and selection processes with a comprehensive audit management module, which was a more efficient risk-based audit selection system. Similarly, Tanzania's tax administration adopted a risk-based audit management module to replace its manual system. In both countries, the switch to risk-based audit management had positive effects on revenue collection and tax administrations' ability to detect and penalize fraud, tax avoidance, and tax evasion (Vellutini 2011).

In addition to the appropriate technology tools, improving auditing capacity depends on efficient statistical and information processing capabilities, as well as on having the appropriate audit selection systems and electronic historical tax return data. Because of human capacity limitations and political constraints, many countries struggle to either develop or make good use of audit management software and therefore to implement effective risk-based audit systems (Bird and Zolt 2008; Kangave et al. 2016).

This capacity gap inhibits revenue authorities from conducting advanced or just basic analytical and data mining work, thereby limiting the scope for enforcement even when the necessary data are being collected and shared (Mikuriya and Cantens 2020). Analytical capacity also strengthens the deterrent effect of auditing by increasing taxpayers' expectations that avoidance or evasion will be discovered and punished. Without the appropriate IT tools and complementary human capacity, the revenue authorities in low- and middle-income countries will continue to have difficulty obtaining and analyzing the vast quantities of data necessary for tax enforcement (Awasthi et al. 2019).

Enhancing Data Sharing

In principle, digital technologies and IT can automate and facilitate data sharing across departments, which can improve identification of tax noncompliance. A key determinant of audit capacity is the extent to which revenue authorities have access to multiple sources of information both within and outside the tax administration. Outside, this access might involve commercial banks, customs, subnational authorities, or the central bank sharing data with the revenue authority (Dogan 2011; Moore 2020). In practice, however, effective data sharing requires more than a functioning IT system. It also depends on both conducive administrative processes and a political commitment to ensure collaboration between the relevant agencies and departments.

On the process and technical side, effective data sharing requires linking systems within and across government and having clear, unified identifiers and parameters that permit data matching and interoperability. It also requires developing information systems and processes capable of maintaining and distributing accurate and complete data about taxpayers. A vital consideration here is building effective data-sharing procedures, while simultaneously protecting taxpayers' data and confidentiality.

On the political side, data sharing can undermine the interests of actors within the relevant agencies or otherwise threaten the interests of those who are avoiding taxes. As a result, there may be political resistance to authorizing the level of data sharing that IT systems can facilitate.

Moreover, a narrow focus on strengthening tax enforcement through improved IT tools for data sharing can backfire. Although in Ecuador third-party information resulted in businesses declaring more revenue, it also induced them to claim larger deductions, thereby limiting the positive effect on tax revenue and demonstrating the importance of complementary investments in facilitation and trust (Carrillo, Pomeranz, and Singhal 2017).

Nevertheless, many countries have made notable progress in improving data sharing and audit management, with vital lessons for other revenue authorities in low- and middle-income countries. In the Philippines, customs and internal revenue databases have been linked on the back end and used to verify VAT declarations and imports successfully. In Peru and South Africa, sophisticated data mining tools have been employed to reduce customs fraud and tax evasion by up to 14 percent (Bird and Zolt 2008). In Chile, a randomized study of over 400,000 firms found that better access to and use of third-party information on VAT compliance had positively altered VAT compliance and the firms' audit probability (Pomeranz 2015).

Meanwhile, evidence from a World Bank study in Madagascar demonstrated that third-party information was somewhat effective in curbing customs fraud but insufficient to counteract entrenched perverse incentives. The study found that providing better third-party information to customs inspectors increased the probability of inspection by 10.3 percentage points and fraud detection by 21.7 percentage points (Chalendard et al. 2020). This improvement was especially noticeable for inexpensive and lower-stake declarations that did not offer lucrative opportunities for collusion. Even better, more precise information also increased tax revenue sizably, by 5.2 percentage points.

However, this positive effect was neutralized because officials had greater incentives to collude than to enforce taxes and use the available information. The officials themselves were poorly monitored, and honesty was seldom rewarded (Chalendard et al. 2020). Overall, Madagascar's efforts to combat customs fraud reinforces the importance of political economy factors and behavioral incentives, in addition to direct technical or technological interventions.

Uganda's experience further illustrates that even where technological solutions have been put in place to facilitate data sharing, improvements in practice are often more limited. The Uganda Revenue Authority (URA) developed an in-house data warehouse, e-Hub, to facilitate data sharing and decision-making between its two core systems: e-tax (for domestic tax purposes) and ASYCUDA World for customs management (Mayega et al. 2019). E-Hub also manages data from the URA's temporary road user licensing database (TEVIES), its e-procurement system, its fleet management system, and its enterprise resource planning (ERP) system. Nonetheless, despite being a positive development, the e-Hub platform has not necessarily improved the quality of data sharing within the URA or its ability to use this information for enforcement purposes (Mayega at al. 2019).

The URA has also invested heavily in other interagency data-sharing initiatives to enhance its capacity to tax high-net-worth individuals (HNWIs). It has entered a tripartite arrangement—the Taxpayer Register Expansion Program (TREP)—with the Kampala Capital City Authority (KCCA) and the Uganda Registration Services Bureau (URSB) to improve data sharing between the respective agencies. It has also automated internal and external services, upgraded its electronic tax system's functionality, established a Joint Compliance Committee (JCC), and reengineered its business processes. These efforts have yielded some successes: URA has better identified and taxed HNWIs, and work is well under way to improve data sharing both within and outside the URA. However, more evidence is needed to determine the effectiveness of these efforts (Kangave et al. 2016).

Meanwhile, difficult political realities and challenges continue to curtail data sharing internally and between the URA and other key organizations, including the Bank of Uganda and the Ministry of Lands (Kangave et al. 2016). Various URA departments have misaligned priorities and performance targets and therefore compete in ways that create counterproductive silos and an inherent unwillingness to collaborate. Furthermore, the URA's ability to access third-party information is still severely limited despite positive reforms. It struggles to collaborate with commercial banks because of a combination of legal and political factors, with the banks either refusing to share data or colluding with customers. Even when structural barriers are less pronounced, such as between the KCCA and the URA, information sharing is still constrained by incompatible information systems, inaccurate or incomplete registries, and limited staff capacity to analyze the available data (Kangave et al. 2016).

Relative to Uganda's efforts, Turkey has successfully implemented several digital tools for enforcement, compliance and risk management, data mining, data sharing, and data warehousing—especially regarding the VAT. Its warehousing system effectively collects information from both public and private organizations (including commercial banks) to combat VAT fraud and misreporting.

Turkey's success stems, in part, from its ability to conduct extensive data-matching exercises (often in real time) using the appropriate digital tools and processes, as well as a permissive cross-agency administrative environment. The results have been noteworthy. In June 2008, up to 140,000 registered taxpayers had omitted credit card sales information from their VAT returns, with the system flagging discrepancies in 20 percent of transactions from 60,000 taxpayers and in up to 5 percent of transactions from 100,000 taxpayers.[5] But within only two months of data matching and risk management facilitated through the data warehouse, a substantial reduction in discrepancies occurred. By June 2009, fewer than 20,000 taxpayers had a discrepancy rate of greater than 20 percent (Dogan 2011). Turkey's experience illustrates the potential of IT-enabled risk management and data sharing to transform compliance management and tax enforcement more broadly.

Improving Access to Electronic Transactions Data
Many revenue authorities in low- and middle-income countries have invested heavily in IT solutions that improve access to electronic transactions data but with a minimal impact on revenue performance or administrative efficiency. These efforts have often focused on VAT enforcement, which has been driving revenue gains in many of these countries. For example, countries have invested in technologies that enable customs authorities to track and monitor goods coming through their borders. However, not much is known about the extent to which these technologies are successful. Some evidence points to their positive impact on VAT compliance, but a broader scan of the literature suggests that the results are mixed (Ali et al. 2015; Pomeranz 2015).

Technologies such as electronic fiscal devices (EFDs), electronic billing machines (EBMs), and electronic invoices have been introduced in several low- and middle-income countries to simplify enforcement and compliance. These devices automatically transmit business transaction information to revenue authorities and are critical for curbing the shadow economy and informality and for collecting and enforcing the VAT (Fjeldstad et al. 2018).

However, despite the advantages of even well-intentioned, well-conceived efforts to propagate EFD use, such efforts are often hampered by high costs of adoption, low levels of digital literacy, and broader administrative challenges that prevent the productive use of data from EFDs. For example, evidence from Tanzania indicates that the government's introduction of EFDs did not improve VAT collection as expected. The growth rate of VAT collection ranged from 13.5 percent in 2010 to 21.7 percent in 2017, and the average growth rate of 16.8 percent fell below the expected 18 percent during the same period (Fjeldstad et al. 2018).

These results mirror those from other countries that have introduced EFDs, and even when significant increases in VAT revenue were recorded, these gains were almost always below expectations (Casey and Castro 2015). The Tanzania study found that the "last-mile problem" of the VAT limits the effectiveness of EFDs. Customers at the end of the supply chain have few incentives to request VAT receipts, which, in turn, gives businesses and suppliers few incentives to request VAT receipts themselves (Fjeldstad et al. 2018).

In Ethiopia, the Ethiopian Revenue and Customs Authority (ERCA) recorded higher VAT and income tax revenue after the introduction of electronic sales registration machines (SRMs). But these gains were limited by two factors: (1) ERCA's low capacity to use data from the SRMs to enforce tax laws and (2) strategic adjustments in taxpayer behavior to evade enforcement (Mascagni, Mengistu, and Woldeyes 2018).

More positively, the Rwanda Revenue Authority (RRA) introduced EBMs in 2012, and by 2014 close to 80 percent of all VAT-eligible firms had registered and activated an EBM, raising VAT payments by an average of 5.4 percent. Nevertheless, other research found significant discrepancies in taxpayers' VAT declarations to the RRA (Mascagni, Mukama, and Santoro 2019). Many taxpayers found the EBMs either challenging or simply too difficult to use, and they had poor perceptions of the RRA's capacity to process information and discover discrepancies. These challenges also reflect more general administrative constraints within the RRA, especially regarding record keeping and information management.

The experiences in Tanzania, Ethiopia, and Rwanda demonstrate the limitations of enforcement capacity in many low- and middle-income countries as well as the broader complexities of even well-conceived IT projects.[6] They also highlight the importance of situating otherwise isolated technology investments—such as EFDs—within comprehensive tax compliance and enforcement reforms. An International Monetary Fund (IMF) study of 19 tax administrations that introduced EFDs concluded as much: EFDs were successful in contexts where they were aligned with broader compliance improvement strategies and complementary investments in developing the administrative capacity to act on EFD-generated data (Casey and Castro 2015).

Beyond EFDs and indirect taxes, many revenue authorities are increasingly availing themselves of sophisticated data analytics tools to detect income tax evasion (for more on new and emerging technologies, see box 7.2). For example, in 2016 India initiated Project Insight, a robust data analytics and compliance management system provided in collaboration with Larsen & Toubro Infotech, an Indian IT firm. The program combines data integration, warehousing, management, and analytics with extensive data exchange arrangements between the Income Tax Department and other government departments and agencies. Project Insight also provides a centralized compliance processing center and portal to support taxpayers, encourage voluntary compliance, and inhibit noncompliance. Although the project is still in its early stages and thus little is known about its effectiveness, it embodies the ever-growing role of advanced data analytics for enforcing taxation (*Economic Times* 2019).

BOX 7.2

The Promise of New and Emerging Technologies

The onset of new technologies such as digital identification (ID), artificial intelligence, big data, and blockchain present many new opportunities—and challenges—for e-government and domestic resource mobilization. What are the promises and limitations of some of these technologies, especially in low- and middle-income country contexts?

Digital ID systems could change the way revenue authorities and national identification agencies handle the identification and registration of taxpayers, enabling people to access taxpayer services who otherwise could not. In many middle- to high-income countries—including Albania, Belgium, Estonia, France, India, the Republic of Korea, Moldova, Pakistan, and Singapore—digital ID technologies have all but replaced legacy physical ID systems and are being used to support social welfare programs, human resources, and election administration.

(Continued)

The Promise of New and Emerging Technologies *(continued)*

In many lower-income countries, however, adoption remains low. Only 18 percent of these countries have a digital ID scheme for identification alone. Fifty-five percent have some form of digital ID system for specific services such as voting, cash transfers, or e-health. Only 3 percent have functional and cross-governmental digital ID systems that enable citizens to access a wide variety of public services. To capitalize on the potential of digital ID, the revenue authorities and governments of low- and middle-income countries will need enabling legal and regulatory frameworks and a clear strategy for interconnectivity and interoperability across various government agencies and databases.

Big data and advanced analytics could improve the way revenue authorities process and analyze the data at their disposal. These technologies can enhance governments' capacity to provide real-time information to taxpayers, improve audit selection criteria and execution, and better target specific taxpayer needs to improve service delivery and guide tax compliance. Ultimately, big data and advanced analytics could enable revenue authorities to extract greater value from existing information, while providing new tools to augment enforcement and detect tax avoidance, evasion, and fraud.

So far, low- and middle-income countries have been unable to capitalize on this promise. Revenue authorities must, then, invest in their data processing, automation, and data management capacity. They also must invest in building a data-driven administrative environment (backed by improved horizontal collaboration within the tax administration) and training staff to build the necessary analytical capacity.

Blockchain and other distributed ledger technologies also offer much potential for e-government generally and tax administration specifically. Blockchain use has emerged across government services, including information security, land registration, evidence and identity validation, transfer payments, voting, and tax administration and tax compliance. By providing immutable distributed ledgers, blockchain could reduce transaction costs, mitigate fraud and security risks, and speed up information sharing and transaction processing.

For tax administration, this could have specific implications for filing, refunds and payments, registration and identity management, auditing, third-party data sharing, and value added tax enforcement, among other functions. However, evidence on the utility of blockchain for revenue administration, particularly in low- and middle-income countries, is scarce. It is also unclear whether blockchain offers any benefits to tax authorities beyond those of a centralized, traditional database.

Sources: Baisalbayeva et al. (2019); OECD (2016); World Bank (2016).

Facilitation: Better Digital Services to Reduce Compliance Costs

Even though enforcement remains the bedrock of reform strategies, revenue authorities have committed significant reform resources to facilitating tax compliance. This is a shift in thinking from the last two decades that now recognizes taxpayers as customers and revenue authorities as service providers.

Compliance reforms tend to involve initiatives to simplify filing, refund, and payment procedures and provide taxpayers with better information about the tax system and their tax liabilities. These efforts often aim to (1) reduce the costs to taxpayers of meeting their tax obligations; (2) manage administrative burdens for revenue authorities; and (3) limit the scope for corruption and harassment of taxpayers.

Digital technologies have been at the forefront of compliance facilitation initiatives. Most notably, many revenue authorities, including those in low- and middle-income countries, have invested heavily in taxpayer portals that enable electronic registration, automated tax management, and e-filing and e-payment services. Thirty-two percent of low- and middle-income countries had introduced e-filing by 2015, and many more have done so since then (figures 7.3 and 7.4), while 84 percent of countries globally have automated tax management systems. E-filing and e-payment systems are the most characteristic feature of tax reforms in low- and middle-income countries (Kochanova, Hasnain, and Larson 2016; Okunogbe and Pouliquen 2018; World Bank 2016).

Introducing E-filing and E-payments

Moves toward greater automation in several countries indicate that e-filing and e-payment platforms do indeed improve revenue performance across various types of tax (IMF 2020):

- *Kenya* introduced its iTax system in 2014, fully integrating and automating the Kenya Revenue Authority's domestic tax functions and providing new electronic avenues for settling tax liabilities. By some metrics, Kenya's iTax has been a success. It has reduced revenue collection costs and has enabled real-time revenue and audit monitoring (Ndung'u 2019).

FIGURE 7.3 Diffusion of E-filing and E-payment Services in Low- and Lower-Middle-Income Countries, 2017

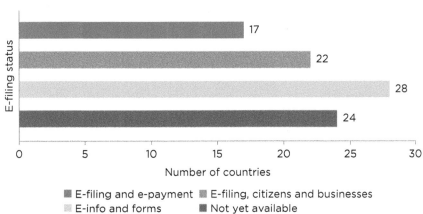

Source: World Bank Public Financial Management Systems and eServices Global Dataset, https://datacatalog.worldbank.org/dataset/public-financial-management-systems-and -eservices-global-dataset (last updated 2017).

FIGURE 7.4 **Global Diffusion of E-tax Systems, by Type, 1984–2017**

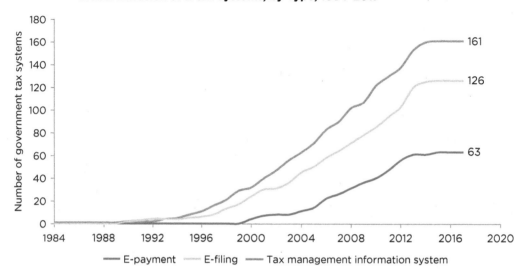

Source: World Bank Public Financial Management Systems and eServices Global Dataset, https://datacatalog
.worldbank.org/dataset/public-financial-management-systems-and-eservices-global-dataset (last updated 2017).

- *South Africa* introduced e-filing and improved automation, which reduced red tape and temporal expenses related to tax assessments and customs evaluations (CIAT 2020; IMF 2020).

- *Guatemala* initiated BancaSAT, an e-filing and payment system, in 2001 with support from the World Bank. Within a year, BancaSAT accounted for 84 percent of Guatemala's tax revenues, while also reducing its revenue authority's administrative burden and improving overall service delivery (Jacobs et al. 2013).

- *Georgia and the Republic of Korea* (box 7.3), among other countries, have also successfully implemented e-registration, e-filing, and e-payment platforms (Awasthi et al. 2019; Bukia 2019).

And yet despite significant investments in taxpayer-facing services such as e-filing and e-payments, many low- and middle-income countries have yet to realize many of the purported benefits, reflecting broader institutional, infrastructural, and technological challenges (Kochanova, Hasnain, and Larson 2016). In the Philippines, a study found that prior offline experiences with the revenue authority, trust in government broadly, and underlying trust in the technology itself had significant effects on taxpayers' propensity to enroll in the country's e-filing and e-payments platform. Propensity was also determined by the quality of information on the platform; the quality of both the system and the service being provided (e-filing, e-payments); and the overall usefulness of—and user satisfaction with—the interface (Bhuasiri et al. 2016; Jengchung et al. 2015).

BOX 7.3

HomeTax Service: Getting Taxpayer Services Right in the Republic of Korea

The Republic of Korea's National Tax Service (NTS) initiated its HomeTax Service (HTS) in 2002, enabling taxpayers to file, report, and pay their tax liabilities via the internet. HTS was born out of user discontent with its predecessor, the Tax Information System (TIS). Korea's experience with the HTS illustrates the challenges and benefits of integrated taxpayer portals and, more important, the role they can play to improve tax enforcement capacity, facilitate quasi-voluntary compliance, and build trust between taxpayers and government.

The NTS began drawing up plans for the TIS in 1994. Between 1994 and 1996, it conducted various feasibility studies and gathered user and system requirements, and in 1997 it launched the TIS with a mandate to improve enforcement efficiency and the accuracy of taxpayer information. Introduction of the TIS was accompanied by significant regulatory and legislative reforms, most notably the nationwide Framework Act on Informatization Promotion (1995), the national information and communication technology (ICT) strategy, and the National Informatization Promotion Plan (1996).

The NTS also embarked on various organizational reforms and business process reengineering efforts to improve professionalism, efficiency, and transparency within the agency. Despite these efforts, the TIS and its accompanying reforms were met with strong opposition. The most salient push-back came from tax officials themselves. They were not happy with the TIS's requirement that they manually file and process taxpayer payments by entering information into a terminal. They found this work to be monotonous and beneath their level of skill and expertise.

In response to the TIS's shortcomings, the NTS initiated the HTS in 2002, phasing in discrete modules and components with a small number of taxpayers before rolling it out to the wider population. The HTS completely digitalized taxpayer services (including filing, reporting, payments, and notices) and made other improvements to administrative protocols and service quality. The NTS also committed resources to outreach, sensitization, and taxpayer education, both during the pilot stage and after the final rollout.

With the HTS, the NTS shifted its focus from enforcement only to providing good taxpayer services and easing compliance costs for individuals and businesses. Korea also produced legislation—the Act on Submission and Management of Taxation Data (2000)—compelling local governments, other government agencies, financial institutions, and various businesses to provide the NTS with 92 types of taxation data. Although the HTS provided the technological portal to automate and process information, it was this legislative change, coupled with a uniform national ICT strategy, that set the stage for improved data sharing and accuracy of taxpayer information.

The results have been positive. Although uptake was slow in the beginning, over 90 percent of taxpayers now file and report their taxes through the HTS. By 2008, 74.1 percent of value added tax returns were filed through the HTS, and annual user experience surveys reveal that up to 80 percent of users are satisfied with the system. Notably, the HTS has improved administrative efficiency, reduced tax compliance costs, reduced tax noncompliance, and eased the administrative burden on the NTS and its staff.

The HTS's success is attributable to a few factors:

- The NTS's ICT goals and strategy were well defined and scoped at a national level and aligned with the central government's ICT policies.
- This approach created room for senior NTS leadership to support the process and enabled a whole-of-government approach, along with early, sustained outreach and engagement efforts.
- Korea's relatively mature foundational IT infrastructure (internet, electricity, and digital literacy) also played an important role in providing a strong basis for the NTS's IT reform efforts.

Source: Awasthi et al. (2019).

An experimental study in Tajikistan highlights the complicated relationship between e-filing, e-payments, and corruption. It found that the degree of adoption of the technology was reliant on firms' risk profiles, prior relationships with tax authorities, and the depth of training and logistical support they received. If firms had been more likely to collude with tax officials (via face-to-face contact), the e-filing system disrupted that behavior, resulting in higher payments from such firms. However, these firms were also more likely to stop using the e-filing system. At the same time, those firms less likely to collude with tax officials actually paid less in taxes after signing up for e-filing because they no longer had to deal with extortionary tax officials who were prone to hiking firms' tax liabilities outside due process (Okunogbe and Pouliquen 2018).

Some research points to the importance of jointly implementing a comprehensive filing and payment program. E-filing systems implemented without also introducing e-payment functionality do not significantly reduce tax compliance costs in the short to medium term. By contrast, systems initiated with e-payment functions lessen both the frequency of tax payments and the time required to prepare returns and pay taxes (Kochanova, Hasnain, and Larson 2016). Although it may seem self-evident, many tax administrations have introduced e-filing systems without embedding accessible e-payment solutions (see figure 7.4).

Other studies have also emphasized the steep costs and learning curve that taxpayers—uniquely individual taxpayers and small businesses—must overcome before using various electronic taxpayer services. This finding suggests that many of the benefits of technologies such as e-filing may remain elusive in the short to medium term (Yilmaz and Coolidge 2013). It also suggests that increasing the adoption of these technologies is likely to require concrete investments in building taxpayers' trust of and competence in using the system, in addition to providing direct incentives to encourage uptake (Bhuasiri et al. 2016; Mas'ud 2019).

Addressing E-registration Issues

The difficulties with taxpayer-facing digital services extend to e-registration. In theory, e-registration should substantially reduce the registration costs for both taxpayers and revenue authorities and simplify the process of bringing informal vendors and taxpayers into the formal tax net. However, although evidence is still limited, increasingly compelling findings suggest that these e-registration initiatives have been mainly unsuccessful, especially in Sub-Saharan Africa. The hyperfocus on registration, which stems from the belief that the informal sector is to blame for revenue shortfalls, often leads to bloated registries with inaccurate or incomplete information and a high number of inactive taxpayers (Moore 2020).

Fostering Taxpayer Engagement

Revenue authorities in low- and middle-income countries have also invested in technology aimed at improving taxpayer education and creating new avenues for communication between government and taxpayers. Singapore's tax authority uses short messaging service (SMS) notifications to provide taxpayers with enhanced services and nudges, reminding them of their tax obligations and providing pertinent information about the tax system. Of the 6 million taxpayers who signed up for these SMS notifications, 96 percent reported that the service was timely and met their needs (OECD 2016). Evidence from Rwanda suggests that electronic communication modes can be highly effective in increasing tax compliance (Mascagni, Nell, and Monkam 2017).

The World Bank's Mind, Behavior, and Development Unit (eMBeD) has conducted several randomized trials in various countries looking into the effects of email and SMS reminders on tax compliance (World Bank 2021a):

- In Costa Rica, a study of 50,000 nonfilers found that email reminders alone improved tax compliance by 20 percentage points within five weeks, with sizable increases in both firms' filing rates and the likelihood they would file third-party reports about other firms with which they do business.

- In Latvia, email messages sent to purported noncompliant shadow economy taxpayers led to sharp increases in tax declaration submission rates.

- In Kosovo, emails and SMS reminders increased personal income tax (PIT) revenue by 2–4 percentage points within just one month of transmission.

Although electronic reminders alone are unlikely to transform tax administration, they are relatively low-cost and offer good value for money. A World Bank field experiment in Madagascar demonstrated this cost-effectiveness. Researchers selected over 15,000 late income tax filers and sent a series of SMS reminders to a sample of them. The intervention resulted in 9.9 percent of late filers in the treatment group filing a tax return before the deadline, compared with only 7.2 percent in the control group, which did not receive SMS reminders. Although this difference may appear small, every dollar spent sending the SMS reminders yielded US$329 in revenue, with an overall return on investment of 32,800 percent—a staggering figure (Peixoto et al. 2019).

Expanding Mobile Money Technologies

Many low- and middle-income countries, especially in Sub-Saharan Africa, have made remarkable progress toward mobile communication penetration, which has given rise to a proliferation of mobile e-government portals and a rapidly growing mobile money ecosystem. Overall, the number of countries that developed mobile e-government portals doubled from 25 in 2012 to 48 in 2014 (World Bank 2016). In Africa, mobile phones, not the internet, drive connectivity. A survey of 12 African countries revealed that, although only 5 percent of individuals used the internet to interact with government, over 60 percent used their mobile phones to do so (IMF 2020; World Bank 2016). Meanwhile, mobile money platforms have the potential to expand financial inclusion and bring large swaths of the informal sector into the formal financial system, with conceivably significant implications for tax administrations (Logan 2017).

Several governments have begun capitalizing on the potential of the mobile money system by using mobile payments to facilitate government-to-business (G2B), government-to-person (G2P), B2G, and P2G transactions (GSMA 2014). Mobile money payments could reduce the scope for fraud, increase transparency, and reduce the tax compliance costs associated with settling tax liabilities, especially in countries with high mobile penetration rates:

- In Tanzania, the Tanzania Revenue Authority recorded decreases in tax avoidance one year after enabling mobile money payments for property taxes and personal income taxes (GSMA 2014).

- In Mauritius, the Mauritius Revenue Authority, in collaboration with the State Bank of Mauritius, enabled mobile money payments for income taxes, resulting in a 12 percent increase in returns filed within one year (GSMA 2014).

- In Cambodia, a GSM Association (GSMA) study found that the introduction of mobile money as a payment option increased the Ministry of Public Works and Transport's revenue from US$14.8 million to US$37 million in 2019 (Fichers and Naji 2020).

- In Kenya, the Philippines, Rwanda, and Uganda, among other countries, mobile money payments were enabled for one or more types of taxes (GSMA 2014; Wasunna and Frydrych 2017).

Although evidence about the link between mobile money payments and tax compliance is still limited, there is reason to be cautiously optimistic. Coupled with complementary institutional and process reforms, mobile technology could considerably ease the collection difficulties that revenue authorities in low- and middle-income countries face.

Trust: Digital Technologies and IT Solutions to Engender Trust

Technology can, in theory, play a vital role in bridging the gap in trust between taxpayers and tax authorities, yet evidence of its usefulness remains relatively thin. Moreover, technology can even undermine trust and is ultimately subordinate to the broader political, administrative, and socioeconomic determinants of trust and tax morale (Lindgren et al. 2019). To maximize the impact of technology on trust-building, IT projects should be situated within wider, whole-of-government coordination that adequately addresses fairness, equity, reciprocity, and accountability. This section discusses how revenue authorities in low- and middle-income countries can use technology to improve trust and provides an overview of existing research on why these efforts may or may not succeed.

Trust of tax administrations' use of technology has two distinct but related dimensions. The first is taxpayers' trust in and acceptance of the government-sanctioned technology tools and services with which they interact. This dimension covers, among other things, the user-friendliness of taxpayer portals; taxpayers' perceptions of the accuracy and utility of information provided electronically; and their sense of how robust the security and privacy safeguards are on the electronic platforms through which they interact with the tax administration.

The second dimension is more broadly concerned with taxpayers' trust of their tax administration and of government. Tax administrations are often only able to influence this dimension of trust to the extent that they can reduce the compliance burden on taxpayers, administer the tax system competently and impartially, and ensure that tax burdens are distributed equitably.

Increasing Perceived Transparency

In many countries, revenue authorities use various digital communication tools—harnessing social media, mobile technologies, and ever-rising internet penetration rates—to bolster taxpayers' comprehension of their tax liabilities and the tax system. The effect of digital communication depends on the quality and usefulness of the information being provided and on the depth of transparency. Used well, digital communications could both facilitate compliance and enhance the trustworthiness of the tax system. For example, evidence from Rwanda found that SMS messages to taxpayers about public services led to substantial increases in taxes declared, and they were a cost-effective mode of engaging with taxpayers for whom mobile technology is the prevailing mode of communication (Mascagni, Nell, and Monkam 2017).

Other efforts to improve transparency—such as by digitally linking revenue collection to service delivery, using digital tools to facilitate participatory budgeting, and systematically publishing open data to encourage civil society engagement—could potentially have sizable effects on all four elements of trust: fairness, equity, reciprocity, and accountability. Many low- and middle-income countries now routinely publish national budgets and other financial information online and through open-data portals. In Nigeria, such digital data disclosure has given birth to civil society platforms such as TrackaNG and BudgIT, which provide and analyze information about public finances and expenditures.

Several governments (both national and subnational) in low- and middle-income countries are also members of the multilateral Open Government Partnership, although it is unclear to what extent this has improved transparency or accountability.[7] A study of the open-data initiatives of several Organisation for Economic Co-operation and Development (OECD) countries—including those that regularly publish budgetary information—concluded that although the government-published information did increase perceptions of transparency, it did not affect public participation levels (Pina, Torres, and Acerete 2007; Pina, Torres, and Royo 2010).

When implementing IT projects, revenue authorities could benefit from investing in various e-participation platforms to facilitate taxpayer education and encourage greater taxpayer involvement in decision-making processes, policy development, and service design (IMF 2020). To build trust, these transparency initiatives need to meet taxpayers wherever they are in terms of both the content of the information shared and the platforms and methods used to share the information. Information shared with taxpayers should be accessible, interactive, and citizen-friendly rather than one-dimensional and authoritative (van den Boogaard et al. 2020).

Building Trust in Taxpayer Services

Anticorruption potential of digitalized systems. As noted earlier, investments in digital taxpayer services could minimize face-to-face interaction between taxpayers and tax officials, thereby limiting opportunities for harassment and corruption. A recent IMF study on taxation, corruption, and trust in Sub-Saharan Africa found that higher digital adoption lessened taxpayers' perceptions of corruption by 4.2 percentage points and notably increased their confidence in tax officials by 2.5 percentage points. However, this effect was significantly dampened when governments shut down the internet or limited social media use (Ouedraogo and Sy 2020).

Digitalized taxpayer services can also create greater clarity within the tax administration about who pays taxes and whether tax officials administer the system according to the rules. For example, in manual systems it can be challenging to determine whether wealthy individuals are paying taxes at all.

Digitalized systems make it much easier to find information about individual taxpayers, nil-filers,[8] nonpayers, and nonfilers. Similarly, it is easier for corrupt officials to artificially reduce (or increase) the tax liabilities of a given firm or individual in a manual system than in an automated system with a digital paper trail.

Portals that boost accountability and reciprocity. Digital technologies may further enable revenue authorities to provide real-time information to taxpayers about their tax accounts and potentially enable taxpayers to contest the veracity of the government's information about them. Tax administrations have also employed digital technologies to improve accountability by implementing digital complaints and appeals processes as well as robust digital taxpayer feedback portals.

In addition to engendering trust between taxpayers and the revenue authority, such digital services could improve data quality and reduce the potential for inaccuracies. In India, for example, taxpayers can view their tax payments and information about taxes deducted at the source online and in real time. Similarly, in the Russian Federation taxpayers have a single digital taxpayer account that shows data about their sources of income, including properties, real estate, and other assets in their possession. They also have access to an online portal so they can directly provide their local tax office with feedback about their property assessments (Ouedraogo and Sy 2020).

Pros and cons of prepopulated forms. Tax administrations are better placed to engender trust if they can positively shift taxpayers' perceptions about their ability to deliver taxpayer services and administer the tax system (Chen, Grimshaw, and Myles 2017; CIAT 2020). For example, technological tools can enhance third-party data collection, which, in turn, can be critical for improving enforcement. Better access to third-party data can also facilitate compliance, including by providing taxpayers with prepopulated forms to facilitate self-assessment, tax filing, and payment.

Although prepopulated forms may not be feasible in the near to medium term in low-capacity contexts, many revenue authorities worldwide have begun experimenting with them to varying degrees of success. Prepopulated forms not only transfer risk from taxpayers to the revenue authority but can also reduce compliance costs and, more broadly, limit the scope for errors and omissions. However, taxpayers' perceptions of how competently tax officials provide this service will either enhance or constrain the potential of technology to improve filing, assessment, and access to third-party data.

Moreover, tax authorities' overreach in terms of what they can deliver can also easily lead to adverse outcomes. Forms prepopulated with incorrect information—for example, overestimating or underestimating tax liabilities—may have negative effects on tax morale and on perceptions of the tax system's competence, integrity, and fairness.

Minding Privacy, Security, and Misuses of Technology

The use of industry standard security and privacy controls is critical to building trust between taxpayers and the government. A failure to do so, such as through leaks of personally identifiable information, could have devastating effects on IT projects and on taxpayers' trust and confidence in their revenue administration.

Security and privacy are even more pressing challenges in countries where citizens are already highly mistrustful of the government holding vast amounts of personal data. Just as technology can be used to enhance trust, it can also reinforce governments' ability to restrict, control, or surveil citizens, with unfavorable consequences for technology investments and tax reform efforts broadly (Lindgren et al. 2019; Zuboff 2019).

Ultimately, there are limits to what technology can do to build trust, and more empirical evidence is needed to determine those limits. Much of the work to improve fairness, equity, reciprocity, and accountability can—and probably should—be carried out without relying heavily on digital tools, the benefits of which can be illusory. Improving trust in revenue authorities requires a whole-of-government framework for good digital governance (box 7.4). Such an approach would account for broader institutional and political factors and recognize that technological advancements can sometimes be at odds with the incentives that drive governments to be accountable or unaccountable.

BOX 7.4

Situating Tax Administration IT Projects within Broader Whole-of-Government ICT Strategies

Several African countries have implemented national digital or information and communication technology (ICT) strategies:

- Côte d'Ivoire launched its E-impôts portal in 2018, following a national ICT strategy, to improve taxpayer services and strengthen data collection and enforcement.
- In Ghana, the Ministry of Communications is leading a digitalization strategy with initiatives focused on a digital property valuation and taxation process; a paperless port system at the country's main ports; biometric national identification; and whole-of-government e-service provision (driver's licenses, passport renewal, and census, among other things).
- Launched in 2019, Kenya's Digital Economy Blueprint is being led by the Ministry of Information, Communications, and Technology and includes initiatives to digitalize taxpayer services; improve digital connectivity and underlying information technology infrastructure; build digital literacy; and strengthen legal and regulatory frameworks for data protection, privacy, and consumer protection.
- Niger initiated a national digitalization strategy in 2017, targeting smart villages, skills and training, and whole-of-government e-services, including e-filing and e-payment taxpayer portals.
- Rwanda has initiated several digital strategies since the turn of the century, including three national ICT infrastructure plans and two ICT sector strategic plans. Rwanda's "SMART Rwanda 2020" master plan was drafted in 2015 to inform the development of e-government services and to enhance digital connectivity, internet penetration, and cybersecurity.

Source: IMF (2020).

Conclusion

Despite the scope for digitalization to transform tax administration, IT projects have, in practice, often had disappointing outcomes. The severity of challenges to digitalization and implementation of IT projects depends in large part on the maturity of both the tax administration and the tax compliance culture. Countries in the early stages of maturity may be constrained by weak accounting practices; low levels of digital literacy; inadequate legal, regulatory, and institutional frameworks; tax departments organized by type of tax rather than by function; and a lack of internet and mobile connectivity. Countries with more advanced maturity levels are characterized by relatively acceptable (electronic) accounting practices; high levels of digital literacy and data sharing; enabling legislative and regulatory frameworks; a functional organizational model; and high levels of both internet and mobile connectivity.

Many low- and middle-income countries fall somewhere in the middle of the maturity spectrum—not quite mature enough to embark on whole-of-government, integrated digital initiatives but well placed to center reform efforts on automation and systems integration; development of more user-friendly taxpayer services and responsive taxpayer engagement platforms; performance of business process reviews and reengineering; and adoption of less-rigid software procurement and development models.

A clear understanding of the revenue administration's capability and maturity enables decision-makers to circumvent the pitfalls of poor sequencing and costly, overambitious, oversophisticated, or unusable digital technologies. Depending on the context, effective sequencing of reform could begin with investing in technology tools to register taxpayers and bring them into the tax net, followed by simplifying data-sharing protocols within and beyond the revenue authority; enhancing audit and case management functions; and, finally, improving internal data management and risk management protocols. For technology to contribute positively to trust, IT projects must also build in robust security and privacy controls, in adherence with privacy-by-design principles, to ensure that taxpayers' data remain safeguarded and that they trust the government to use their data ethically. The absence of these safeguards can have drastic effects on trust-building.

IT projects are also less likely to succeed if decision-makers fail to account for broader regulatory and administrative constraints, even though some of these factors are outside the control of the revenue authority. They should prioritize process reengineering and improved inter- and intra-agency cooperation and carefully consider the administration's capacity, directing technology investments accordingly.

Especially in low-capacity contexts with weak connectivity and digital literacy rates, IT projects should fully account for the potential transition costs (and negative externalities) faced by taxpayers and tax officials. Phasing in digital tools gradually and testing iteratively could be one approach. Solutions should be genuinely aligned with reform objectives and responsive to administrative requirements and users' dynamic needs.

Ultimately, political constraints may prove to be the most intractable hindrance to the digital transformation of tax administration. From the outset, IT projects should map out the relevant political interests and embed strategies to confront or circumvent them when implementing digital transformation initiatives. There are various ways to approach this, depending on the core objectives of reform. For example, technology investments could focus on low-cost solutions—such as improved interagency cooperation and data sharing within tax departments—that may be politically challenging but not technologically sophisticated. Even if unsuccessful, such efforts can yield the benefit of signaling the degree of political will among various stakeholders before more expensive or complex reforms are undertaken.

Other approaches to overcoming political obstacles could involve using digital technologies in ways that give taxpayers, elites, and government officials incentives to buy into reforms. This effort could include extensive engagement with stakeholders early in the process to better understand their needs and reservations. It could also include investments in communication tools and strategies to align IT projects with the challenges in providing public services. There also may be benefits to concerted outreach efforts led, if possible, by local and national champions or a reliance on local vendors who may be more culturally competent than their international counterparts.

Although low- and middle-income countries have made substantial investments in IT systems and technologies in recent years, evaluations of these systems' effectiveness in improving tax compliance remain relatively few, while evidence of their role in building (or undermining) broader trust and confidence in government remains even scarcer. Research that would support better cost-benefit analysis of IT investments is a priority. Insights into the potential for more exotic new technologies such as blockchain and artificial intelligence in lower-capacity contexts would also be interesting as their use expands in many countries. Meanwhile, as open government efforts around the world prioritize the use of IT systems to boost transparency and engagement, more empirical evidence on what has worked or failed in different contexts could help guide governments in prioritizing IT investment vis-à-vis lower-tech approaches.

Successful digitalization efforts recognize that technology is a means to solve a defined problem, not an end in itself. Particularly in low-capacity contexts, would-be reformers need to emphasize the need for simplicity and local ownership, while investing in proper project and change management to ensure that IT investments are well implemented and sustainable. Meanwhile, navigating political barriers requires a deep understanding of the enabling environment and identification of opportunities to generate momentum and broad-based support for reform both within and outside the government. If employed effectively to facilitate the work of tax authorities and provide tangible value to taxpayers, technology can play an essential role within a broader framework for building trust and tax morale.

Notes

1. Although many low- and middle-income countries, including those in Sub-Saharan Africa, are becoming more digitalized, there are still fundamental challenges with connectivity and digital depth. Many countries with advanced technology for tax administration experienced a capability development curve spanning more than 25 years.

2. Countries such as Cabo Verde, Ghana, Rwanda, and the Seychelles have made significant improvements in internet penetration and mobile connectivity.

3. However, as Prichard (2014) points out, local procurement poses risks of politicization. This has indeed been the case with Remita's prevalence in Nigeria because of the now-discredited corruption allegations against SystemSpecs.

4. See Gerhardt, Maki, and Headd (2019) for an overview of the trade-offs between COTS and other alternatives and the more specific technical factors governments should consider before locking into a COTS solution.

5. In other words, 60,000 taxpayers had discrepancies flagged in 20 percent of their transactions, while 100,000 taxpayers had discrepancies flagged in at least 5 percent of their transactions.

6. A few well-documented VAT enforcement IT projects, most notably from the Republic of Korea, where investments in ETI, an ETI-backed early warning system to identify suspicious transactions and combat fraud, and Tax Incentives for Electronically Traceable Payments (TIETP) have yielded positive benefits for VAT collection and compliance (Awasthi et al. 2019).

7. The Open Government Partnership (OGP), formed in 2011 by eight countries (Brazil, Indonesia, Mexico, Norway, the Philippines, South Africa, the United Kingdom, and the United States), is a multilateral initiative to secure concrete government commitments to promote open government, empower citizens, fight corruption, and harness new technologies to strengthen governance. Its membership now comprises 78 countries (representing 2 billion people), a growing number of local governments, and thousands of civil society organizations. For more information, see https://www.opengovpartnership.org/.

8. A nil-filer is a taxpayer who files a tax return, thus abiding by the law, but reports zero business income and zero income tax.

References

Adelmann, F., J. A. Elliott, I. Ergen, T. Gaidosch, N. Jenkinson, T. Khiaonarong, A. Morozova, N. Schwarz, and C. Wilson. 2020. "Cyber Risk and Financial Stability: It's a Small World After All." Staff Discussion Note No. 2000/007, International Monetary Fund, Washington, DC.

Ali, M., A. Shifa, A. Shimeles, and F. Woldeyes. 2015. "Information Technology and Fiscal Capacity in a Developing Country: Evidence from Ethiopia." Working Paper No. 31, International Centre for Tax and Development, Brighton, UK.

AlphaBeta and BMGF (Bill and Melinda Gates Foundation). 2018. "Digital Innovation in Public Financial Management (PFM): Opportunities and Implications for Low-Income Countries." Research report by AlphaBeta, Singapore, for BMGF, Seattle.

Awasthi, R., H. C. Lee, P. Poulin, J. G. Choi, W. C. Kim, O. J. Lee, M. J. Sung, and S. Y. Chang. 2019. "The Benefits of Electronic Tax Administration in Developing Economies: A Korean Case Study and Discussion of Key Challenges." World Bank, Washington, DC; KDI School of Public Policy and Management, Sejong City, Republic of Korea.

Baisalbayeva, K., E. van der Enden, V. Ion, H. Tsavdaris, D. Deputy, F. van der Vlist, T. Bohsali, and C. Aygun. 2019. "Blockchain for Tax Compliance." White paper, Microsoft, Seattle; PricewaterhouseCoopers, Amsterdam; Vertex Inc., King of Prussia, PA.

Barbone, L., A. Das-Gupta, L. De Wulf, and A. Hansson. 1999. "Reforming Tax
  Systems: The World Bank Record in the 1990s." Policy Research Working Paper
  2237, World Bank, Washington, DC. doi:10.1596/1813-9450-2237.

Bhatnagar, S. C. 2009. *Unlocking E-government Potential: Concepts, Cases and
  Practical Insights*. New Delhi: Sage Publications.

Bhuasiri, W., H. Zo, H. Lee, and A. Ciganek. 2016. "User Acceptance of
  E-government Services: Examining an E-tax Filing and Payment System in
  Thailand." *Information Technology for Development* 22 (4): 675–95. doi:10.1080
  /02681102.2016.1173001.

Bird, R. M., and E. M. Zolt. 2008. "Technology and Taxation in Developing
  Countries: From Hand to Mouse." *National Tax Journal* 61 (4): 791–821.

Bukia, I. 2019. "Supporting Tax Policy for Small Business in Georgia." *Economics and
  Business* XI (1): 122–26.

Carrillo, P., D. Pomeranz, and M. Singhal. 2017. "Dodging the Taxman: Firm
  Misreporting and Limits to Tax Enforcement." *American Economic Journal:
  Applied Economics* 9 (2): 144–64. doi:10.1257/app.20140495.

Casey, P., and P. Castro. 2015. "Electronic Fiscal Devices (EFDs): An Empirical Study
  of Their Impact on Taxpayer Compliance and Administrative Efficiency."
  Working Paper No. 15/73, International Monetary Fund, Washington, DC.
  doi:10.5089/9781475521023.001.

Chalendard, C., A. Duhaut, A. M. Fernandes, A. Mattoo, G. Raballand, and B. Rijkers.
  2020. "Does Better Information Curb Customs Fraud?" Policy Research Working
  Paper 9254, World Bank, Washington, DC. doi:10.1596/1813-9450-9254.

Chen, J., S. Grimshaw, and G. D. Myles. 2017. "Testing and Implementing Digital Tax
  Administration." In *Digital Revolutions in Public Finance*, edited by S. Gupta,
  M. Keen, A. Shah, and G. Verdier, 113–45. Washington, DC: International
  Monetary Fund. doi:10.5089/9781484315224.071.

CIAT (Inter-American Center of Tax Administrations). 2020. *ICT as a Strategic Tool
  to Leapfrog the Efficiency of Tax Administrations*. Seattle: Bill and Melinda Gates
  Foundation; Panama City: CIAT.

Dogan, U. 2011. "Tools for Risk Management: The Case of Turkey." In *Risk-Based
  Tax Audits: Approaches and Country Experiences*, edited by Munawer Sultan
  Khwaja, Rajul Awasthi, and Jan Loeprick. Directions in Development Series.
  Washington, DC: World Bank.

Dunleavy, P., and L. Carrera. 2013. *Growing the Productivity of Government Services*.
  Cheltenham, UK: Edward Elgar Publishing. https://ideas.repec.org/b/elg/eebook
  /14497.html.

Economic Times. 2019. "No Country for Evaders: This April 1, India Enters
  Uncharted Tax Territory." March 26, 2019. https://economictimes.indiatimes
  .com/news/economy/policy/no-country-for-evaders-this-april-1-india-enters
  -uncharted-tax-territory/articleshow/68574891.cms.

Engelschalk, M. 2000. "Computerizing Tax and Customs Administration." *PREM
  Notes* 44, Poverty Reduction and Economic Management Network, World Bank,
  Washington, DC.

Fichers, N., and L. Naji. 2020. "Digitalizing Person-to-Government Payments:
  Leveraging Mobile to Improve Government Revenue and Access to Public
  Services." GSMA, London.

Fjeldstad, O-H., C. Kagoma, E. Mdee, I. H. Sjursen, and V. Somville. 2018.
  "The Customer Is King: Evidence on VAT Compliance in Tanzania." Working
  Paper No. 83, Institute of Development Studies, Brighton, UK. doi:10.1016/j
  .worlddev.2019.104841.

Fountain, J. E. 2001. *Building the Virtual State: Information Technology and Institutional Change*. Washington, DC: Brookings Institution Press.

Gerhardt, L., N. Maki, and M. Headd. 2019. "When to Use Commercial Off-the-Shelf (COTS) Technology." 18F Blog, March 26, 2019. https://18f.gsa.gov/2019/03/26/when-to-use-COTS/.

Gnangnon, S. K., and J.-F. Brun. 2018. "Impact of Bridging the Internet Gap on Public Revenue Mobilization." *Information Economics and Policy* 43: 23–33. doi:10.1016/j.infoecopol.2018.04.001.

GSMA (GSM Association). 2014. "Paying Taxes through Mobile Money: Initial Insights into P2G and B2G Payments." Mobile for Development (blog), December 4, 2014. https://www.gsma.com/mobilefordevelopment/programme/mobile-money/paying-taxes-through-mobile-money-initial-insights-into-p2g-and-b2g-payments/.

GSMA (GSM Association). 2019. "The State of Mobile Internet Connectivity Report." GSMA, London.

Gupta, S., M. Keen, A. Shah, and G. Verdier. 2017. *Digital Revolutions in Public Finance*. Washington, DC: International Monetary Fund.

Heeks, R. 2003. "Most eGovernment-for-Development Projects Fail: How Can Risks Be Reduced?" iGovernment Working Paper No. 14, University of Manchester, UK.

IMF (International Monetary Fund). 2020. "Digitalization in Sub-Saharan Africa." In *Regional Economic Outlook: Sub-Saharan Africa, April 2020. COVID-19: An Unprecedented Threat to Development*. IMF, Washington, DC.

Jacobs, A., D. Crawford, T. Murdoch, C. Lethbridge, D. Osinski, S. Hinsz, Y. Hodges, G. Jimenez, D. Pulse, and A. Kamenov. 2013. "Detailed Guidelines for Improved Tax Administration in Latin America and the Caribbean." Leadership in Public Financial Management (LPFM) Series, United States Agency for International Development (USAID), Washington, DC.

Jengchung, V. C., R. J. M. Jubilado, E. P. S. Capistrano, and D. Yen. 2015. "Factors Affecting Online Tax Filing—An Application of the IS Success Model and Trust Theory." *Computers in Human Behaviour* 43: 251–62. https://doi.org/10.1016/j.chb.2014.11.017.

Joia, L. A., and J. C. Vinhais. 2017. "From Closed Source to Open-Source Software: Analysis of the Migration Process to Open Office." *Journal of High Technology Management Research* 2 (28): 261–72. https://doi.org/10.1016/j.hitech.2017.10.008.

Junquera-Varela, R. F., M. Verhoeven, G. P. Shukla, B. Haven, R. Awasthi, and B. Moreno-Dodson. 2017. *Strengthening Domestic Resource Mobilization: Moving from Theory to Practice in Low- and Middle-Income Countries*. Directions in Development Series. Washington, DC: World Bank. doi:10.1596/978-1-4648-1073-2.

Kangave, J., S. Nakato, R. Waiswa, and P. L. Zzimbe. 2016. "Boosting Revenue Collection through Taxing High Net Worth Individuals: The Case of Uganda." Working Paper No. 45, International Centre for Tax and Development, Brighton, UK.

Kochanova, A., Z. Hasnain, and B. Larson. 2016. "Does E-government Improve Government Capacity? Evidence from Tax Administration and Public Procurement." Policy Research Working Paper 7657, World Bank, Washington, DC. doi:10.1596/1813-9450-7657.

Ligomeka, W. 2019. "Assessing the Performance of African Tax Administrations: A Malawian Puzzle." African Tax Administration Paper No. 14, International Centre for Tax and Development, Brighton, UK.

Lindgren, I., C. Ø. Madsen, S. Hofmann, and U. Melin. 2019. "Close Encounters of the Digital Kind: A Research Agenda for the Digitalization of Public Services." *Government Information Quarterly* 36 (3): 427–36. doi:10.1016/j.giq.2019.03.002.

Logan, S. 2017. "Regulating Mobile Money to Support Scale-Up." Synthesis brief, International Growth Centre, London.

Mascagni, G., A. T. Mengistu, and F. B. Woldeyes. 2018. "Can ICTs Increase Tax? Experimental Evidence from Ethiopia." Working Paper No. 82, International Centre for Tax and Development, Brighton, UK.

Mascagni, G., N. Monkam, and C. Nell. 2016. "Unlocking the Potential of Administrative Data in Africa: Tax Compliance and Progressivity in Rwanda." Working Paper No. 56, International Centre for Tax and Development, Brighton, UK.

Mascagni, G., D. Mukama, and F. Santoro. 2019. "An Analysis of Discrepancies in Taxpayers' VAT Declarations in Rwanda." Working Paper No. 92, International Centre for Tax and Development, Brighton, UK.

Mascagni, G., C. Nell, and N. Monkam. 2017. "One Size Does Not Fit All: A Field Experiment on the Drivers of Tax Compliance and Delivery Methods in Rwanda." Working Paper No. 58, International Centre for Tax and Development, Brighton, UK.

Mas'ud, A. 2019. "Acceptability of E-filing of Taxes by Micro-Entrepreneurs in Northwestern Nigeria." Working Paper No. 96, International Centre for Tax and Development, Brighton, UK.

Mayega, J., R. Ssuuna, M. Mubajje, M. I. Nalukwago, and L. Muwonge. 2019. "How Clean Is Our Taxpayer Register? Data Management in the Uganda Revenue Authority." African Tax Administration Paper No. 12, International Centre for Tax and Development, Brighton, UK.

Mikuriya, K., and T. Cantens. 2020. "If Algorithms Dream of Customs, Do Customs Officials Dream of Algorithms? A Manifesto for Data Mobilisation in Customs." *World Customs Journal* 14 (2): 3–22.

Moore, M. 2020. "What Is Wrong with African Tax Administration?" Working Paper No. 111, International Centre for Tax and Development, Brighton, UK.

Morozov, E. 2013. *To Save Everything, Click Here: The Folly of Technological Solutionism.* New York: Public Affairs.

Ndung'u, N. 2019. "Digital Technology and State Capacity in Kenya." Policy Paper No. 154, Center for Global Development, Washington, DC.

OECD (Organisation for Economic Co-operation and Development). 2016. *Technologies for Better Tax Administration: A Practical Guide for Revenue Bodies.* Paris: OECD Publishing. doi:10.1787/978926446439-en.

OECD (Organisation for Economic Co-operation and Development). 2019. "Introducing a Commercial Off-the-Shelf Software Solution: The Experience of the Finnish Tax Administration." Forum on Tax Administration report, OECD, Paris.

Okunogbe, O. M., and V. M. J. Pouliquen. 2018. "Technology, Taxation, and Corruption: Evidence from the Introduction of Electronic Tax Filing." Policy Research Working Paper 8452, World Bank, Washington, DC. doi:10.1596/1813-9450-8452.

Ouedraogo, R., and A. Sy. 2020. "Can Digitalization Help Deter Corruption in Africa?" Working Paper No. 2019/68, International Monetary Fund, Washington, DC. doi:10.5089/9781513545691.001.

Paulson, J. W., G. Succi, and E. Eberlein. 2004. "An Empirical Study of Open-Source and Closed-Source Software Products." *IEEE Transactions on Software Engineering* 30 (4): 246–56. https://doi.org/10.1109/TSE.2004.1274044.

Peixoto, T., H. A. Fanomezantsoa, F. Sjoberg, and J. Mellon. 2019. "How Mobile Text Reminders Earned Madagascar a 32,800% ROI in Collecting Unpaid Taxes." Governance for Development (blog), July 23, 2019. https://blogs.worldbank.org /governance/how-mobile-text-reminders-earned-madagascar-32800-roi -collecting-unpaid-taxes.

Pina, V., L. Torres, and B. Acerete. 2007. "Are ICTs Promoting Government Accountability? A Comparative Analysis of E-governance Developments in 19 OECD Countries." *Critical Perspectives on Accounting* 18 (5): 583–602. doi:10.1016/j.cpa.2006.01.012.

Pina, V., L. Torres, and S. Royo. 2010. "Is E-government Leading to More Accountable and Transparent Local Governments? An Overall View." *Financial Accountability and Management* 26 (1): 3–20. doi:10.1111/j.1468-0408.2009 .00488.x.

Pomeranz, D. 2015. "No Taxation without Information: Deterrence and Self-Enforcement in the Value Added Tax." *American Economic Review* 105 (8): 2539–69. doi:10.1257/aer.20130393.

Prichard, W. 2014. "Using Local IT Solutions to Improve Local Government Tax Reform." Policy Briefing No. 58, Institute of Development Studies, Brighton, UK.

Prichard, W., and P. Fish. 2017. "Strengthening IT Systems for Property Tax Reform." Summary Brief No. 11, International Centre for Tax and Development, Brighton, UK.

Prichard, W., A. B. Kamara, and N. Meriggi. 2020. "Freetown Just Implemented a New Property Tax System that Could Quintuple Revenue." *African Arguments*, May 21.

van den Boogaard, V., W. Prichard, R. Beach, and F. Mohiuddin. 2020. "Strengthening Tax-Accountability Links: Fiscal Transparency and Taxpayer Engagement in Ghana and Sierra Leone." Working Paper No. 114, International Centre for Tax and Development, Brighton, UK. doi:10.19088/ICTD.2020.002.

Vellutini, C. 2011. "Database and IT Framework for Risk Analysis." In *Risk-Based Tax Audits: Approaches and Country Experiences*, edited by Munawer Sultan Khwaja, Rajul Awasthi, and Jan Loeprick, 57–64. Directions in Development Series. Washington, DC: World Bank.

Wasunna, N., and J. Frydrych. 2017. "Person-to-Government (P2G) Payment Digitisation: Lessons from Kenya." Case study, GSM Association, London.

World Bank. 2016. *World Development Report 2016: Digital Dividends*. Washington, DC: World Bank.

World Bank. 2021a. "Behavioral Insights for Tax Compliance." Policy note, World Bank, Washington, DC.

World Bank. 2021b. *World Development Report 2021: Data for Better Lives*. Washington, DC: World Bank.

Yilmaz, F., and J. Coolidge. 2013. "Can E-filing Reduce Tax Compliance Costs in Developing Countries?" Policy Research Working Paper 6647, World Bank, Washington, DC. doi:10.1596/1813-9450-6647.

Zuboff, S. 2019. "Surveillance Capitalism and the Challenge of Collective Action." *New Labour Forum* 28 (1): 10–29. doi.org/10.1177/1095796018819461.

CHAPTER 8

Conclusion

A Framework for Tax Reform

Innovative approaches are needed to overcome the persistent technical, political, and social barriers to improving tax compliance. Traditionally, tax reformers have aimed to strengthen compliance through investments in enforcement and facilitation of tax payments, drawing heavily on technical best practices from across countries. This approach has achieved important successes across countries in recent decades, yielding sustained progress in strengthening revenue collection, rationalizing tax policies, and improving tax administration. Yet those reform efforts have also fallen short of their ambitions in a variety of ways.

This reform pattern is something of a puzzle. Reform efforts may seem highly promising—and there have been many successes—yet across time and space the overall progress has been uneven. Revenue improvements have been steady but also relatively slow. Collection of more progressive taxes on income and property remains weak. Both multinational companies and wealthy individuals continue to benefit from the weaknesses in the international tax system. The adoption and deployment of new technologies have been uneven. And the heavy, often informal burdens of revenue collection on smaller taxpayers remain common.

Even seemingly simple measures to improve performance have frequently proven difficult to enact. Governments have seemed reluctant to adopt the types of policy experiments and simplification reforms that are consistent with recent research and appear to hold substantial promise. Meanwhile, tax agencies remain among the least-trusted government entities in many countries, with lack of trust in tax systems undermining compliance and the potential for building broader political support for reform.

The Conceptual Framework

To address these challenges, this report proposes a conceptual framework for understanding why reform efforts have often fallen short of their goals and how outcomes may be improved moving forward. The framework is based on three central elements:

- *Political support for reform.* The importance of understanding the political barriers to tax reform and developing concrete strategies to identify, navigate, and address those challenges.

- *The social contract.* An emphasis on trust-building, alongside enforcement and facilitation, as part of a holistic vision for tax reform. This vision would reflect the importance of trust not only for encouraging quasi-voluntary tax compliance but also in mobilizing political support for reform and laying the foundation for a stronger social contract.

- *Context-specific strategies.* Reform strategies tailored to the needs, circumstances, and constraints of each country context.

The framework's key contribution lies in unifying relatively siloed and fragmented strands of research and practical insight that have emerged in recent years. No individual component of the framework is particularly novel or transformative. However, this report embeds discrete research findings into a holistic framework for reform.

Although the best reform programs already do much of what is proposed here—albeit often in more ad hoc ways—the framework lays the groundwork for the development of tools to consistently transform these research insights into operational outcomes and provides a platform for conducting systematic research into the effectiveness of these approaches.

The Thematic Applications

The thematic chapters in this volume seek to illustrate the application of these ideas within specific areas of tax reform, highlighting the concrete ways in which the framework may shift understanding of both the reform challenge and the kinds of reform strategies adopted. Rather than being organized around individual tax types, the chapters are organized around distinct taxpayer groups: individuals and households, high-net-worth individuals (HNWIs), large corporations, small and medium enterprises (SMEs), and subnational taxpayers. Despite the overlap across those categories, as well as the diversity within them, each has distinct characteristics with respect to technical challenges, political barriers, and the dynamics of trust-building.

By focusing on taxpayer segments rather than on specific tax types, the framework emphasizes the need to establish where the biggest revenue gaps and opportunities lie and the broader distribution of tax burdens across groups of taxpayers. The final thematic chapter describes the cross-cutting role of technology in tax reform programs. It reflects not only the centrality of technology across reform initiatives, but equally the importance of paying more attention to politics, trust-building, and locally tailored reform strategies so that the introduction of new technologies is more consistently successful.

This concluding chapter pulls together insights from those individual thematic chapters. What follows returns to each central component of the conceptual framework—politics, trust-building, and adopting locally appropriate solutions—drawing illustrations from the thematic chapters.

Navigating the Politics of Reform

Recent developments in public administration research stress the need to think and work politically when pursuing reform (McCulloch and Piron 2019; World Bank 2017). Put most simply, the most important barriers to successful tax reform in many contexts are political rather than technical. Reformers often know what could and should be done to improve outcomes, but political resistance has prevented them from taking those steps (Prichard 2020).

Political Barriers
Vested interests. Tax reform confronts powerful and organized vested interests. It depends on securing resources from relatively small groups of wealthy and frequently well-connected taxpayers and firms, while the benefits of taxation are more widely disbursed and long term. Tax administrators have historically proven to be complex participants in reform. Some have been vocal champions of reform and better performance, but others may resist reforms that curtail opportunities for collusion and corruption.

Meanwhile, political leaders themselves have conflicting incentives. On the one hand, they need to expand revenue to deliver improved services to citizens and voters. On the other, they are often part of the very elite who benefit from weak tax enforcement. They profit personally or politically from enabling tax evasion by powerful interests or by preserving space for informality and corruption in policy and administration.

Weak governmental coordination. The political complexity of tax reform is also revealed in the frequent lack of cooperation across government. Effective tax policy and administration require coordination across a variety of government agencies, including ministries of finance, tax administrations, business registries, investment promotion agencies, and the judiciary. For example, data sharing across government is critical for identifying tax avoidance and evasion. Yet, in practice, such data sharing is often sharply limited—including poor data sharing within tax agencies themselves—because of institutional rivalries, resistance to greater transparency and enforcement, and inadequate systems.

Coordination between national and subnational governments can be critical as well, but also ineffective in practice. For example, small firms often pay taxes and fees to both national and subnational authorities, exacerbating the heavy tax burdens on relatively low-income groups and undermining equity. Moreover, efforts by subnational governments to strengthen property taxation are often stifled by central government control of key aspects of policy and administration.

Political Strategies

Building coalitions. In the long term, countering the headwinds created by vested interests requires building winning coalitions for sustained reform. These coalitions may center on a wide taxpayer base or on a consensus among elites or other stakeholder groups. However, lack of trust in the government's intentions or effectiveness may make it difficult to build a grassroots coalition, even if a broad swath of taxpayers is interested in increasing tax collection among large firms and the wealthy.

Striking elite bargains. Another option is to strike an elite bargain, perhaps starting with those who already pay their fair share of taxes and would prefer that their peers do the same. Such a bargain could promise fair and equitable treatment of all taxpayers, as well as improved provision of public goods and services, in exchange for greater compliance. Relatively large informal firms that would benefit from formalization could form a constituency for appropriate reform of SME taxation focused on simplifying compliance and increasing the benefits of formality.

In each tax segment, strengthening the incentives that motivate tax officials to enforce the law diligently and evenly—and limiting face-to-face interactions between taxpayers and tax collectors that create opportunities for corruption—will likely be important.

Marshaling existing support. Because of the difficulties faced in building broad popular support for taxation, reform programs have often sought instead to identify environments where sufficient political support appears to exist ex ante. This strategy makes sense, but it also faces important challenges and limitations.

The first challenge is that reformers may struggle to identify adequate, sustainable political support for reform. Prospective reformers have strong incentives to claim that there is support for reform, even where such support is limited or fragile. Clearer strategies are needed for identifying and assessing genuine political support for reform—for example, by looking for evidence of government willingness to undertake technically simple but politically costly reforms.

The second challenge is that adopting more politically expedient targets for reform risks excluding reform priorities that are politically more challenging and yet critical to strengthening revenue, equity, trust, and the social contract. Most obviously, past reform efforts have sought to strengthen the value added tax, broaden the tax base, and tax the informal sector, while shying away from more politically contentious areas of reform, including taxation of the wealthy, property taxes, and problematic tax exemptions. Yet these areas exhibit the largest current gaps in revenue collection, while also increasing inequity and undermining trust in tax systems. Reformers need strategies to support these more politically contentious types of reform.

The Critical Foundation: Trust

Working politically means, in part, trying to design incentive-compatible reform programs—that is, programs designed, to the extent possible, to minimize key sources of resistance and maximize support. But there are limits to such strategies, and in the medium term strengthening trust among taxpayers is likely to be a central pillar of efforts to overcome political barriers to tax reform. That said, building broad popular support for tax reform is notoriously difficult. Tax reformers often ask taxpayers to bear a heavier burden of taxation in the short term based on the promise of future improvements in public spending.

Few taxpayers are willing to actively support such efforts where trust in government is limited. Distrust of government service delivery is often reinforced by broader distrust of the fairness and equity of tax systems. As described throughout this volume, research indicates that significant shares of taxpayers view tax agencies as corrupt and untrustworthy, with many taxpayers having experienced harassment and abuse. Likewise, it is an open secret that the powerful and well connected often escape paying the taxes they owe. Few taxpayers will support paying more taxes if they do not believe that others are paying their fair share. Recent research as well as historical experience highlight how essential it is to address these sources of mistrust while also pointing toward strategies for doing so.

Building Trust to Underpin Successful Reform

The conceptual framework advanced here identifies efforts to build public trust in tax systems as a critical but historically overlooked aspect of strengthening tax reform. Building trust relies on three distinct pathways:

- *Broadening political support.* Greater public trust in tax systems is critical to building broader political support for tax reform, as the preceding section describes.

- *Building tax morale.* A rapidly expanding body of research offers evidence that increased public trust in tax systems can drive stronger tax morale and the expansion of quasi-voluntary tax compliance (see, for example, Ali, Fjeldstad, and Sjursen 2013).

- *Strengthening the social contract.* Measures that increase trust in tax systems—including more equitable enforcement, greater transparency, and expanded forums for taxpayer–government engagement—can also empower taxpayers to demand reciprocity and accountability from governments, thereby strengthening the broader social contract (Prichard 2015; van den Boogaard et al., forthcoming).

There is extensive evidence that nonpecuniary drivers of compliance (tax morale) rooted in ethics, social norms, and perceptions of tax systems are important determinants of tax compliance (Luttmer and Singhal 2014). The conceptual framework argues more specifically that four drivers of trust play a role in efforts to strengthen broader tax morale: fairness, equity, reciprocity, and accountability. Fairness and equity are direct products of the tax system itself—so-called tax system outcomes. Reciprocity and accountability are outside the direct control of tax administrations, although tax reforms can be designed in ways that aim to enhance reciprocity and accountability.

The importance of trust-building is increasingly well accepted in popular discussions of taxation and tax reform. Yet a focus on trust-building appears to remain marginal in most reform programs. The framework developed here aims to provide an approach to operationalizing these ideas.

Impediments to Building Trust

Perceived unfairness and inequity. The starting point for efforts to build trust is to address taxpayers' concerns (supported by cross-country data and evidence) that others are not paying their fair share and that systems are regressive and skewed in favor of the powerful and well connected. There is mounting evidence that perceptions of such unfairness and inequity undermine tax morale and support for reform (Mellon et al. 2021).

However, unfairness and inequity remain widespread. At the macro level, collection of progressive income and property taxes is less effective than any other major type of tax collection, while distrust of tax authorities remains extensive. Enforcement is particularly ineffective among the best-off because of weak taxation of nonsalary incomes and the lack of progressivity and enforcement in most property tax systems. Meanwhile, at the micro level trust is undermined by common features of tax systems in low-income countries such as widespread informality, significant risks of harassment by tax officials, limited transparency and taxpayer education, and few mechanisms for appealing unfair treatment.

Perceptions of such unfairness and inequity undermine willingness to pay and may also create a vicious cycle by creating incentives for individuals and firms to seek to escape formal taxation. For example, in countries where wealthy individuals realize that compliance is highly uneven, they may be reluctant to pay not only on equity grounds but also for fear of being singled out for stricter enforcement or harassment by authorities if they are forthcoming.

Similar dynamics are at play among firms. Wherever firms believe that their competitors are paying less in taxes than they are—owing to incentives and exemptions, uneven administration, or avoidance or evasion via international tax systems—they are more likely to try to reduce their tax burdens and to invest in securing similar preferential treatment for themselves.

Weak accountability and reciprocity. In addition to concerns about whether enforcement is fair and equitable, tax morale is driven by the extent to which taxpayers believe the government is putting public resources to good use. On a broad level, this is an opportunity for governments: a growing body of highly intuitive evidence indicates that where governments can draw clear links between tax collection and public services, taxpayers are more likely to be compliant and to support reform (Ali, Fjeldstad, and Sjursen 2013). Similarly, a small but growing body of evidence reveals that where citizens have a voice in shaping tax systems and broader government priorities, tax morale improves (Touchton, Wampler, and Peixoto 2019).

That said, it is also important to remember that priorities may vary across time and space, as well as across groups of taxpayers. Taxpayers differ in the services they value and whether their concerns revolve around services or political voice. For example, firms (particularly large corporations) focused on profitability may be interested only in the small subset of public services that directly affect them, while individual taxpayers may define self-interest more broadly. For SMEs, perceptions of reciprocity can be bolstered by providing firms with the benefits of formality, such as legal protection. And the perceived extent of corruption and the general degree of responsiveness to constituents' priorities shape taxpayers' views on government accountability more generally.

Design of Trust-Building Policies

Building trust is likely to be particularly important in low-capacity settings because of the difficulties and costs of effective enforcement—and frequently the very low baseline levels of trust in tax systems. Strategies to build trust may have a significant impact in these settings. In many low-income countries, and particularly across Sub-Saharan Africa, survey evidence suggests a high willingness, in principle, to pay taxes but very low levels of trust in the tax system (Aiko and Logan 2014). This finding may indicate that particularly explicit trust-building policies such as tax earmarking may not be needed where there is greater trust in government.

That said, it is critically important to recall that enforcement and trust are complements rather than substitutes: public trust and political support are necessary to underpin more effective enforcement, while effective, rules-based enforcement is a critical aspect of ensuring fairness and equity (Kirchler, Hoelzl, and Wahl 2008).

Balancing priorities. Reform strategies to improve trust may be aimed broadly, but they are often likely to target a particular tax segment or dimension of trust in pursuit of specific reform objectives—and in hopes of triggering more virtuous cycles of improved trust. For example, increasing tax collection among self-employed professionals (possibly by levying presumptive taxes as a second-best solution) may be a relatively straightforward way to improve general perceptions of equity. Highly visible enforcement efforts among HNWIs may have a similar effect, so long as those efforts do not appear to be targeting political opponents.

Elsewhere, the trade-offs may be starker. Different types of services are likely to be priorities for different groups of taxpayers. Efforts to expand political voice and accountability will inevitably target some taxpayer constituencies more than others. Governments thus should balance competing priorities in building trust among targeted constituencies while also ensuring equity more broadly.

Empowering taxpayers. Finally, building trust is fundamentally about empowering taxpayers. A common concern is that newly collected revenues will not translate into improved services for taxpayers. Yet tax policy makers and administrators have no direct control over those public spending decisions. Even so, tax reformers can seek to design tax reform in ways that make reciprocity and accountability more likely—that is, a "governance-focused tax reform agenda" (Prichard 2010). Part of such a strategy lies in drawing explicit links during the design of tax reforms between new revenue and the delivery of broader benefits. This approach may take the form of commitments to particular expenditures, increased transparency, or new forums for taxpayer engagement.

Such a strategy should also involve designing tax reform programs in ways that explicitly empower taxpayers to push for responsiveness and accountability from their government. Historically, the expansion of taxation has often played an important role in spurring the broader expansion of accountability precisely because of its potential to mobilize and strengthen public demand making (Moore 2008; Prichard 2015). But such outcomes are not guaranteed, and they depend, among other things, on the design of tax systems and tax reforms. By emphasizing features of reform that contribute to expanded trust—including fairness, equity, transparency, and the creation of forums for engagement with government—tax reformers can help create an enabling environment for bottom-up demands for accountability.

Despite the growing research on building trust and public discussions about tax reform, the extent to which those insights have been translated into concrete reform efforts is less clear. There is a continuing need to adopt concrete strategies to enhance trust, rooted in a detailed understanding of local concerns and priorities as well as the broader political dynamics of reform.

Tailoring Reform to Local Contexts: Binding Constraints Analysis

Central to this volume are two interconnected arguments. First, to succeed, tax reformers need strategies for better navigating the political barriers to successful reform in both the short and longer term. Second, a greater emphasis on trust-building in reform efforts will enhance compliance, build political support for reform, and empower taxpayers to demand greater reciprocity and accountability. Overall, investments in trust-building are likely to be a critical aspect of any strategy to build greater political support for reform.

However, reform strategies must be tailored to context-specific capacities, political dynamics, and priorities. Historically, tax reform, perhaps more than many other areas of reform, has emphasized best practices—an approach reflected in references to a "global tax reform agenda" in the literature (Fjeldstad and Moore 2008). Yet research and experience highlight the need for solutions that are tailored to the technical, political, and social contexts of specific jurisdictions.

Technically, the approaches being pursued must match the technical capacity that is realistically available. Politically, the strategies adopted must be not only technically appropriate but also compatible with political constraints, bearing in mind possible resistance from taxpayers, from political leaders, and from within tax administrations. Finally, reforms should be tailored to the local trust environment—not just the extent of public trust but also the key drivers of distrust and potential strategies for building trust.

One strategy for prioritizing reform options within resource-constrained environments, and for tailoring solutions to the particular needs of specific contexts, is a binding constraints analysis.[1] It is not the only strategy that could be deployed for prioritizing and tailoring reform. Other approaches, such as problem-driven iterative adaptation (PDIA), may achieve similar goals. But a binding constraints approach is, in general, well suited to the technically detailed, data-rich character of effective tax policy and administration. The approach has five broad steps:

1. Draft a clear problem statement—for example, the need to strengthen ineffective taxation of wealthy individuals.

2. Develop a decision tree that lays out all potential causes of suboptimal performance.

3. Systematically identify which causes are most important in the specific context.

4. Among these, identify the likely binding constraints on improved performance.

5. Develop potential strategies for addressing those challenges that are feasible in light of technical and political constraints.

Identifying Problems and Their Causes

Application of the binding constraints approach begins by identifying the central problem to be solved. The examples that follow seek to illustrate the ways in which a binding constraints analysis may guide tailored reform priorities and strategies.

Technology and data. A common challenge within tax administrations is low-quality data and weak data sharing across departments and agencies, which together limit the potential for identifying tax avoidance and evasion or for implementing risk-based audits. A binding constraints analysis asks reformers to assess the multiple potential explanations for poor data quality, data sharing, and analysis.

One possibility is that information technology (IT) systems lack interoperability. However, other possibilities include (1) ineffective processes for frontline data collection; (2) legal constraints on collecting or sharing key data; (3) administrative resistance to greater transparency; (4) administrative resistance to wider use of IT for fear of job losses; (5) elites' political resistance to greater transparency and more effective enforcement; and (6) inadequate skills to analyze data effectively.

Sophisticated IT systems may or may not solve the problem of poor data and data sharing. A corresponding need is to understand specific drivers of underperformance in specific places and to target reform accordingly.

Taxing HNWIs. The same kind of analysis can be applied in combining technical, political, and trust-building logics to assess the taxation of HNWIs. Technical assessments of the challenge of taxing HNWIs tend to point to the limitations of third-party data in identifying avoidance and evasion and to the capacity challenges in auditing wealthy taxpayers. Yet a binding constraints analysis asks whether these are, in fact, the root causes of ineffective taxation. Recent evidence suggests that in many contexts they are not. Research from Uganda, for example, makes clear that many tax administrations are entirely capable of identifying HNWIs and developing evidence of noncompliance using existing data and systems (Kangave et al. 2018).

Instead, weak taxation in many places appears rooted in political resistance to more effective taxation, low trust and compliance, and the difficulties posed by wealth held offshore. Analysis of binding constraints could imply a very different approach to reform, based on building political support among elites and tax administrations, strengthening trust to build broad-based taxpayer support, and pushing to reform international rules.

Taxing corporate income. Across a range of tax challenges, mismatches between policy and administrative strategies, on the one hand, and technical capacity (and political feasibility), on the other, have hampered successful reform. This has been true, for example, of efforts by low-income countries to prevent tax avoidance and evasion by wealthy individuals and multinational firms via the international tax system.

The most common explanation of poor performance has been inadequate capacity, which has pointed to a corresponding need for expanded capacity-building programs. An alternative explanation is that the existing rules are too complicated, either because they exceed the realistically available technical capacity or because they offer too much scope for political interference or administrative corruption. The latter analysis of the problem points to very different reform strategies focused on simplifying existing rules (both nationally and internationally) and increasing transparency.

Perhaps the greatest challenges facing low-income countries are related to the international tax system. Despite recent reforms, many low-income countries still struggle to administer existing rules. The introduction of Automatic

Exchange of Information (AEOI) rules was designed to improve access to data on bank accounts held overseas by wealthy individuals. But, in practice, low-income countries have struggled to access that international data because they have been unable to collect data in their home jurisdictions adequate to meet data exchange reciprocity requirements. Although reforms may seek to improve domestic data collection, a growing chorus of observers has argued that a more likely solution lies in pushing for reform of international rules to facilitate participation by low-income countries.

Taxing property. Countries are frequently plagued by incomplete, out-of-date property registers and weak compliance, which, in turn, undermine revenue collection and equity. Historically, a common prescription has been to invest in building more complete property cadasters, expand valuation capacity, and develop new IT systems. Yet such investments have frequently disappointed. An alternative assessment of the binding constraints on reform calls for simplifying property registration and valuation, emphasizing basic process reform to strengthen enforcement capacity, and building trust with taxpayers through strategies such as small-scale participatory budgeting to generate sustainable political support for reform.

An additional benefit of the binding constraints approach is that it can highlight ways in which tax reform may be constrained by barriers beyond the specific jurisdiction pursuing reform—with important implications for designing context-specific reform strategies. In property tax reform, a frequent challenge for subnational governments is that reform efforts are dependent on, and sometimes constrained by, central governments. For example, central governments may control the process of property registration or valuation in ways that make action prohibitively expensive or impossible for local governments to execute on their own.

Alternatively, legislation in many countries limits the use of simplified strategies or available enforcement tools because the central government is often reluctant to create opportunities for greater subnational fiscal autonomy. In these cases, an appropriate reform process may combine subnational pilot projects to illustrate the potential of new models, coupled with efforts to achieve facilitation of reform at the national level. Alternatively, where national reform is impossible, it may be necessary to adapt local-level reform strategies to the particular technical and political constraints of individual countries.

Developing Strategies for Addressing Problems

Ultimately, the goal of a binding constraints analysis is to ask: What reform target and strategy are most likely to improve outcomes given the technical, political, and social constraints in a given context? Each case will be unique. That said, the preceding examples illustrate that greater reliance on binding constraints analysis is likely in many cases to point to three broad directions for reform:

- *Simplifying reform* to align policy and objectives with technical and political constraints

- *Paying greater attention to politics,* which is frequently the most important constraint on improved outcomes

- *Developing strategies to enhance trust* in order to build political support for reform and overcome pervasive challenges with compliance.

Innovations in Tax Compliance

Conclusion

Central to the framework laid out in this report is the belief that tax reform efforts have historically been too narrow, focusing on technical solutions to the question: How can governments raise more revenue? That focus on technical solutions remains critically important and has contributed to important gains. But the persistence of key reform challenges suggests that this focus, while useful, is not enough. An emphasis on technical solutions related to *enforcement* and *facilitation* overlooks the political determinants of successful reform; the diversity of potentially appropriate technical solutions in different contexts; and the importance of *trust* to compliance, to the political sustainability of reform, and to strengthening the social contract.

Incorporating these elements has significant implications not only for designing reform programs but also for reframing the broader goals of reform: shifting from a comparatively narrow effort to tax *more* in favor of taxing and spending *better*. The ultimate goal of any tax reform program is not simply to achieve short-term increases in revenue. It is also to achieve sustainable revenue increases, collected fairly and equitably, that translate into benefits for citizens. This is widely understood. Yet, in practice, these broader objectives are less consistently reflected in the design of reform programs. The framework presented here highlights both why taxing better is so important and how reform may more fully prioritize those goals.

The sustainability of reforms demands that they be rooted in durable policy and administrative improvements. In technical terms, sustainability depends on reform strategies that are tailored to the realities of the local technical capacity and constraints. The persistent challenges encountered in adopting and implementing new technologies and sustaining them over time is indicative of an important disconnect between reform objectives and reform approaches. Sustainability also requires durable political support from administrators, political leaders, and taxpayers—support that is likely to rely on both designing reform in politically viable and sustainable ways and investing in building trust and broader pro-reform coalitions.

As important, the social benefits of taxation turn critically on the extent to which expanded taxation contributes to improved public services, less inequality, and a stronger social contract between the state and taxpayers. To a significant extent, those outcomes are beyond the control of tax reformers, who cannot control how tax revenues are ultimately spent. But the design of tax reform does have an important role to play. Strengthening fairness and equity depends on which kinds of reform objectives are prioritized and on the extent to which the reform is designed to tax *better* or to simply tax *more*. Tax reformers can also seek to link revenue-raising, service delivery, and broader citizen voice in the design of reform programs, instead of allowing those elements to be an afterthought.

Those kinds of measures may not only improve the social benefits of taxation, but also foster trust, compliance, and political support for reform. And, finally, they can help empower taxpayers to engage and bargain with states, thereby raising the likelihood that taxation will go beyond extraction and contribute to strengthening the social contract and taxpayers' broader well-being.

Note

1. This strategy was introduced briefly in the introduction to this volume and is reflected in the operational toolkit developed in parallel to it.

References

Aiko, R., and C. Logan. 2014. "Africa's Willing Taxpayers Thwarted by Opaque Tax Systems, Corruption." Policy Paper No. 7, Afrobarometer, Accra, Ghana.

Ali, M., O-H. Fjeldstad, and I. Sjursen. 2013. "To Pay or Not to Pay? Citizens' Attitudes toward Taxation in Kenya, Tanzania, Uganda, and South Africa." *World Development* 64: 828–42.

Fjeldstad, O-H., and M. Moore. 2008. "Tax Reform and State-Building in a Globalised World." In *Taxation and State-Building in Developing Countries: Capacity and Consent*, edited by D. Brautigam, O-H. Fjeldstad, and M. Moore, 235–60. Cambridge, UK: Cambridge University Press.

Kangave, J., S. Nakato, R. Waiswa, M. Nalukwago, and P. Lumala Zzimbe. 2018. "What Can We Learn from the Uganda Revenue Authority's Approach to Taxing High Net Worth Individuals?" Working Paper No. 72, International Centre for Tax and Development, Brighton, UK.

Kirchler, E., E. Hoelzl, and I. Wahl. 2008. "Enforced versus Voluntary Tax Compliance: The 'Slippery Slope' Framework." *Journal of Economic Psychology* 29 (2): 210–25.

Luttmer, E., and M. Singhal. 2014. "Tax Morale." *Journal of Economic Perspectives* 28 (4): 149–68.

McCulloch, N., and L-H. Piron. 2019. "Thinking and Working Politically: Learning from Practice." *Development Policy Review* 37 (S1): 1–15.

Mellon, J., T. Peixoto, F. M. Sjoberg, and V. Gauri. 2021. "Trickle Down Tax Morale: A Cross-Country Survey Experiment." Policy Research Working Paper 9507, World Bank, Washington, DC.

Moore, M. 2008. "Between Coercion and Contract: Competing Narratives on Taxation and Governance." In *Taxation and State-Building in Developing Countries: Capacity and Consent*, edited by D. Brautigam, O-H. Fjeldstad, and M. Moore, 34–63. Cambridge, UK: Cambridge University Press.

Prichard, W. 2010. "Taxation and State Building: Towards a Governance Focused Tax Reform Agenda." Working Paper No. 341, Institute of Development Studies, Brighton, UK.

Prichard, W. 2015. *Taxation, Responsiveness and Accountability in Sub-Saharan Africa: The Dynamics of Tax Bargaining.* Cambridge, UK: Cambridge University Press.

Prichard, W. 2020. "Tax, Politics, and the Social Contract in Africa." In *Encyclopedia of African Politics*, edited by N. Cheeseman. Oxford, UK: Oxford University Press.

Touchton, M., B. Wampler, and T. Peixoto. 2019. "Of Governance and Revenue: Participatory Institutions and Tax Compliance in Brazil." Policy Research Working Paper 8797, World Bank, Washington, DC.

van den Boogaard, V., W. Prichard, R. Beach, and F. Mohiuddin. Forthcoming. "Enabling Tax Bargaining: Supporting More Meaningful Tax Transparency and Taxpayer Engagement in Ghana and Sierra Leone." *Development Policy Review*.

World Bank. 2017. *World Development Report 2017: Governance and the Law.* Washington, DC: World Bank.